THE FEDERAL TRUST
for education & research

THE EUROPEAN REPUBLIC

Reflections on the Political Economy of a Future Constitution

by

Stefan Collignon

in association with the Bertelsmann Foundation

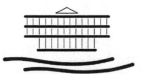

Bertelsmann Foundation

This book is published by the Federal Trust whose aim is to enlighten public debate on issues arising from the interaction of national, European and global levels of government. It does this in the light of its statutes which state that it shall promote 'studies in the principles of international relations, international justice and supranational government.'

The Federal Trust conducts enquiries, promotes seminars and conferences and publishes reports and teaching materials. It is the UK member of the Trans-European Policy Studies Association (TEPSA), a grouping of fifteen think-tanks from member states of the European Union.

Up-to-date information about the Federal Trust can be found on the internet at www.fedtrust.co.uk

© Federal Trust for Education and Research 2003

ISBN 1 903403 51 0

The Federal Trust is a Registered Charity No. 272241

7 Graphite Square, Vauxhall Walk,

London SE11 5EE

Company Limited by Guarantee No.1269848

Marketing and Distribution by Kogan Page Ltd

Printed in the European Union

For Fabian

Who was born on 12 May 2000, when Joschka Fischer gave his path-breaking speech on Europe's Constitution at the Humboldt University in Berlin.

Contents

List of Figures and Tables

Foreword

Change and continuity are the two opposite poles between which European integration has veered for more than 50 years. Currently we are experiencing a period of especially rapid change. Both the single market and the euro are signs of the progress which has been made to weld the EU member states into a community with shared values and a common destiny. A further milestone in the history of the unification process is the constitution which the European Convention is currently preparing for the next Intergovernmental Conference in the second half of 2003. Its aim should be to improve Europe's ability to act both internally and externally, and to enhance its democratic legitimacy. If the constitution meets these requirements, it will transform the European Union into a political system that resembles that of a state.

Stefan Collignon's study on 'The European Republic', describes the way in which this can be achieved by defining core requirements of a future constitution for the wider Europe on the basis of a political economy approach and the theory of collective goods. The author analyses the reasons for the serious lack of democracy in the European Union in its present form and its inefficient decision-making structures from a political theory and economic perspective. Collignon then describes a way of overcoming this impasse that is both feasible and ambitious. The study clearly constitutes a signal contribution to the current debate about the future of Europe.

The Bertelsmann Foundation and the Center for Applied Policy Research have for many years shadowed the process of reforming the European Union, and have commissioned the present study in the framework of their joint "Consequences and Implications of the Euro" project. In The Federal Trust we have acquired a competent partner who has supported us in making the present study available to a wider European public.

Finally I should like to thank Stefan Collignon for his valuable reflections on the future shape of Europe. I am particularly grateful to The Federal Trust for the care with which the publication has been prepared.

Professor Dr Werner Weidenfeld

Member of the Executive Committee of the Board, Bertelsmann Foundation, Guetersloh; Director, Center for Applied Policy Research, University of Munich

Guetersloh/Munich, 2003

Preface

We all want to live in peace and prosperity. Why don't we? This question has intrigued mankind from the beginning. Many solutions have been tried and often failed. European integration has been a success story over the last half-century, but in terms of history, this has been a short period. After the end of the Cold War, new challenges have to be faced. Has European integration simply been an instrument to resist Soviet domination? Or has it been the fruit of collective learning? Is the liberal democratic consensus, on which the European Union is built, a solid foundation for future developments, or will Europe revert to warring states as it has previously done for 350 years? These are questions, which loom in the background of the work of the *European Convention*, which is presently deliberating a Constitution for the European Union (EU). But the immediate task is to find institutions, which will allow efficient policy-making for decades to come. Today an intransparent web of institutions, procedures, rules, committees, governments, parliaments, etc. contributes to a wide range of policy outcomes, but this method is no longer coherent with the values and norms that Europe's polity proclaims to adhere to, nor is it likely to produce efficient results.

This book aims to contribute to the ongoing debate on Europe's future. It takes a political economy approach to analyse some of the underlying issues and argues that collective action problems require a courageous step forward in creating coherent governance structures for the Union. *The European Union needs a proper government and full democratic legitimacy by its citizens.* This does not necessarily mean that the EU has to become an oppressive Leviathan. But in the course of the last 50 years, a large number of European collective and public goods have been created which affect the daily life of each and every European citizen. It has to be recognised that their governance has become a 'public thing', a *res publica*. Hence, a constitution will establish a European Republic which one may also call a European Democracy. Today it has become essential to give European citizens their democratic right to political autonomy. It is time to take the European 'common concern' out of the sole hands of national governments. For Europe does not belong to governments. It belongs to its citizens.

I would like to thank all those who have contributed to my reflections over the recent months, especially Keith Lehrer, Daniela Schwarzer, Susanne Mundschenk, Sebastian Dullien, Eleni Katirtzoglou and Maria Joao Rodriguez. I am especially grateful to Holger Friedrich and Thomas Fischer from the Center for Applied Policy Research and the Bertelsmann Foundation for the intellectual and financial support, including the stimulating discussions at the seminar in Gütersloh and the SommerAkademie Europa 2002 in Seeon. Christopher Herrick has been a solid rock as my assistant. I am indebted to my colleagues at the LSE, notably Paul Taylor, Meghnad Desai, Charles Goodhart and Waltraut Schelkle, but the greatest treasure have been my students. I also have benefited from discussions with many policy makers. The visits by Giuliano Amato and Paul Nyrup Rassmussen to the LSE and our conversations were particularly helpful. Heinz-Joachim Neubürger's support cannot be overestimated. I also have learned from the discussions at the InterAction Council meetings. I would like to acknowledge Helmut Schmidt, who has inspired me for over 35 years. His generous support over recent years has strengthened my conviction that we can make a difference by standing up for our beliefs.

Paris, March 2003

Abbreviations

CAP	Common Agricultural Policy
DPEF	Documento di Programmazione economico-finanziara; the Italian Growth and Stabilisation Program
EC	European Community
ECB	European Central Bank
Ecofin	Economic and Financial Affairs Council
EMU	European Monetary Union
EP	European Parliament
EPP	European Peoples Party
ERM	Exchange Rate Mechanism
EU	European Union
FAO	Food and Agriculture Organisation
GDP	Gross Domestic Product
GDR	German Democratic Republic
IMB	Individual Marginal Benefits
LSE	London School of Economics
MEP	Member of the European Parliament
OECD	Organisation for Economic Cooperation and Development
SGP	Stability and Growth Pact
SMB	Social Marginal Benefits
TARGET	Trans-European Automated Real-Time Gross Settlement Express Transfer
UK	United Kingdom
US	United States
USA	United States of America
VAT	Value Added Tax
WWF	World Wildlife Fund

Introduction

The European Union is not a state. Nor is it a nation. But what is it? A supranational community? A federation? Burgess (2000:29) affirms: 'Whatever the EU is, it is *not yet* a state'[1]. And McKay (1999:3) claims: 'When eleven countries of the European Union officially adopted the euro on January 1st 1999, few commentators doubted that the EU had embarked on a major step towards the creation of a federal system of government.' Even if one does not fully subscribe to this statement, it is certain that European Monetary Union (EMU) has structurally transformed the European economies in many ways. By complementing the single market with the euro, economic integration has essentially been completed, but political integration is still lagging behind. With one single currency, the monetary economy of the participating member states has effectively become one unit. On the other hand, economic rules and regulations are still highly fragmented, even if European legislation has achieved some harmonisation with respect to the single market. This poses problems of efficiency. My concern in this book is that there are too many cooks in one kitchen. Governments conduct their policies primarily according to national objectives, while concern for the potential impact on others is frequently overwritten. I will show that this disequilibrium between Economic and Political Union is the Achilles heel of European integration.

In this context it is not surprising that doubts are also frequently voiced about the appropriateness of the present political arrangements for the monetary constitution of Euroland. Hardly a European Council passes without the EU requesting or promising better policy co-ordination. But the measures, which are agreed at these summits, are only meaningful for a small group of bureaucrats, mostly in the national capitals. The growing prominence of policy co-ordination issues in Euroland is a sign that existing policy-making rules are not optimal. There is little transparency about intergovernmental European policy-making, both in matters of content and procedures. For ordinary citizens the summit communiqués sound like incomprehensible Chinese.

Hence, European unification has reached a critical stage. After the successful introduction of the euro as the single currency for more than 300 million citizens, new tasks and modes of economic governance are becoming the focus of attention. By integrating a potentially large number of new countries into the European Union, many of whom have had only a relatively short experience with market economies and liberal democracy, the quality of European policy-making will change. In many EU member states, new populist movements are voicing discontent and signal a divorce between policy elites and disenfranchised sections of the population. Will European integration face up to these challenges?

My principal focus is on constitutive rules for policy-making, with particular emphasis on the economic aspects of a European Constitution. This implies looking at how politics affect economic outcomes, but also how economics affect politics. Thus, my task stands in the tradition of political economy, but I will also touch on some deeper, political and philosophical issues. The reason is that with the creation of a unified monetary economy, Europe has consciously or unconsciously also opted for a model of society. Money is not neutral. The institution of money has a normative content, which requires a broader institutional context in order to achieve its welfare-enhancing qualities. My basic argument is simple: *the European Union needs a full-fledged government, which draws its authority from European citizens.* In a context of ongoing globalisation, near-complete economic integration and the enlargement to a large number of new member states, *European intergovernmental policy making is no longer efficient.* Authority can no longer be derived from national governments alone. It needs the legitimacy of a European democracy.

This proposition is controversial. For example, the British Foreign Secretary Jack Straw declared in a speech in Edinburgh (27/08/02):

> 'There is a case for a constitution which enshrines a simple set of principles, sets out in plain language what the EU is for and how it can add value, and reassures the public *that national governments will remain the primary source of political legitimacy.* This would not only improve the EU's capacity to act; it would help to reconnect European voters with the institutions which act in their name.'

I will show that the stated objectives of the EU can only be achieved if the primary source of the EU's political legitimacy is its citizens and not its governments. I will therefore explain why a European government would improve European welfare. I will also have to clarify the intellectual background, which may have led other observers to different conclusions. In order to find a *terrain d'entente* I will refer occasionally to some abstract concepts and theories, but I will always try to bring their relevance back to European policy making.

Plan of the Book

In Chapter One, I will first look at the motivations for European integration and some basic concepts about policy-making and social consensus, which are important because they are the foundation of any European Constitution. In the next chapter, I will give a cursory glance at the changing environment of European policy making that will ultimately force the EU to take the next step in political integration – or to perish. Chapter Three sets the intellectual framework for my discussion of a European Constitution. I will then look at specific forms of European constitutional rules. Federalism is the most frequently used system of ideas, when Europe's Constitution is discussed. Chapters Four and Five will analyse different manifestations of federalism. First I look at the political concept, which has two different traditions. The anarcho-communitarian approach, which is today expressed in the principle of subsidiarity, goes back to the 16th century and reflects a holistic and exclusive vision of society. I will show that it is inconsistent with the explicit normative content of the Treaty on the European Union. By contrast, the liberal-democratic approach, as reflected in the US constitution, has transformed this traditional view of federation into a modern republican constitution. I will show that this approach is coherent with the economic constitution of European Union as it was established by the Maastricht Treaty. In Chapter Five, I will analyse in-depth economic federalism, which is a theory to determine the optimal regional organisation of government within one state. I will discuss efficiency criteria with respect to subsidiarity in the context of globalisation and deeper European integration. It turns out that collective action problems are likely to prevent the provision of a large class of European collective goods through voluntary intergovernmental co-operation between EU member state governments. A larger Union will increase the probability that the EU will turn from a 'privileged' into a 'latent' group, to use Olson's (1971) famous concept. This means that subsidiarity and EU enlargement risk undoing European integration. Hence, competences for supplying these goods need to be delegated to the European level, to a European government with full democratic legitimacy by its citizens. Chapter Six focuses on the macro-economic policy mix as a case study for the complexities linked with the provision of collective goods in Europe. I conclude that only a full, democratic constitutional consensus would be able to give European stabilisation policies the coherence they need. The last chapter summarises some of the main arguments developed in this book and discusses some practical applications.

Chapter One.
The Essence of European Integration

The Motives for European Unification

European integration has been a continuous process of piecemeal institution building for over half a century. Scholars of European integration have sought to identify the causes and motives behind this process. Intergovernmentalists are insisting on the interests of states and governments (usually the two are assumed to be identical) in creating commitment devices through institutional co-operation in order to overcome conflict and improve welfare (Moravcsik, 1998). Neofunctionalist theories emphasise the functional spillovers resulting from previous integration steps, thereby pushing the process forward.[2] These theories seek to explain the 'objective' reasons why political actors chose European integration and voluntarily gave up rights to sovereignty and ceded authority and power over crucial aspects of domestic policy to common institutions. Without any doubt, they provide useful insights. In particular the rational choice framework whereby self-interested politicians, voters and interest groups seek to maximise their net benefits derived from policy choices are intuitively convincing. While I do not dispute their validity, I wish to go one step further and question how preferences are formed and derived interests articulated. It may therefore be useful to return to the subjective motives of Europe's Founding Fathers, as they are anchored in the continent's collective experience and handed down to new generations through the normative content of European ideologies, practices and institutions.

The early men of European unification had drawn lessons from the economic and political instability, which previously had led to two world wars. They sought to preserve peace, freedom and prosperity by creating conditions of trust and mutual respect. In the words of Jean Monnet the purpose was 'to unite men, to solve the problems that divide them, and to persuade them to see their common interest'. His fundamental question was, 'how can people be persuaded to approach the problems in the same way, and to see that their interests are the same, when men and nations are divided'.[3] Monnet found the answer in a two-step procedure: The first aim of this was to change the context in which conflicts were traditionally set and, second, to give this new context a solid form by creating new institutions.

Changing the context for policy-making was important because individuals' particular attitudes, perceptions and preferences, but also the values and norms they followed were legitimate only according to specific contexts. Monnet here intuitively anticipated what has since been developed as a major rethink in social science,[4] usually called the 'linguistic turn' (Rorty, 1992). I will come back to this in the next section. Monnet believed that by changing people's daily practices, the context within which they perceive their interests and desires will also change. By integrating economic structures by functions such as steel and coal industries (the 'war machine'), but also by creating a single market, sharing the same currency and providing multiple points of interaction in daily life, people would develop a sense of common interest, if not a European identity. However, this functionalist approach led him to favour an 'elitist' conception of the European construction that later gave rise to the 'democratic deficit' (Featherstone, 1994). Economic integration played a functional role in 'unifying men' (Monnet) by creating a shared background and knowledge. This change in European context was not rapid or instant. It had to be gradual, step-by-step, 'like for a man climbing a mountain who sees the perspective changing minimally, but exorably all the time' (Duchêne 1994:375-6).

Yet, changing individual attitudes by transforming their life context was not sufficient, although necessary to ensure stability. Contexts change all the time. If peace was to be sustained, people's attitudes towards co-operation had to become enduring. For the Founding Fathers of European integration, the normative dimension of their project was based on the lessons they had learned in the first half of the 20th century. But their subjective intentions were not enough:

'The Union of Europe cannot be based on goodwill alone. Rules are needed. The tragic events we have lived through and are still witnessing may have made us wiser. But men pass away; others will take their place. We cannot bequeath them our personal experience. That will die with us. But we can leave them institutions' (Monnet, 1978:384).

Hence, while a changed context would alter people's interests, formal institutions were necessary to ensure the *continuity and persistence* of the transformation of national contexts. As a consequence, the gradual change of context had to be matched by the creation of European institutions.

Today, this approach is manifest in the myriad of amazing processes, strategies, devices and institutions for European integration. But the endogenous change of context through quantitative cumulation of new institutions and processes has now reached a point where a leap to a new quality of European governance is required. Policy-making has become too complex and intransparent. In some respects there seems to be too much Europe, in others too little. In fact, Monnet's method has led to a widening of tasks for the European Union, from the common management of steel and coal industries to the customs union, the single market with a single currency, including now also aspects of Justice and Home Affairs and a Common Foreign and Security Policy. This progress in integration is neither automatic nor irreversible. Although the proliferation of flexible, task-orientated and overlapping institutions of governance partly followed their function (Rosamond, 2000), it also depended on the collective will and intentions by policy-makers as well as citizens, market participants, firms and consumers. These actors realised that the efficient management of common concerns required new forms of trans-border co-operation, and also in many instances the delegation and pooling of sovereignty to common European institutions. However, in addition, the context of European policy-making has also changed exogenously due to the collapse of the Soviet Union and the end of the Cold War. This now also requires that the system of European institutions be adapted to be able to deal with the new environment. I will discuss some of these long-term structural changes in the next chapter. Here, I will first discuss the mechanism through which ideas and preferences get incorporated into institutions. This is of importance for our understanding of constitutions.

Monnet's emphasis on context and institutions opened the possibility to put European policy-making on a normative and ethical foundation, something that had seemed impossible after the atrocities of previous world wars. In many ways he was a visionary and a pragmatist, not a theorist. In recent years, the 'Monnet method' has come under scrutiny (Featherstone, 1994). In his speech at the Humboldt University in 2000, the German Foreign Minister Joschka Fischer has declared it out of date. But no alternative method has been established until now. In order to assess its relevance, I will therefore make an attempt to reframe his method in terms of modern political economy approaches. This will allow me to identify what deserves to be preserved in Monnet's method, namely the emphasis on creating structures of mutual trust, and what needs to be further developed, namely the arrangements of democratic European institutions.

Theory (I): Collective Choice and Policies

Let us start by examining some definitions. Policy-making is about specifying rules for choosing actions. According to modern dynamic decision-making theory (see for example Puterman, 1994) a decision-maker or actor at any point in time observes the state of the world (as far as it is relevant for his decision) and chooses an action. The action choice produces two results: 1) the decision-maker receives an immediate reward (pay-off) and 2) the system evolves to a new state at a subsequent point in time according to a given probability distribution. As this process evolves through time the decision-maker receives a sequence of rewards. A decision rule specifies the action to be taken at a particular time and a *policy is a sequence of decision rules*. For example, a policy of maintaining price stability specifies how the central bank should act at specific moments of interest rate setting. Implementing a policy therefore generates a sequence of rewards, such as low rates of inflation. The policy-making problem is to choose or formulate a policy to maximise the sequence of rewards.

This model has many useful applications in micromanagement. But while it operates in a given context, public policies by governments, states and social institutions are more comprehensive, because they structure the macro-context itself. Public policies are the output of a polity, i.e. the structured system of institutions, norms and rules that are set up by constitutions and represent the decision-making domain. For example, price stability is not only dependent on the central bank, but also on government budgets and wage bargaining. But although these policies can change the context of society, they are also determined by the structural context of their polity. For example, fiscal policies may aim at reducing deficits, but through their spillover on interest rates and effective demand they may also change the general incentives for investment, economic growth and unemployment. Hence, public policy-making is more than choosing a sequence of decisions in a given environment. We have to reflect the context. In applying the standard decision-making model to public policies, we have to consider two implicit *a priori* conditions without which public policies could not function efficiently. One concerns the scope of policies (I), the other their epistemic foundation (II).

(I) First, the assumption that the *decision-maker receives the rewards* from (or pays the costs for) implementing the policy is not always correct. Although the idea of people governing themselves and therefore making decisions about actions that affect themselves is the essence of democracy, in reality there are many areas where decisions are made that affect people who had no opportunity to participate in the decision-making process. The challenge comes from asymmetric information and agency problems and also from a large class of externalities, i.e. asymmetric fall-outs (spillovers) from decisions. To start with, there is a *principal-agent relationship* between voters and governments. The modern theory of public choice assumes that politicians and voters act in self-interest, the former maximising power and seeking rents while the latter are preoccupied by their own welfare (Downs, 1957). Thus, the rewards for principal and agents are not the same. However, it can be argued that in democracies, the politician's (agent's) rewards are systematically linked to the people (principal) through the constitutional social contract, and are therefore expressing either a general policy consensus or at least the median voter's preference. This does not necessarily solve all problems of asymmetric information, notably time inconsistent policy actions, but it does point at the need to share information, make politics transparent and create common knowledge. These are epistemic ingredients of democracies.[5] They are not always respected in the European Union.

But even if the interests and rewards of the principal and agents were identical, there is still the problem of *externalities*.[6] Particularly in the age of globalisation, there are a growing number of cases where the rewards or consequences of a policy decision affect not only the decision-makers and those they represent, but also other individuals, firms or groups. The well-known examples are pollution and environmental policies, but the phenomenon of externalities is far more universal. In the European Union, the problem of externalities appears when the decisions by one member state have consequences in other jurisdictions without these members having been involved in the policy-making process. The incongruity between the decision-making sphere and those affected by the consequences of those decisions, without having been asked or been able to contribute to the decision-making process, is one of the central policy issues in Europe today.

I will discuss the consequences in the following chapters. Here, I am developing the analytical tools for our analysis in later chapters. The theory of fiscal federalism has established the principle of *fiscal equivalence* (Olson, 1969) which can be applied to a wide range of policies. In its classic formulation it says that the geographical incidence of the benefits of a public program should coincide with the jurisdiction of the government operating and financing the program. I suggest that we interpret these public programs as the provision of collective goods of all kinds, including policy decisions. I also propose, for lack of any better words to call the set of all persons affected by a given policy the *policy domain*. Insofar as individuals live in space, the policy domain is close to the concept of 'geographical incidence of benefits'. It follows, that different collective goods have different policy domains. For example, the policy domain of municipal parking regulations are all car owners in that town. Financial markets are the policy domain of financial regulation or monetary policy measures etc. Yet, it is clear that if there are spillovers from policies pursued by one jurisdiction onto another, these externalities prevent a clean correspondence between a given polity and its policy domain. Hence the polity does not correspond neatly with the policy output.

The equivalence, or congruence between policy deciders and their incidence is not sufficient for the efficient provision of collective goods. Difficulties also arise from preference heterogeneity. Decisions are made in the decision-making domain, i.e. in the context of a given *polity*. A polity consists in the political organisation of individuals who are bound into a political entity (a jurisdiction) by their institutions and by their wish to determine their public affairs. In standard policy-making models, as in the political theory of the nation-state, the polity and the decision-making domain coincide. This is the principle of jurisdictional congruence (Fischer and Schley, 1999), to which we will return in Chapter Five. Governments make decisions for their 'countries' through the constitutional rules, which structure their polity. In democracies these rules aim to ensure that policy decisions reflect collective preferences of the government's constituency. But if the polity's structure reflects only partial preferences, i.e. those of a subset of the decision-making domain, policy externalities occur. In this case it is the input into the polity that does not correspond with the decision-making domain. Policy decisions emerging from the structures of a given polity will then have consequences beyond the decision-making domain. Figure 1.1 illustrates these relations.

Figure 1.1 The Policy-making Process

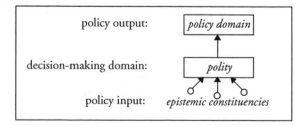

One of the main reasons for European integration is derived from the realisation that there is a growing range of collective goods and policy issues where the decisions taken by one government affect all or many others. Efficiency can be achieved by co-ordinating such policies in order to maximise the welfare of the policy domain, thus incorporating these externalities. This can be achieved by developing a joint decision-making structure in a polity that matches the policy domain. This implies that in order to build a European polity, a European Constitution must define the structures of policy-making for the entire European policy domain.

(II) Second, all policies need solid epistemic foundations. The standard model of decision-making assumes *a priori* that the expected value of rewards from a policy is known before choosing an action (Puterman, 1994:20).[7] Ideally this requires complete information, no 'unintended consequences' and also an external standard of evaluation, which is most easily achieved when the pay-off can be measured in monetary or quantifiable terms. For example, most people can agree that higher income is better than lower, etc. However, there are policy areas, where the measurement of rewards is far from obvious. How do we assess the nuisance of pollution? Does the use of military force produce more or less security? Are unemployment benefits improving or worsening the opportunity to find new jobs? Is the right to grant asylum a positive or negative reward for a society? Economists call the subjective evaluation of rewards 'utility'. Individuals are assumed to be able to rank the expected utilities of their actions and choose those, which produce the highest utility. Similarly, they can rank policies, which produce different outcome sequences. But this approach, developed and perfected for single autonomous actors, is highly problematic for actions with collective rewards (Arrow 1963, Basu 2000). Conflicts may arise either because of disjunctive preferences over the distribution of outcomes, or because actors disagree over the evaluation.[8] Overcoming diverging views about the world requires consensus on theory and analysis. In order to make coherent collective choices, there has to be collective *agreement on the values of potential pay-offs* from a chosen policy. Without this epistemic dimension, policy-options would be incommensurable. Thus, making a choice about distributive issues implicitly requires an epistemic consensus over evaluative issues. I will call the group of individuals that share the evaluation consensus the *epistemic constituency* of policy-making. An epistemic constituency does not necessarily have to agree unanimously on specific evaluations, but its members are sufficiently connected and trust each other to learn rapidly from each other.[9]

In the European context, this fact is of utmost importance. As long as policy preferences are formed exclusively or primarily in the context of national polities, it is unlikely that they will share similar cognitive foundations. People 'see' policy issues differently in different national contexts. These individuals do not share the same common knowledge on which national policies and/or institutions of policy-making are based. Hence, different institutions usually have different epistemic constituencies. In the European context this means, of course, that each nation-state has its own political and ideological traditions and policy preferences are derived from it. However, a given polity may also receive input from different epistemic constituencies.[10] For example, even in well-established nation-states there exist particular epistemic constituencies, which express their specific regional identities (Bavarians in Germany, the Basques or Catalonians in Spain, Protestants and Catholics in Northern Ireland etc.). Epistemic constituencies and polities are not always the same. This is even more so the case in European policy-making, where a 'fragmented polity' reflects the strong epistemic heterogeneity of EU member states.

Full *epistemic consensus* does not necessarily imply agreement on the evaluative *choices* or the distribution of rewards, but simply that there is an accepted standard to evaluate them. The common knowledge regarding these standards is what keeps individuals together and is therefore one of the most elementary foundations of society.[11] If Europe is to be united, it will have to construct institutions, which allow the emergence of such European consensus. The consensus within an epistemic constituency also does not eliminate possible dissent and conflict over policy issues of a distributive nature as we will see below. Such distributive problems are the focus of game theory. Epistemic consensus simply means that all members of the epistemic constituency refer to the same valuations, even if they may wish to distribute them differently. For example, as a standard of value the euro represents an epistemic consensus in Europe insofar as millions of citizens refer to it in evaluating economic choices - even if they think they never have enough euros!

Consensus emerges from epistemic constituencies. My concept of the epistemic constituency bears some resemblance with Habermas' 'public sphere'. However, I use a different notation to emphasise that the epistemic constituency is held together by the evaluative consensus, the conditions of this I will clarify below. If these conditions are not met, epistemic disagreement can cause a more fundamental conflict than distributive issues. It can lead to the break down of rational choice because of the incommensurability of policy options. It is in fact impossible to pick 'the best' option when agents disagree on how to evaluate what is best. In game theoretic terms, some players in a game may not only have different pay-off functions, but because they use different numeraires, any form of strategic interaction is excluded. For example, if one part of the population thinks nuclear energy is a blessing, and the other considers it a curse, a coherent and rational evaluation of the best nuclear policy is impossible.

Disagreement will need to be solved differently in order to make a decision.[12] The worst scenario to solve conflict is decision by brute physical force: one party imposes its will and its standard on another. Not surprisingly, this approach seems to enjoy highest respectability in international relations. For Clausewitz, *war* was the 'continuation of politics with other means', that is to say, forcing a decision when diplomacy broke down. He did not necessarily mean the complete *annihilation* of the enemy, but at least forcing the other party to *accept* a solution (Aron, 1987:102). War is unavoidable, when an evaluative consensus between different polities is non-existent, the policy domains overlap (so that interests could clash) and no agreement on procedures is available to solve the conflict.[13]

Alternatively, a more peaceful solution for overcoming disagreement is possible, if agreements on procedures can be concluded. This is what institutions are about. I understand *institutions* with Searle as 'a cluster of related constitutive rules or practices' (Fotion, 2000:192) that creates social reality. Hence, government institutions stipulate rules which allow decision-making under disagreement, provided there is agreement on the procedures. For example, if I prefer nuclear energy (x) over windmills (y) and you do the opposite, a consensual rational choice whereby our utilities are both maximised is impossible.[14] However, if we can agree on a procedure (z) on how to make a decision, and this procedure will realise either your preference or mine according to a given probability distribution, then the value of this procedure is always higher than my and your worst outcome.[15] Hence, it is rational to agree on a procedure, which protects both you and me, against the worst scenario, i.e. against the *certainty* of having our preferences overruled.[16] What matters here is that individuals may 'agree to disagree' on distributive issues, because they *agree on some higher order choice rule*.[17] Today's cognitive dissonances between different epistemic constituencies may become tolerable if the political process keeps the option open, that collective preferences and choices may change over time, or simply because they are considered to be fair with respect to some external standard.[18]

Thus, agreement on decision-making procedures is crucial for policy-making. It is the foundation of all constitutions. It is therefore essential that we understand how such agreement comes about if we want to design a European Constitution. *Constitutions* are sets of rules by which economic and political processes operate over time.[19] The time dimension implies that these rules are repeatedly re-enacted and therefore generally accepted. Philpott (1999:145) has pointed this out with respect to the constitution of international society:

> 'A constitution of international society is a set of norms, mutually agreed upon by polities who are members of the society, that define the holders of authority and their prerogatives, specifically in answer to three questions: Who are the legitimate polities? What are the rules for becoming one of these polities? And, what are the

basic prerogatives of these polities? Constitutions of international society are both legitimate – that is, sanctioned by authoritative agreements – and practiced, generally respected by all polities, which are powerful enough regularly to violate it.'

The value of a constitution is determined by the expected utility of policy outcomes that it is likely to produce. But acceptance of and agreement on a constitution is itself dependent on the epistemic consensus regarding the probability distribution of likely policy outcomes. Societies with entrenched and closed epistemic constituencies easily become prey to rebellion and civil war, if the minority expects a zero-probability of ever seeing its own preferences prevail. Hence, the epistemic consensus on decision-making procedures is more fundamental than consensus on the evaluation of substantial and distributive issues. This conclusion is highly relevant for European policy-making, for it implies that in a European society different epistemic constituencies can coexist as long as they can agree on policy procedures. To summarise, we may define a *polity as an epistemic constituency that agrees on a constitution* for procedural policy-making rules, although it may split into different epistemic constituencies on the evaluation of substantial and distributive issues.

Policy-making in Europe

The classical policy-making models for the nation state assume that epistemic constituency, polity and policy domain all cover the same set of individuals. Congruence between the three spheres guarantees that governments act as the agent for the 'people' who are their principal. This is the essence of Abraham Lincoln's famous definition of democracy as 'people's government, made *for* the people, made *by* the people and answerable *to* the people'. Hence, policy decisions are efficient and legitimate. But as far as policy-making in the European Union is concerned, our two *a priori* conditions for coherent policy-making - congruence between the policy domain and the polity, and between the polity and the epistemic constituency - are only partially fulfilled. The policy domain is significantly larger than national polities and the epistemic constituencies reflect national debates rather than the entire European policy domain. Hence, they are smaller than the European polity. This is a fundamental difference with the classical nation-state model of democracy. No doubt, in the European Union citizens are also bound together by their wish to determine European affairs, but the lack of a proper constitution with decision-making procedures, which involve European citizens directly in policy choices, keeps epistemic constituencies apart. *Hence, the European polity remains fragmented and policy disagreements between constituencies (nation-states) persist* for a long time.[20] This fact renders coherent and rational European policy choices more difficult and certainly less efficient than warranted. European policy debates are often not about what would be the right or best policy, that would benefit citizen's welfare, but about positioning entire communities, i.e. 'countries' with respect to whether one or another member states' government will accept a decision ('Does Germany want to do this?' 'Will Britain agree to that?'). The problem with this approach to policy-making is not only that it gerrymanders minority voices out of the national debates by only giving credit to the majority behind the government,[21] but also that it prevents the emergence of genuine European policy preferences, which allow choosing policies that are acceptable to all European citizens. This fact contributes to the general disenchantment with European integration.

We can identify two types of policy-making inefficiencies. The first is related to the incongruence between epistemic constituencies and polity, the second to the gap between polity and policy domain. I will return to a formal treatment of these inefficiencies in Chapter Five. Here I would like to focus attention on two related issues. First, the relative congruence between national and the incongruence between European epistemic constituencies and the polity is one reason why constitutional consensus is strong in national polities but weak in the European polity. This can be seen from the way different national polities deal with controversy. Lijphart (1999) has emphasised the ways of handling conflictuality in different models of policy-making. He drew a distinction between the conflictual nature of the majoritarian, Westminster model of parliamentarianism versus the consensual model, represented by federations like Switzerland or Belgium and also by the European Union. I would argue that the observed conflictuality of the Westminster model is only sustainable because there is a strong consensus behind the (unwritten) constitution of Westminster. Hence, the polity is highly coherent in Britain, despite dissent on policy issues. The same is largely true in France. In the European Union the existence of many epistemic constituencies prevents such constitutional consensus, and *as a consequence, decision-making institutions in the European polity are weak.* On the European level, greater emphasis is therefore put on consensus about substantial policy issues. European politicians love projects, programs, and grand schemes because it seems easier to achieve consensus on these 'practical' issues than on an underlying framework of values and norms.[22] Political cleavages in the EU are hidden behind the multi-party pro-European coalition, which often embraces the major government and opposition parties of member states. Dissent appears primarily through multi-level governance, when member state governments represent their national epistemic constituency but have to bargain for a compromise with other governments at the European level. If the Convention on Europe's Future is to produce a European Constitution, it must also ensure that it is backed by a strong consensus from its citizens. And even if that does not exist from the beginning, it must create structures that will permit such consensus to emerge. I will discuss this point at greater length in the last chapter.

Second, in the European Union the set of those individuals who are affected by a policy decision and those who are involved in or legitimising these decisions do not coincide. *Policy domain and polity are incongruous* and *this causes externalities*. As their scope is widening, the impression grows that the nation-state and democracy are no longer capable of fulfilling their functions. But this is not just a consequence of the world's 'increasing complexity'; it is also the self-made cause of the EU's incapacity to act, of Europe's loss of power. There is nothing predetermined or inevitable about this development. What is required from a logical point of view to overcome the problem is the creation of a fully integrated European polity, so that a comprehensive policy consensus allows coherent policies for all Europeans affected by them.[23] From a practical point of view, these two points imply, as we shall see, the setting up of institutional structures for public deliberation, mutual respect and communication between the national and cultural communities in the European Union with a focus on relevant policy issues that affect all European citizens.

Theory (II): Values, Norms and Consensus

European integration is a political project, based on democracy. At least that is the claim. A European Constitution will not only affirm this orientation, it will also have to create institutions, which allow European citizens to practice their democratic rights. In recent years, the theory of democracy has taken a 'deliberative turn'. Increasingly, democratic legitimacy is seen in terms of the ability or opportunity to participate in effective deliberation on the part of those who are subject to collective decisions (Dryzek, 2000:1). I will now turn to the question how policy deliberation can contribute to the emergence of European collective preferences and a constitutional consensus.

How does agreement and consensus on policy evaluations and constitutions come about? Without going into the theoretical depth of the problems related to amalgamating individual preferences into collective ones, I will here use the *model of stochastic consensus*, as first presented in Collignon and Schwarzer (2003) and further developed in Annexe 1. In this model, stochastic consensus, i.e. the potentially unanimous agreement on policy choices, reflects an *equilibrium* of preferences which is a weighted average. While deviations from equilibrium are possible, actual consensus, i.e. unanimity, would only be achieved after an infinite sequence of policy deliberations where all members of a group take each other's preferences, reasons and arguments into account. However, the concept of stochastic consensus does not require that unanimity is actually achieved. It simply describes the equilibrium towards which all individual preferences would converge if the process of deliberation went on long enough.[24] Hence, at any given point in time one can observe individuals who have not yet been convinced by the arguments of others and therefore have divergent preferences, but who will get closer to the equilibrium of unanimity at each subsequent exchange of arguments. In this respect the model of stochastic consensus is fundamentally different from *deterministic consensus*, as for example in Buchanan and Tullock (1962). Deterministic consensus assumes unanimity a priori, while stochastic consensus is concerned with getting there. What matters in this model of preference formation are the conditions under which an equilibrium can emerge. We can describe them in three steps. (I) Individuals have naturalistic preferences, which are derived from cultural contexts and conventional values. (II) These immediate preferences are re-valued in light of new empirical evidence and more abstract norms and reasons, leading to rational preferences. (III) Collective preferences are established through dialogue, deliberation and higher order beliefs where individuals evaluate other individuals' views.

(I) Individuals have immediate or *naturalistic preferences*, also called needs and desires. They may arise from biological foundations, such as thirst and hunger, but at a higher level they are derived in the context of communities in which people live, and the social practices, cultural traditions and social understandings they share (Smith, 2001).[25] They reflect individuals' 'sense of self' in relation to their immediate environment, their idea of identity (Kymlicka, 1993). What individuals believe to be right or wrong, preferable or objectionable, depends largely on how their views are framed by their 'life world', i.e. by the background of cognitive structures and beliefs which seem to have been 'always there' (Habermas, 1987). One may also call these structures *conventions* (Lewis, 1969). They consist of linguistic and cultural resources, ideologies, sciences, arts or religions, but also of the practical knowledge about 'how to do things' or in shared memories of history. In order to operate effectively in the world, any actor has to be able to rely on a large set of background conditions, which give orientation not only to himself, but also to all others who share this common knowledge. This context is their 'culture,' which provides the framework for their collective identity. The background conditions, which allow individuals to distinguish what actions are desirable and worthwhile, I will call *conventional values*. Hence values establish a one-to-one relation between cultural context and *naturalistic* preferences.[26] Political philosophers of the School of 'communitarianism' have focussed on this dimension of preference formation, which they call the 'politics of the common good' (Kymlicka, 1993:369). I believe that peoples' attachment to a false self that is programmed by a predetermined context is the cause of much human conflict and suffering. But it is a fact that we need to take into account.

In most societies the immediate context that shapes traditional values is the family and local communities like schools, religious institutions and other small associations. They are the background of providing aid to the poor and deserving. On a more abstract level, the nation-state has become the dominant context for the definition of political preferences in Europe. Most people identify strongly with their nationality, even if they are aware of the larger European context. 44 per cent of all European citizens identify only with their own nationality while 53 per cent feel also to some extent European. Fewer than 10 per cent give priority to their European identity (Eurobarometer, 56, 2001). This is not surprising, given that cultural traditions have been transmitted through the institutions of nation states (Ferry, 2000). Hence *l'Europe des patries* is a fundamental cultural foundation of peoples identities. Yet, this does not exclude that there is also a sense of common European identity, based on a common culture in the narrow term like religion, philosophy, literature, music, painting, architecture and science. The European culture also includes awareness of common ideas regarding the economic order (money, markets, welfare, freedom, equality, solidarity) and the political experiences of European history. In Chapter Four I will describe how specific historic events have contributed to shaping European ideas on federalism. Helmut Schmidt (2000:211) rightly pointed out, that the common influence of cultural developments in European nations was largely responsible for the emergence of a European identity. Whether one 'belongs to Europe' depends less on geography than on the cultural context, on the historic role of Romanism, Gothic, Renaissance, Scholastic, Humanism, Baroque, Enlightenment, Classicism, Romantic, human rights, democracy and the welfare state. Not all countries who wish to become members of the European Union share this part of Europe's cultural identity.[27]

(II) Secondly, human beings do *not only* act as background-conditioned Pavlov's dogs, but they are also capable, through linguistic references and communicative processes, to reflect on their own context, to learn from experience and to determine rules for judging their desires and will (or cognition and feeling). I will call these rules *rational norms*. They permit the transcendence through reason and deliberation of context-bound conventions, values and naturalistic preferences. We are here talking about the ethical dimension of preference formation. As rational actors, human beings are capable of transforming their cultural background (or life world) by referring to 'reason'. Kant's categorical imperative is an example for this. Their 'sense of identity' is elevated to a more abstract and universal form of solidarity, social integration and ethics. This transcendence of naturalistic into rational preferences belongs to the universalistic tradition of modern Enlightenment and inspires political liberalism until today. I call *rational preferences* the transformed desires, which are derived from a given context, but re-evaluated by normative considerations.[28]

European integration is an impressive example for transcendence of 'naturalistic' national preferences. The unification of nations with their own identities, history and language, the voluntary delegation of sovereign powers to common institutions without war, repression and violence is unique in the history of mankind. Helmut Schmidt (1998:236) has also made the point that French willingness for reconciliation with Germany after the war was 'a *moral act* of greatest importance'.[29]

Yet, the transcendence of 'naturalistic' preferences is not always easy. Many European citizens feel a conflict between their national identity, their patriotism and the reasonableness of the large trans-national project of the European Union. Giving up their currency was painful, not only in Germany. Creating the single market meant giving up many national protections. Most member state governments reflect the 'natural' preferences and conventional views of their constituencies because that is the context in which they operate. Similarly, members of the European Parliament (EP) usually represent the ideologies of the political parties at home that are the basis of their career. However, in the European context of policy-making, they often go beyond these familiar ideas, because they have to take into account their partners' views, and the evidence provided by experiences in other countries. The European Commission facilitates the dissipation of such evidence. However, the process of preference adjustment at the European level remains largely confined to a small elite. What is missing are structures for the exchange of information and the deliberation of policy options that involve the European policy domain, i.e. European citizens at large. This would require genuine decision-making power to be given to the European Parliament and Commission. I will return to this issue at the end of this book.

(III) The third step is to amalgamate these rational individual preferences into *collective consensus*. This requires introducing communication into our model. Following de Groot (1974), Lehrer and Wagner (1981) have provided the theory and an algorithm for doing this. Individuals determine their preferences not only with respect to their own, but also to other individuals' beliefs. They learn from each other. They also make second order evaluations about other individuals' capacities to evaluate beliefs. It so turns out that if all individuals in a group or community are connected through a chain of communication and mutual respect and process all information rationally, consensus emerges as the steady state equilibrium in the stochastic process of persuasion and deliberation after a significant (ideally infinite) number of deliberative iterations. Mutual respect means that members of a group give a positive weight to their own opinion and to that of some other members. However, it does not imply 'reciprocity' in respect.[30] It is sufficient that the group 'communicates respect' (Lehrer and Wagner, 1981:21) in the sense that each member of the group is connected to every other through intermediation by other members.[31] Though the iterative updating of their rational preferences with respect to other people's views (and not to new factual evidence, which belongs to step II) individuals' views will ultimately converge to the equilibrium of unanimous or consensual beliefs and preferences. The consensus on collective preferences is therefore dependent on individual rational preferences and on the relative weight that individuals attribute to each other in a world that is connected through communication. Hence, consensus does not require public information to be available to anyone, nor does it require 'ideal' conditions of deliberation as Habermas assumes, but simply the existence of 'higher order beliefs', i.e. the evaluation by each individual of some other individuals' information and beliefs, provided these individuals are connected through mutual respect.

This model is less ambitious than Habermas' *Theory of Communicative Action* (1987) and related theories of deliberative democracy. Stochastic consensus does not require that collective beliefs and decisions be justified by public reasons that are 'generally convincing to *everyone* participating in the process of deliberation' (Bohman, 1996:5). It is sufficient that there is a 'chain of respect', i.e. that the conditions of mutual respect and connectedness be fulfilled. I take a large view on how preferences are changed by deliberation that includes all sorts of discourses going on in a society. In Chapter Six I give an example of how this process works in forming fiscal policy preferences. Consensus emerges because each individual adjusts his/her own beliefs and preferences in view of what some others think, mostly in their own immediate social environment. The reasons for this adjustment are not really relevant for the consensus process. They may be Socratic ethos, trust, superior information or strategic advantage (Sen, 1970:26; Buchanan and Tullock, 1962). The point is that in the process of communication individuals adjust their views because they respect each other's cognitive capacities. This assumption is nowadays widely shared by theories of deliberative democracy, although there are different sensitivities in evaluating the conditions of deliberation (Dryzek, 2000). Our model allows us to be generous on the limits of deliberation because the primary condition for consensus to emerge is the existence of a 'chain of mutual respect'. The essential point of the model is that without mutual respect and a chain of connectedness through communication policy consensus is impossible and conflict will prevail. This aspect is highly relevant for European integration.

Overcoming conflict, deepening integration, efficient policy-making all require structures to connect European citizens and build mutual respect.

The model of stochastic consensus does not imply that everyone 'thinks alike'. For example, a left wing militant may 'agree' that a right wing politician becomes President because he won the elections, but she may still personally 'prefer' her own candidate. As pointed out before, the reason for her acceptance may be agreement on the constitution in the epistemic constituency. The preference may then take the form of passing silence over her 'private,' non-public preferences (Kuran, 1995) and by acting in accordance with the consensual collective preferences because they reflect 'how the world is'. In that sense, consensus subordinates individuals to collective evaluations; yet, the model assigns primacy to individuals as the basic elements from which consensus is built up.

Stochastic consensus is a non-holistic model of consensus.[32] It is different from deterministic consensus because it does not assume or postulate unanimity, but defines consensus as the weighted average of all opinions. It includes individual dissent as the deviation from potential or ultimate unanimity. This distinction is also relevant for understanding the difference between a liberal 'society' and organic or holistic 'communities'. The conceptual distinction between *Gesellschaft* (society) and *Gemeinschaft* (community) goes back to Tönnies (1881:2001) who described *Gemeinschaft* as a single, organic whole, whose members (!) share language, custom and beliefs 'by birth' (Tönnies 2001:18), while *Gesellschaft* is seen as a mechanical aggregate or rational construction with 'individuals living alongside but independently of each other' (p. 19). According to Michael Taylor (1982:26) community is defined by 'almost complete consensus', direct and many-sided relations between members and reciprocity. In terms of the stochastic consensus model, this concept of community implies conditions where the assignment of mutual respect is effectively identical for every group member.[33] But this posits the existence of consensus *ex-ante;* it does not explain the process of getting there. Hence 'community' is defined by deterministic consensus.

Three further implications can be derived from our model. First, it is important to bear in mind that once consensus or unanimity has been attained, it becomes part of the cultural context or background. The common knowledge allows expectational regularities, which form the basis for conventions (Lewis, 1969). Hence naturalistic preferences change over time as new evidence becomes available and criticism is voiced (step II). Collective deliberation then shifts the consensus to a new equilibrium. For profound normative and constitutional issues, this process may take a long time. For example, the idea of the modern nation-state, which emerged only in the 16th century, has transcended the traditional world of hierarchical tribal communities, but agreement on its normative content with popular sovereignty has only appeared as the 'natural' framework for policy-making in the 20th century - at least in Europe (Sørensen, 1999:174).

Second, an important distinction implied by our model concerns dissent and conflict. Assuming rational behaviour, the emergence of consensus requires, (1) that individuals have respect for their own beliefs and those of at least one other (condition of mutual respect) and (2), that there is a chain of respect that connects each individual in the consensus domain (connectedness condition). It is this connectedness condition that is the constitutive characteristic of an epistemic constituency in policy-making. If either of these *conditions is not fulfilled*, no equilibrium is possible and *conflict* arises. However, if both conditions are fulfilled, but the iterative process of higher order evaluations has not yet converged to full equilibrium, we observe *dissent*.[34] Hence, conflict and dissent are fundamentally different phenomena. Conflict is defined as the impossibility of agreement; dissent gravitates around consensus. Conflict is an obstacle to making coherent public choices; dissent is compatible with it. Furthermore, it is the existence of dissent which makes a society 'liberal' and tolerant and distinguishes it from 'holistic' conformist communities.

Conflict arises when intolerant, dogmatic or dictatorial attitudes prevent members of the group from respecting other members of the group and lead them to insist that they alone are 'right' and only their own preferences deserve to be chosen. Hence, even 'compromise' is impossible, let alone persuasion and conviction. Therefore conflict leads to war in the sense discussed by Clausewitz (Aron, 1987). Dissent implies 'agreement to disagree' because even if there is no unanimous consent, different members respect each other sufficiently to adapt their own views, attitudes and preferences at least marginally. Because this respect is mutual, the adjustment narrows the difference of opinion until unanimity is reached. Therefore a tolerant society may have a high degree of dissent, but little conflict. An intolerant society is marked by a high degree of conformism between insiders (within 'communities') and conflict with outsiders (between communities).

Third, our model of stochastic consensus has implication for the concept of 'community' which has recently found new interest in philosophy and political science and which will become relevant for our discussion of federalism. According to Michael Taylor (1982:26), there exist three characteristics possessed in some degree by all communities: (1) The set of persons who compose a community have beliefs and values in common and 'there is typically an *almost complete consensus* on a wide range of beliefs and values.'[35] (2) Relations between members should be direct and many-sided. (3) The relation of reciprocity. This last attribute describes a strong constraint on the condition of mutual respect. The second is a manifestation of connectedness, but the emphasis on direct unmediated relations keeps communities small in size (Taylor 1982:32). Finally, the essential attribute of 'almost complete consensus' implies that community preferences are close to naturalistic or conventional preferences. Therefore in communities conformism dominates, but shocks lead easily to the withdrawal of reciprocity, violent retaliation, ostracism and excommunication (Taylor 1982:83), hence to conflict and scission (Dumont 1980:198-200).

Policy Consensus in Europe: Communitarian or Rational?

How does this model relate to policy-making in Europe? Clearly, the purpose of European integration was to overcome conflict, as I have defined it, between nations and individuals. Monnet's method consisted of convincing policy-makers of new ideas (step II in our model), hoping that their acceptance by highly respected policy-makers would create a broader consensus, which in turn would gradually transform the evaluative background for individual and public decision-making. Legal rules and democratic decision-making merely offered ex-post endorsement of an already existing reality (Bellamy and Castiglione, 2000:66). Yet, the purpose was not to abolish dissent in the sense defined by the stochastic consensus model.

One manifestation of dissent about European policies is the constitutional debate between sovereignists and integrationists. It is mirrored in the academic debate about intergovernmentalism versus supranationalism. Both schools of thought can be related to the re-emerging philosophical controversy between communitarianists and universalists (Rasmussen, 1990; Barry, 2001). But the intellectual disagreement goes effectively back to the emergence of modernity in Europe during the 16th and 17th Century (See Chapter Four). This dissent relates to the first two steps of our stochastic consensus model. Sovereignists and communitarianists are emphasising the role of cultural background and values and the sense of identity, community and trust (Taylor, 1995; Walzer 1983, 1994; Kymlicka, 1993), hence step I. By contrast, integrationists and universalists focus on context-transcending general norms, such as equality, liberty and individual rights (step II).[36] From the perspective of our model of stochastic consensus, communitarians start with the *result* of step III, i.e. with the consensus equilibrium, which becomes part of the background, while for universalists, consensus is the final outcome of a rational *process*.

This debate between philosophers can clarify some relevant questions in the European context, which affect the emergence of a constitutional epistemic constituency. A European constitutional consensus requires that all European citizens can agree on procedures for policy-making. Sovereignists and eurosceptics reflect the communitarian attachment to values, which are derived from national cultural backgrounds, while integrationists refer to a different set of norms. Consensus building requires dialogue between the two constituencies. I will show the difficulties of such dialogue by using a typical British euroceptical argument. Hindley and Howe (2001:37-38) provide a perfect example for preferences unreflectedly derived from background:

> 'An important matter underlying the economic costs and benefits of EU membership is an apparent cultural difference in attitudes to free markets between the 'Anglo-Saxon' and the 'continental' approaches. The latter exhibits a propensity to favour regulation over free markets. A more federal structure would allow this propensity freer rein, creating what many British voters, even enthusiasts for the single market, might regard as a noxious mixture. (...) However, the problem is real even within the present European structure. Two examples suffice to illustrate the underlying issue. The first is a report in *The Times* (8 December 1993) in the run-up to the 1994 elections for the European Parliament, under the headline: 'Tories embarrassed by European allies'. The allies are the European Peoples Party (EPP), with which the Conservatives are associated in the European Parliament. The problem lay in the draft EPP manifesto for the elections. One sentence conveys the flavour of the manifesto and explains the embarrassment. It says that 'governments must ensure that the functioning of the market remains subordinate to the general welfare and social justice'. (...) That free markets are better for the general welfare than political processes is, of course, the central proposition of classical liberal thought. British Conservatives do not always apply it in full, but few of them would deny its force or fail to pay it at least lip service. That their continental counterparts refuse even lip service reveals an intellectual gulf. Reflected in policy, it could become a political chasm'.

Here, policy preferences for the free market are an unmitigated function of the national British context as it had emerged from the Thatcher years. There is no consideration of market failure arguments, nor is there any respect for the reasons why 'continental counterparts refuse even lip service'. Reference to national cultures and particularities justifies using the nation-state as the procedure for making collective choices, but at the same time it reinforces the sense of national identity by confining communication and policy deliberation to the national community (i.e. to a national epistemic constituency).

Integrationists, on the other hand, refer to liberal universalistic norms of freedom, equality and legal rights amongst individuals that are often anchored in economic structures like the single market. They may well agree to the 'central proposition of classical liberal thought', but their concern is that deregulation of national laws may require re-regulation at a European level to ensure the equal and efficient functioning of the market. Hindley and Howe (2001:44-45) refer to this possibility:

> 'A 1994 Directive relating to the packaging of goods seeks to curb the unnecessary use of packaging and generation of packaging waste on environmental grounds. It is complex and has needed to be transposed onto voluminous implementing regulations in the UK and in other member states. It is a 'framework Directive,' which provides for the making at the European level of further detailed subordinate legislation. It will impose substantial burdens on producers, as well as administrative costs; however, if producers comply with its provisions, then (in theory at least) their products should be free to circulate into other member states without being hindered by other locally differing packaging regulations.
>
> Is the UK better off within this regime or outside it? For producers who do not export to other EC member states, these regulations represent an unnecessary cost. For producers who do export there, it avoids the potential necessity to produce goods with two different standards of packaging, one for the home market and one for the EC.'

The Packaging Directive had considerations on environmental externalities as its normative content. These are collective goods of a universal nature and therefore require regulation in all member states. They would not only facilitate free circulation of goods, as Hindley and Howe acknowledge, but supposedly they would also protect Europe's environment. This fact is not recognised by the authors. It is, of course, legitimate to dissent from the European consensus. But by refusing respect for the norms contained in the Directive ('unnecessary cost'), the European polity becomes segregated into different epistemic constituencies (the 'free' UK market and the administratively overburdened European market). Hence, the lack of mutual respect is not only a source of conflict in Europe, but it also inhibits a rational debate about what would be 'best' policies for the single market, or for the European political domain in general. A rational European policy, in the sense of what can be agreed to be best, is not possible because the choice of preferences has already been made by national conventions before European deliberation took place. These multilevel policy choices contribute crucially to the inefficiencies of European policy making. Communitarians find it difficult to accept that the shared social practices in an integrated economy will transcend national communities and thereby transform traditional values into European social and legal norms. For integrationists 'European construction' contributes to the emergence of a European identity by integrating, i.e. preserving *and* reformulating national identities.

Whether collective policy preferences are more strongly influenced by European sovereignists or integrationists, will depend on the process of deliberation, i.e. the relative weights attributed by the individuals of a given society to the different arguments and norms. Hence, it will result from step III in our model. Lehrer (2001:108) has emphasised that it is the aggregating process of individual views, which makes converging views, and, I would add, phenomena like European integration possible:

> 'I propose that we confront the paradox of individual sovereignty and social identity as a paradox that should be treated initially as a problem of explaining how we can offer an account of a sovereign individual with a social identity and how within the social situation we can have a sovereign individual. How can we resolve the conflict between individual autonomy and social identity? How can the interests of the individual conform to the interests of the social groups to which he belongs without the group co-opting the interests of the individual? How can the interests of the social group conform to the interests of the individual without decomposing in the conflict of individual interests? The answer to all these questions is that individual interests may converge toward consensus at the same time in the ideal case and by the same process that the consensus socially defines the identity of the individual. We do not need to suppose, at least in the ideal case, that there is a chicken and egg problem of whether the egg of individualism comes before the chicken of communitarianism or *vice versa*. The individual and society fry and fly together. The society is defined by a consensus aggregated by individuals and individuals are defined by the consensus they aggregate. The truth of communitarianism is to be found in the aggregate, the truth of individualism in the aggregation.'

The conditions for creating consensus on the constitutional philosophy behind European policy-making have important implications for the nature and future of European integration. If individuals treat each other with equal respect, societal consensus is reached fairly rapidly. Yet, by definition, communitarians value collective identity and autonomy highly and therefore they give great weight to themselves (i.e. members of their community) and little to others. The consequence is a high degree of dissent in society[37] or segregation into different homogenous sub-societies.[38] However, as the degree of dissent rises, possibly even approaching conflict, coherent policy-making becomes increasingly more difficult. Because the acceptance of policy preferences is dependant on the legitimising force of belonging to a community (nation), communitarian ideologies have a tendency to become exclusive. Hence, the predominance of sovereignist perspectives, even in the weak form of intergovernmentalism, implies a high degree of dissent and potential conflict about policy choices between governments and nations.

This is exactly what Jean Monnet and the other European Founding Fathers sought to overcome. Their integration policies focussed on the material and substantive transformation of the European cultural background by integrating the economy. This method proved surprisingly successful, well beyond their expectations at the time. However, they gave little attention to the deliberative structure of consensus formation (Step III) necessary to provide legitimacy and ultimately public acceptance of European policy choices. A European Constitution will have to address these issues. Before we deal with them, it is, however, useful to review some of the major changes in the material context for European policy-making.

Chapter Two.
The Changing Context of European Unification

The global context, within which European integration has taken place, is gradually changing. As a consequence, international power relations will also shift. Some transformations are of a fundamental economic and social character, others are more related to the strategic positions in international relations. A Constitution for Europe's integration will have to take these changes into consideration. The most fundamental structural transformation is population growth, followed by technological progress especially in communication. Politically the world has changed because the bipolar system of international relations has disappeared. Europe's governance will also be challenged by EU enlargement to Central and Eastern Europe.

Globalisation as a New Context

Trends in world population determine not only economic power in the world, but they also set the long-term political agenda. While at the end of World War II 2.5 billion people lived on this planet, today there are more than 6 billion. In 2050 this figure will be in excess of 9 billion (See Table 2.1). Hence, population density in many parts of the world will increase significantly. These men and women need to be fed, while arable space is shrinking. The claims on resources will intensify. WWF-International has calculated that worldwide 20 per cent more natural resources are presently consumed every year than could be regenerated (WWF 2002). By 2050, on present trends, humans would consume roughly twice the Earth's biological capacity. The land area required to sustain consumption averages 2.3 hectares for each of the

6 bn people on the planet today. But the 'biological capacity', i.e. exploitation levels consistent with replenishment of resources is estimated at no more than 1.9 hectares.

Moreover, resource use is highly unequal, with North Americans using 9.6 hectares per person, Western Europe 5 hectares, 2.2 for Latin America and 0.8 hectares for low-income countries and Africa. Hence, the United States use nearly five times and Europe more than twice the amount of resources that are biologically sustainable. Europe's population will remain stagnant, as in most industrialised countries, while dramatic increases will take place in less developed countries. The need for economic growth and new investment will therefore be high in the poorer and younger parts of the world, and they will need a larger share of the worlds 'natural capacity'. The richer and ageing societies will also be confronted with new distributional issues at home: fewer people in the working age group will have to support more dependent and retired people. Both developments are likely to increase social envy, questions of fairness and the need to overcome conflict.

In addition, deteriorations in the environment and climatic changes, partly man-made, will require large-scale research efforts to meet the world's rising energy needs and to replace coal, oil and other fossil fuels if the generation of heat-trapping greenhouse gases is to be avoided. To supply energy needs 50 years from now without further influencing the climate, up to three times the total amount of energy generated today from these resources will have to be produced from new technologies (*Science*, November 2002). This is a collective task which has been compared to the Apollo moon landing program. But even if determined policies were to tackle this issue, environmental issues are likely to translate into natural catastrophes such as flooding, droughts and desertification. Hence distributional disputes over natural resources like water, food, oil, forests, etc. will intensify, probably in a shock-like fashion. Already in recent years military conflicts of this sort, especially about mineral resources, have become more frequent (Figure 2.1). Migration across countries and continents will increase as a consequence, thereby challenging traditional cultures and reinforcing defensive reflexes. Wars, armed conflicts and terrorist rebellion will not only become more prominent in the future, but their nature will also change. Of the 56 major armed conflicts registered between 1999-2000, only three were of state-against-state military nature, while all others reflected internal conflicts, even if outside forces sometimes did intervene (FAO, 2002). Whereas human-induced disasters have contributed to about 10 per cent of total world emergencies in 1984, by the end of the century they were a determining factor in more than 50 per cent of cases. With an increase in distributional conflict, normative issues of culture and morality and the 'clash of civilisations' will also

Table 2.1: Global Population Distribution

	1950		2000		2050	
Regional Population	millions	percent	millions	percent	millions	percent
WORLD	2,519.5	100.00	6,056.7	100.00	9,322.3	100.00
Africa	221.0	8.77	794.0	13.11	2,000.0	21.45
Asia	1,399.0	55.53	3,672.0	60.63	5,428.0	58.23
Latin America & Caribbean	167.0	6.63	519.0	8.57	806.0	8.65
Europe	548.0	21.75	727.0	12.00	603.0	6.47
North America	172.0	6.83	314.0	5.18	446.0	4.78
Oceania	13.0	0.52	31.0	0.51	47.0	0.50
EU15						
Luxembourg	0.3	0.01	0.4	0.01	0.7	0.01
Ireland			3.8	0.06	5.4	0.06
Finland	4.0	0.16	5.2	0.09	4.7	0.05
Denmark	4.3	0.17	5.3	0.09	5.1	0.05
Austria	6.9	0.28	8.1	0.13	6.5	0.07
Sweden	7.0	0.28	8.8	0.15	7.8	0.08
Portugal	8.4	0.33	10.0	0.17	9.0	0.10
Belgium	8.6	0.34	10.2	0.17	9.6	0.10
Greece	7.6	0.30	10.6	0.18	9.0	0.10
Netherlands	10.1	0.40	15.9	0.26	15.8	0.17
Spain	28.0	1.11	39.9	0.66	31.3	0.34
Italy	47.1	1.87	57.5	0.95	43.0	0.46
France	41.8	1.66	59.2	0.98	61.8	0.66
United Kingdom	50.6	2.01	59.4	0.98	58.9	0.63
Germany	68.4	2.71	82.0	1.35	70.8	0.76
Total EU15	**293.2**	11.64	**376.5**	6.22	**339.3**	3.64
Malta	0.3	0.01	0.4	0.01	0.4	0.00
Cyprus	0.5	0.02	0.8	0.01	0.9	0.01
Estonia	1.1	0.04	1.4	0.02	0.8	0.01
Slovenia	1.5	0.06	2.0	0.03	1.5	0.02
Latvia	1.9	0.08	2.4	0.04	1.7	0.02
Lithuania	2.6	0.10	3.7	0.06	3.0	0.03
Slovakia	3.5	0.14	5.4	0.09	4.7	0.05
Bulgaria	7.3	0.29	7.9	0.13	4.5	0.05
Hungary	9.3	0.37	10.0	0.16	7.5	0.08
Czech Republic	8.9	0.35	10.3	0.17	8.4	0.09
Romania	16.3	0.65	22.4	0.37	18.1	0.19
Poland	24.8	0.99	38.6	0.64	33.4	0.36
Total Accession	**78.0**	3.10	**105.3**	1.74	**85.0**	0.91
Accession + EU15	371.2	14.73	481.8	7.95	424.3	4.55
Turkey	20.8	0.83	66.7	1.10	98.8	1.06
EU15+Accession+Turkey	392.0	15.56	548.5	9.06	523.1	5.61
Accession+Turkey/EU15		33.71		45.68		54.16

Source: United Nations Population Division

gain prominence. If they take a military form, these conflicts are likely to further disrupt food and other production creating a vicious cycle of conflict leading to poverty, leading to more violence.

Technological innovation may help to master the ecological and economic challenges, but at the same time it is transforming the nature of conflicts. The increased efficiency and lower cost of transport and communication, the generally rising levels of education in the world which underpin the increases in production, but also the victorious expansion of monetary market economies, they all contribute to the individualisation of mankind. Increasingly, men and women are becoming aware of their autonomy and emancipate themselves from their more traditional cultural contexts. As a consequence large migrations across countries and continents take less the form of organised conquest and more of individual migration. But at the same time, these developments exert disintegrating pressures on traditional cultural contexts, such as families, ethnic and religious groups. Xenophobic and fundamentalist reactions are likely to gain importance, unless alternative forms of socialisation and integration are found.

Furthermore, technological change is also transforming the form and nature of public governance. The dramatic falls in transport costs for ideas and people, which are the hallmark of globalisation (Overman, 2001), also affect the provision of collective goods. In the past, many collective goods could only be provided at high cost and this 'jointness of supply' necessitated that they were produced by public administrations. One of the strengths of the modern nation-state consisted in the set-up of efficient public services over the whole national territory. Hence the nation-state was like a club that excluded non-citizens and provided public goods and services to its members. With improved technology more, although not all, collective goods can be produced non-jointly and they can be treated like private goods in the market (see Chapter Five). Prominent examples are Post and Telecommunication, electricity supply etc. But the same is also true for certain levels of weapon technology, which opens a whole new field for warfare such as terrorism. These tendencies require new forms of governance within nation-states and between them.

Figure 2.1 Military Conflicts in the World

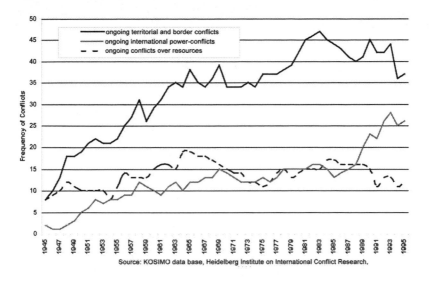

Source: KOSIMO data base, Heidelberg Institute on International Conflict Research.

New forms of global governance have to anticipate, regulate and avoid violent conflicts of interests. Many of the lessons from Europe's history - democratic governance, justice and fairness, the conditions of successful economic development and the reduction of poverty - may prove useful in this context. I certainly do not claim that Europe should or could be a model for the world. But as the region where modernity in its economic and ideological dimensions was first invented in the 16th century, Europe has also been the first to struggle with the painful transition from traditional subsistence to modern monetary market economies, and with the difficult ideological changes from hierarchical holism to contractual individualism that go in parallel with it.[39] But even if some lessons may be learned from Europe's history, the economic, social and ideological transformation of today's world poses radically new challenges. If conflict in the world is to be reduced, mutual respect in an interconnected world is required. Although a world consensus on policy issues may not be easily perceptible, it must be possible, at least, to transform conflict into dissent. In this context, Europe could act as a 'connecting broker', as a voice of reason. But Europe will only be respected and have an impact on developments elsewhere in the world, if it is capable of speaking with one voice, and can act in a concerted and unified manner. Narrow nationalism cannot produce the answers, for the noise of internal conflict and dissent lowers the credibility of European policy positions and does not allow the build-up of trust and respect from other parts of the world.

Today's 376 million European Union citizens represent 6 per cent of world population, half of the share at the end of World War II. By the year 2050 it will fall to 3.6 per cent (See Table 2.1). Europe is far from the power it held a century ago, politically, technologically, militarily and culturally. Internal conflict will reduce it to insignificance. As Schmidt (2000:15) put it:

'One cannot exclude that we Europeans will fail with our attempt to create a voluntary unification of our democratic sovereign states or that the previous successes of the Union will be lost in coming decades. The European states would become marginalized figures in world politics in this case – and possibly also the victims of world-wide economic, social and power-political conflicts' (my translation).

Hence, the question of Europe's Constitution is of vital importance. Europe will only exert influence and wisdom if it can lead by example. Europe's capacity to act and to protect its interests and values will depend crucially on the institutions by which it will manage its common affairs.

Europe's Fragile Governance

The changes in Europe's policy-making environment require also reviewing the tasks of the nation-state. Population pressure and migration will give increasing prominence to security concerns in a wide sense. As a final step, new responsibilities have been recognised as 'common concern' in the European Union. The 'area of freedom, security and justice' and the construction of a 'European defence autonomy' are added to the traditional economic community (Wallace and Wallace, 2000). But even the economic arena is fundamentally transformed. The completion of the Single Market Program has harmonised many aspects of national legislation, especially for standards and market management. While the original approach insisted on uniform rules, the 1979 *Cassis de Dijon* judgement by the European Court of Justice advanced the concept of mutual recognition of national standards. These developments changed the ways policy-making was implemented in Europe, as Wallace and Wallace (2000) comprehensively document.

However, a qualitative new step has been reached with the creation of European Monetary Union (EMU). The creation of a single currency was an indispensable complement to the single market (Collignon and Schwarzer, 2003). The European Central Bank provides liquidity to financial institutions in all countries at exactly the same terms and conditions. Hence, all economic plans are subject to the same monetary budget constraint.[40] By setting-up an efficient payment system (TARGET), the balance of payment constraint has been eliminated within Euroland - in the same way as regional economies within countries can freely finance the net balance of their sales and purchases through the banking and payment system. Furthermore, monetary policy has one target variable (the harmonised consumer price index) and essentially one instrument - the short-term interest rate.[41] There are no exchange rates within the Union, but only outside with respect to other countries currencies. Hence, from a monetary point of view, Euroland is one country. On the other hand, economic policy-making remains highly fragmented. Structural policies are meant to improve 'national competitiveness', assuming that 'countries' compete with each other in the same way as firms. But this approach overlooks the important externalities which are caused by many public policies. This issue was partly addressed at the European Council in Lisbon, which created the 'Open Method of Co-ordination'. Yet, as I will argue below this method is often deficient in view of the tasks to be accomplished. In the field of budget policies, the excessive deficit procedure in the Maastricht Treaty and the Stability and Growth Pact have set some limits to national deficits, but a conscious and deliberate definition of the proper *aggregate* fiscal policy stance does not take place and therefore prevents reaping the full benefits from EMU.

This national bias in governments' behaviour is not surprising. It is engrained in the ground rules of national democracies. Governments are supposed to respond to, or reflect, the preferences of their voters. This democratic logic excludes by definition other polities and the preferences of those who are not potential voters - such as citizens of neighbouring nations.[42] The question is whether this is causing problems for an optimal design of European policies. If many atomistic individual actors, such as firms and consumers, can create efficient solutions in a market economy where money is the hard budget constraint, why should this logic not apply to many national governments pursuing self-interested objectives? The answer, which we will discuss further in Chapter Five, is that private market participants are modelled as allocating private goods without further externalities, while collective action deals with collective goods implying externalities, which lead to market failure. The competitive market model is therefore not applicable to most European policy actions.

EU Enlargement

The nature of European institutions requires a radical overhaul at the moment when the European Union is preparing itself to accommodate up to 12 or 13 new member countries from Central and Eastern Europe or even from *Asia minor*. The 12 accession countries represent nearly 28 per cent of the EU15 population, and if Turkey is included, enlargement increases the population of the EU by 45 per cent. This is significantly more than the increase after Greece, Spain and Portugal joined or when Germany integrated the former GDR. It inevitably means that the policy preferences of very many individuals will have to change and the process of adjustment, if it takes place at all, will be characterised by high degrees of dissent. The present-day EU institutions had been designed for co-operation among six states only. Gradually, with the enlargement to 15 members, institutions were modified in order to cover new areas of competencies. But at the same time operational efficiency has declined and the gap of democratic legitimacy has increased. Enlargement, if pursued without dramatic institutional reform, will impede the decision-making capability of the entire EU because, as I will show in Chapter Five, today's intergovernmental policy-making is less likely to produce results as the number of member states increases.

Structural heterogeneity will increase. Large differences in per capita income between the old EU 15 and the potential new members exist (see Figure 2.2). Only Slovenia and Malta come close to the two poorest EU countries, Portugal and Greece, while most accession countries' per capita incomes are less than a quarter of EU income. The Eurobarometer for the candidate countries reveals high hopes for improved economic conditions. This contrasts with the assessment by people in EU member states who are more sceptical about improvements of economic standards. It is therefore possible that the population in accession countries might soon feel disappointed by their membership. In addition, political cultures also diverge due to the different shared political experiences over the last half-century. According to Eurobarometer (No 56 and Candidate Countries March 2002) over 40 per cent of all EU citizens had trust in the public institutions of their country (42 per cent without Italy), but only 30 per cent in the 13 accession countries. In the ten former Communist countries, only 27 per cent trust their public institutions. In Lithuania and Slovakia they are even only 18 per cent. This lack of trust does probably reflect the relative inexperience with democratic institutions, but also the lower per capita income (the correlation coefficient is 0.76). One can also show that an improvement in trust of national public institutions improves peoples' opinion that 'membership of the EU is a good thing', while increases in living standards and membership itself actually reduce them.[43] This means that a successful EU enlargement requires a reinforcement of public institutions within the enlarged EU, while the simplistic assumption that people will approve of the EU if they prosper, will turn out to be counterproductive.

Figure 2.2 European Per Capita Income

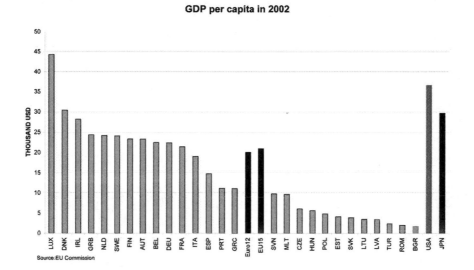

GDP per capita in 2002

Source: EU Commission

Governing by intergovernmental bargaining will also become increasingly more difficult because the complexity of compromise solutions and therefore the cost of decision-making grow exponentially with the number of negotiators.[44] But even introducing qualified majority voting into an essentially intergovernmental system of policy-making does not contribute to an improvement. Bobay (2001) has undertaken a game-theoretic study of the decision-making arrangements, which were discussed and decided by the Treaty revision in Nice in December 2000. He found that the modus of qualified majority voting retained by the European heads of state and government only allowed 'winning coalitions', i.e. decision-making majorities in 2.0 per cent of all possible combinations in an EU of 27 countries. With the pre-Nice system there would have been 2.4 per cent. Alternatively, the European Commission proposed a system with double majority of both people and states, and this would have allowed 35.7 per cent of winning coalitions. Even if Bobay's is a rather abstract approach to decision-making in Europe, it does demonstrate the high cost of present-day institutional arrangements in Europe.

Europe's capacity to act is also hampered by the growing democratic deficit. While the functions and tasks of the European Union have steadily increased over the last 50 years, the resources for carrying them out have not. This is to some degree true with respect to the financial resources of the European Union, which have been frozen at a level below 1.27 per cent of aggregate GDP. But more important is the democratic deficit, because legitimacy is the most fundamental resource for policy-making. No democratic polity can succeed without the support of its citizens and European enthusiasm for the institutions of the European Union has steadily waned. While the Eurobarometer shows support for the EU in early 1990 close to 70 per cent, it had fallen below 50 per cent ten years later. The failed referenda in Denmark and Ireland[45] on major Treaty revisions, but also the persistent europhobia in parts of the British Conservative Party and the re-emergence of populist movements elsewhere in Europe are signs that an increasing number of people feel estranged by the policy decisions taken at the European level.

These inefficiencies in policy-making are cause and consequence of co-ordination failure and require institutional solutions. In order to overcome these difficulties it is no longer sufficient to progress gradually by new steps in integration. One has to leap to a new quality level in European decision-making. This is the *raison d'être* for the Convention on Europe's Future. But what tasks should a constitution fulfil?

The Ideological Context

The debate on improved policy co-ordination takes place in a wider political and ideological context. I understand ideology as a set of ideas of how the world *ought* to be, as distinct from science which is a set of ideas about how the world *is*. Ideologies are ideational representations of cultural and normative background, which give meaning and direction to action and inform the purposeness of human behaviour. Intergovernmentalist pro-European arguments compete with federalist ideas, while national governments seem to defend their own interests against both other governments and against supranational institutions like the European Commission or Parliament. Sovereignists wish to return to less integrated ways of policy-making by re-allocating competencies from the European level back to the national or provincial level. Often these demands are made under the label of 'subsidiarity'. This approach can be justified by the greater proximity of decision-making to citizens. Local and national cultures are more homogeneous than European culture and seem to better reflect the shared values and conventional (naturalistic) preferences of people. Local people seem to know better what they want. Thus, smaller social groups are expected to have a lower degree of dissent and community preferences are more consensual. Hence it is thought that decision-making with less dissent improves efficiency. This theory is guilty of the 'naturalistic fallacy', whereby 'ought' cannot be derived from 'is'.[46] It is therefore logically incoherent. This communitarian approach also overlooks that there is an increasing number of decisions that have consequences far beyond the immediate domain of local polities. For example, the Bavarian Prime Minister Edmund Stoiber has claimed that subsidies for the Bavarian steel plant Maxhütte should be decided in Munich and not in Brussels, because his government knew better how to save local jobs than the distant bureaucracy. Yet, if a provincial administration would provide subsidies for an uncompetitive supplier of goods in the whole European market, it would not only save local jobs, but also contribute to distortions in the single European market which end up endangering jobs elsewhere. These so-called externalities have to be brought under control and that requires policy-making at the European level. I will discuss this argument formally in Chapter Five.

A moderate variant of the communitarian approach is to recognise the need for European regulation of policy externalities, but to take the related decisions primarily through voluntary co-operation between governments rather than involving supra-national European institutions like the Commission and the European Parliament. This can be justified by the argument that national governments are elected by their people and are therefore fully endowed by the democratic legitimacy of their votes. While this is true at the national level, it creates major difficulties for democracy at the European level: If in Europe's multi-level governance policy decisions are the consequence of bargaining between governments, they reflect compromises and second best solutions which are *accepted by governments*, but not necessarily *by the citizens who are clearly excluded* from the decision-making process at the European level. Even the domain of co-decision with the European Parliament is restricted. But the epistemic constituency of national governments is by definition not the same as the ministerial councils of the Union, where European bargains are hammered out, often by unanimous agreement.[47] As a consequence, people's *commitment* to European institutions is necessarily lower than to the national rules and regulations where they have a greater role in the deliberation of policy and where they can vote in selecting a government and formally organise their opposition. This weakness in European policy-making is manifest in the widely-felt perception of a 'democratic deficit' in Europe. The point here is that dissent on distributive issues within nation states rests on, or is tolerated because the national polity shares the constitutional consensus and therefore there is fundamental trust in the fairness of long-term outcomes. But at the European level, there is no such constitutional consensus. Policy decisions are an outcome, which reflects bargaining power and strength. Hence, it inspires distrust. Of course, there will be many decisions where citizens accept European regulations simply out of trust in their elected representatives. But as the range of European decisions widens, the probability of democratic frustration rises as well.[48] To avoid misunderstandings: I do not claim that all decisions must be taken 'by the people'. I simply emphasise the need for open and inclusive *deliberation* in a European epistemic constituency to make collective choices acceptable. A European Constitution must set the rules and institutions whereby this can be achieved.

Chapter Three.
On Rules and Constitutions

The writing of a European Constitution does not start from scratch. It builds on existing Treaties as well as on decades of common experiences in intergovernmental co-operation and the pooling of sovereignty. These formal and informal practices are already describing a 'European Constitution', because 'Europe' could not exist as a social entity without them. The writing of a European Constitution is an exercise in formalising and redefining some of the rules and practices, which have already determined European reality for decades. Many of them have been codified in the Treaties of Rome, Maastricht, Amsterdam, and Nice. The Single European Act, which laid the foundation for the Single Market also had constitutional character, because by eliminating national non-tariff trade barriers and creating the four freedoms[49] it set a new level playing field for Europe's economy. However, the gradual growth of tasks has contributed to the invention of ever more regulative rules, which, due to their complexity, have become intransparent and inconsistent with the context in which they are supposed to function today. This fact undermines the legitimacy of Europe's institutions. The resulting democratic deficit runs the risk of creating disenchantment with European integration that could ultimately undermine the benefits of prosperity, peace and freedom a unified Europe is meant to ensure. We will therefore have to address the question of how to combine economic and institutional efficiency with democratic legitimacy. Before we can do this, we need to first clarify the conceptual context for our discussion. This is particularly relevant as the Convention on Europe's Future frequently seems to amalgamate constitutional issues with programmatic policy objectives and this has hampered the emergence of a European constitutional consensus.

Theory (III): Constitutive and Regulative Rules

What is a constitution? A constitution can be thought of as 'a social contract joining the citizens of the state and defining the state itself' (Mueller, 1996:61). But the European Union does not (yet) count as a state. It is, however, based on a form of social contract, which specifies certain duties, obligations and rights of individuals and public institutions. This fact allows us to talk of a European Constitution. In essence, a constitution is a set of ground rules for policy-making. These rules must be legitimate but also correspond to actual practice. As Mueller (1996:61-63) put it: 'Contracts are *unanimous* agreements among affected parties. Joining a contract is a *voluntary* act [...] A good constitution is one to which all citizens have agreed.' Because constitutions make policy-making possible, they structure a polity (Philpott, 1999). They may be conventionally enacted by repeated social practices, or formalised by written constitutions. For example, the United Kingdom prides itself for not having a written constitution. But there is little doubt that it has a constitution in the sense that policy-making follows rules that assign the status of Queen or King or prime minister to certain people, or give power to parliament, provided the conditions required by the procedures inherent to these institutions have been fulfilled. The relation between legitimacy and constitutions is Janus-faced: Rules set up the enactment of certain practices, but without them being accepted they would not be enacted.

Rules are legitimate when they are perceived to be 'obligatory, worthy of assent, something individuals consider obliged to mutually respect' (Philpott, 1999:152). But, these institutional ground-rules, which Searle (1995:27) called *constitutive rules*, also create the possibility of conducting certain activities, by defining which actions are legitimate. Characteristically, this type of rule has the form: 'x counts as y in the context c'. Examples for such so-called status functions are: 'A person called Elizabeth (x) counts as queen (y) in Britain (c)' or 'this piece of metal (x) counts as one euro (y) in Euroland (c)'. The interposition of such status function allows the social creation of institutions by stipulating who may do what.[50] Like the rules of chess, constitutive rules create the very possibility of playing games. It is important to distinguish constitutive rules from *regulative rules*, which regulate already existing activities. This distinction goes back to Hume but has only become a common place since Rawls (1955) has built on it. Buchanan and Tullock (1962) also emphasised it with respect to constitutions and contracts: there is a difference between agreements on the rules of a game, and an agreement on the outcomes. Constitutive rules therefore provide the background for regulative rules. For example the rule of driving on the right-hand side of the road regulates traffic, but driving can take place prior to the existence of that rule. Hence traffic rules are of different nature than the rules of chess, which are the foundation of the game. With respect to a European Constitution this means that it must fix the rules by which the process of policy-making becomes possible, but it does not stipulate what policy outcomes are desirable. However, as we will see in the next chapter, such process orientation of a constitution does not deny that a European Constitution also has specific normative content.

Constitutions are never 'value-neutral'. All constitutive rules have normative content insofar as they define how the players of a game *ought* to behave in order to remain coherent with the rules of the game. Constitutive rules usually come in systems because they define the coherence between different sets of potential individual actions. By assigning a specific status to objects or actions, they provide the logical foundation and normative content of institutions (Searle, 1995:48). It follows that the form of a constitution (a written bill, an international treaty etc.) is less important than the procedures by which policy-making is set up. Some constitutive rules create games by abolishing rules and creating the freedom to do what is not forbidden. In this sense 'negative integration' by deregulation and the abolition of obstacles to the four freedoms in the single market is part of the constitutional foundation of European freedom, corresponding to Berlin's concept of negative liberty (Gray, 1995). Positive integration is more often dependent on regulative rules where the normative character is more obvious. For example, the social democratic idea of economic equality reflects positive freedom because it seeks to enable the underprivileged. Although the normativity of such regulative rules may be felt as a constraint (as in the quote from Hindley and Howe (see above page 38), they do imply that there is some autonomous force of last resort, a sovereign, that is free to define these rules. Even in Britain, where constitutionalist theorists have argued that the unwritten constitution and Common Law protect individual liberties better than continental codes and catalogues of rights because they leave individuals free to do what is not forbidden by law, there is an implicit constitutive rule that creates the basis for exactly this freedom (Klug et al. 1996).

Territory and the Limits of Europe

One important ground rule of policy-making is the delimitation of the space within which all other rules, constitutive or regulative, are to have validity. States, countries or nations are often associated with a territory. Some would argue that territory is the 'objective' component of a nation, distinguished from 'subjective' elements like will and memory (Hutchinson and Smith, 1994:4). Nationalism as a doctrine of popular freedom and sovereignty assumes that people must be united in a single historic territory, a homeland. But these theories are guilty of the 'naturalistic fallacy' (Moore, 1993:93) because they derive values (such as identity, culture, fraternity) from properties of things. The role of territory in the definition of a nation or state can only be correctly understood as an epistemological relation. In this context, territories are 'linguistic symbols' (Searle, 1995:66), which symbolise something beyond themselves. Because institutional facts, like constitutions, states or governments exist only by human agreement, they require official representation or what Searle called 'status indicators'.[51] Their logical function is expressed in a proposition like: 'the territory from here to there (x) counts as the country, state, jurisdiction (y) in the context of international relations (c_1) or in the context of federal competencies (c_2).' Here, territory is a status indicator which allows to *identify where and to whom a rule is applicable or not.* It is the collective agreement and acceptance of this statement which links territory to people – not nature. The question arises, however, for which rule does 'territory' fulfil the function of a linguistic symbol? Sometimes it stands for cultural community, sometimes it is used to define a nation, sometimes it stands for the delimitation of states. In statements like 'the Welsh are different from the English' or 'Paris n'est pas la France', territory stands for conventional values in a cultural context that has few political implications. However, when the context is the administration of collective goods, the function of territory can take several articulations. First of all, the consumption of public goods may have geographical limits. If territory stands for a given policy domain, it becomes the symbolic delimitation for the reach of a polity. Thus, local governments may be in charge of providing local public goods like schools, sports facilities etc., while national governments are in charge of defending security on the territory. This is the classic use of jurisdictional limitations in federal states.

What matters in this context is policy output, not input legitimacy. The output is the regulation of collective goods and from this perspective Krugman (1991:72) has rightly argued that countries should be defined by their restrictions because government policies affect movements of goods and factors. However, when territories are used as a status indicator not only for what policy rules achieve, but also for who may apply them, they become a symbol for institutional legitimacy. In this context territory stands for constitutive rules. If these rules primarily reflect *conventional values in a given community*, territory symbolises a nation. This is an unfortunate amalgamation (see also Smith, 2001), as *Blut und Boden* ideologies are nearly always at the root of nationalism and lack of respect for others, whether it takes the defence of territory against enemies or simple light-hearted forms such as 'a politician must say nothing critical about his country on foreign soil'. Alternatively, territory can stand for the *modern state*, which is defined by the constitutional consensus of an epistemic constituency. This is what Habermas has called '*Verfassungspatriotismus*'. The distinction between nation and state is important, although it seems to disappear in the concept of the nation-state. For example, Giddens (1985:120) claims: 'A nation [...] only exists when a state has a unified administrative reach over the territory over which its sovereignty is claimed'. However, for most people a nation refers also to the cultural context within which they define their identity. But, as Habermas has frequently explained, the organisational forms of states rarely coincide with the cultural, linguistic and historic life-worlds.[52] The German nation has hardly ever been living under the unified administration over one territory.[53] On the other hand, there are many states, which administer several national groups. Although one may argue that the Austrian-Hungarian empire failed because of its cultural heterogeneity, the United Kingdom demonstrates the successful integration of several nations into a single and even unitary state.

Because Europe does not have a clearly defined polity, the symbolic function of territory remains ambivalent. Is Europe a geographic concept, reaching from the Atlantic to the Urals, as de Gaulle believed? And if Moscow is part of it, what about Novosibirsk and Vladivostok? Is Europe a cultural community, as Helmut Schmidt (2000) has emphasised? Or is it a political-administrative project as neofunctionalist integrationists pretend? Where are Europe's borders? If we consider territory as a linguistic symbol that stands for Europe's polity, and if this polity is founded on a constitutional consensus by European citizens, then the answer is simple: 'Europe' is a political institution, which finds its limits in peoples' willingness to play by its rules. This means that 'Europe' remains an institution that is potentially open to accepting any amount of members. But at the same time the institution must be based on individual acceptance and agreement of its constitutional and normative content, rather than on governments' *raison d'État*. The cultural delimitation of such a European Union is then derived by individual preferences which may reflect conventional values and cultural contexts from both national and European backgrounds, and this increases the probability that individual citizens will accept playing by the rules of a European Constitution. Such constitution is democratically legitimate and the geographic extension of its territory depends on its legitimacy. But there is nothing wrong, or discriminatory, if in some countries citizens reject such constitutional consensus because their attachment to conventional values is too strong. What matters is constructing a constitution that will sustain and deepen a collective acceptance of its constitutive rules.

Theory (IV): Power and Legitimacy

Constitutive rules also *create* power. A European Constitution will therefore invest power into institutions. By exercising this power, institutions make the constitution a reality. This is not the same as 'allocating power between different public authorities.'[54] *Power is defined as the capacity of some persons to produce intended and unforeseen effects on others.*[55] By assigning the status of legitimacy to regulative rules, constitutive rules create the very capacity of producing certain distributive effects. Searle (1995:100) calls this *conventional* power and rightly distinguishes it from brute physical power. I will reserve the term *conventional power* to power, which is legitimised by consensus based on background values (step I in the stochastic consensus model). I will call *institutional power* that, which is founded on normative consensus (steps II and III). Brute physical power may be associated with Hobbes' 'natural state',[56] where individuals live in a state of war.[57] Hobbes defines 'war' as a time when the will of competitors (*voluntas certandi*) obtains satisfaction by the power (*vis*) of words and acts.[58] He then argues that it is a matter of rationality (*recta ratio*) to seek peace by entering contracts, but contract enforcement requires 'civil government'. Hence for Hobbes, institutional power is a way of transcending 'brute physical power'. This insight has been lost by anarchists and modern libertarians. They focus on the coercive power of the State.[59] De Jasay (1998:271) calls this 'discretionary power' which 'permits the state to make its subjects do what it wants, rather than what they want'. This is a violation of liberty, which has given rise of the claim to organise society without a state. However, the problem here is the legitimacy of the state. A state that does not do what its subjects want it to do is illegitimate. A state that is to preserve peace must be legitimate.

The problem re-appears in European policy-making. Given that policy preferences are largely formed in the conventional context of nation-states, a high degree of dissent, if not conflict, on substantive issues prevails in the European polity. Hence, a 'common' European policy decision is easily perceived as 'Brussels imposing something nobody wants'. Rather than creating a 'European super-state', voluntary co-operation between national governments appears as the appropriate method to give legitimacy to European policy decisions. In Chapter Five I will show why this approach will not work efficiently. Institutional power, based on European constitutional consensus, will endogenously create a European Republic.

In civilised societies conventional and institutional power are far more important than brute force. It is true, the power of the state is often discussed in terms of the state's monopoly to use violence. When rules are not adhered to, sanctions may be necessary to enforce compliance. This is the task of the police and military. Yet, the fear of sanctions can never be the main motivation for rule following. One reason is that in an uncertain world, contracts are always incomplete and the normative content of rules provides the orientation for what is not explicit. Another reason is that the costs of policing through brute physical power are too high to be sustainable, as all dictatorial regimes sooner or later found out. Hence, the legitimacy of a state also determines its power.

How is it possible that legitimacy should be able to create power? The answer is contained in a simple logical operation by which all institutional reality is created and constituted. It has the form of the proposition (Searle, 1995:111):

> We collectively accept, acknowledge, recognise, go along with etc., that (S has power, S does A).

This proposition is at the core of constitutive rules. In other words, the collective acceptance of a constitution simultaneously creates legitimacy and the capacity to produce intended effects. Unless rules are considered to be legitimate, they will not be collectively accepted and therefore have no power.

Legitimacy can be defined as *the propensity of members of a group (society) to obey the rules set by a regulator in the absence of either punishments or rewards for doing so.*[60] This poses the question why anyone would do so without immediate rewards.[61] Max Weber has provided an answer by building the concept of legitimacy around the idea that individuals may act *according to the ideas and orientations they derive from a social context (an 'order') in which the normative content is accepted as 'valid'* (Weber, 1972:16).[62] Hence, legitimacy consists of two dimensions: normativity and acceptance.[63] Yet the acceptance (validity) of certain rules depends on the coherence of their normative content with the background of value standards against which they are evaluated. For example, before the Single European Act in 1986, different national approaches to regulation and the pressures on governments from domestic groups with an interest in preserving the status quo (their cultural background) frequently delayed harmonising legislation. When the Commission sought to accelerate the process, it often exacerbated this problem by paying too little attention to the genuine attachment of people to their familiar ways and cultures (Wallace and Wallace, 2000:89). Only when the principle of mutual recognition was accepted, was it possible to advance consensually (including qualified majority voting) with market integration. This example reminds us of the two main sources for the legitimacy of rules which are always present in societies: cultural background and rational deliberation; it also shows that a lack of legitimacy produces a lack of power.

The first source of legitimacy is dependant on the background against which these rules are operating. Personal values and the familiar ways of cultural and linguistic contexts structure human preferences and behaviour 'naturally', i.e. without further reflection. In Chapter One, we called these values 'naturalistic' or conventional. Getting stuck in naturalistic preferences and conventions often leads to invoking 'civilisation' as a term of guidance and legitimacy that subsequently justifies a 'clash of civilisations', where conflict between states will increasingly take the form of normative disputes (see Huntington, 1993; Halliday, 1996). Similarly, thinking that inflation is bad or federalism is good seems as 'natural' to a German, as social responsibility in the framework of the welfare state to a Swede and the freedom to carry arms to an American. The same is true for the acceptance of human rights as a political norm in the Western world or of competition in the context of a liberal market economy. People largely behave the way they do, because they have always done so. This is *legitimacy by convention*. The modern nation-state has been the constitutional framework, within which conventional values have provided legitimacy for policy-making for at least 200 years.[64] It has thereby become an integrated part of the ways we interpret policy-making. But we must not forget that it is only one form of legitimising power - and a very conventional one as well, which may be in need of re-evaluation.

The other source of legitimacy for policy-making rules derives from collective reflection, deliberation and evaluation with reference to some other valid norms. Here, legitimacy is derived on the basis of reason that transcends the immediacy of cultural context. This form of legitimacy holds therefore the claim to universality, while the former emphasises particularity. For example, the creation of the euro as a single currency drew its legitimacy from the existence of the single market with the four freedoms as explicit norms, while opposition to the euro was focusing on the preservation of national currencies as part of tradition and cultural context. Reflection on moderate inflation in the 1970's modified conventional preferences in France or Italy in the light of new evidence and the apparent success of the German model. Similarly, the concept of citizenship, which entitles persons to certain rights, can be based on the ethnic concept of a common background or on the universalistic concept of adherence to shared norms of equality, liberty and individual rights. These are examples for conventional policy preferences being modified or abandoned in favour of new preferences incorporating both, rational arguments and respect for others.

Because most, if not all, rules draw on both sources of legitimacy the character or form of a constitution is largely determined by the relative weight given to these two traditions. However, once full consensus has been established, it becomes part of the conventional background. Habermas has described this process beautifully for the creation of the European nation-state:

'In the nineteenth century, the peoples of Europe - each on its own, of course - were faced with a structurally similar problem. A European identity, which today has to be created from a communicative context stretching over national public spheres, was at that time the product of national elites, and took the form of a double-sided national consciousness. Of course, the idea of the nation in its populist version led to devastating acts of exclusion, to the expulsion of enemies of the state - and to the annihilation of Jews. But in its culturalistic version, the idea of the nation also contributed to the creation of a mode of solidarity between persons who had until then remained strangers to one another. The universalistic reformation of inherited loyalties to village and clan, landscape and dynasty was a difficult and protracted process, and it did not permeate the entire population until well into the twentieth century, even in the classical nation-states of the West. Regarding the political unification of Europe, we now stand, if not in an entirely comparable situation, then certainly before a similar task to the one that our Germanists faced for the political unification of their nation' (Habermas, 2001b:18).

Sovereignty, Constitutions and People

The concept of constitutive rules allows us to clarify the notion of sovereignty, which underlies the debate about a European Constitution. Sovereignty is often discussed in terms of its symbols: the flag, an army, the head of the Queen on a bank note etc. However, although the symbolic features of sovereignty are important because the assignment of status and function in the creation of institutions is impossible without them (Searle, 1995:68), I will focus here on the nature of sovereignty as a *rule of last resort*. This will be useful when dealing with the concepts of federalism and subsidiarity in the next chapter.

We have said that regulative rules usually focus on the distribution of costs and benefits derived from human actions, while constitutive rules make the creation of these costs and benefits possible in the first place. Because constitutive rules govern regulative rules, they have often been assimilated to ultimate or absolute power.[65] *Sovereignty is the power to set the ground-rules and those who can do so legitimately are called 'the sovereign'.* Early political philosophers like Bodin and Hobbes, or at least their followers, did not always distinguish clearly the functional, epistemic aspect of sovereignty as rules of last resort from the individuals who were the ontological carriers of this function.[66] Therefore, all too often sovereignty has been amalgamated with the sovereign. This was certainly so in absolutist France and is still the case in some British concepts of Parliament's authority today.

In modern political theory 'the people' are assumed to be the sovereign. However, this begs the question, what kind of entity 'the people' is. European political thought has been dominated by two different conceptions, a holistic tradition reaching from today's communitarianists back to Hegel, Althusius and Plato, and an individualist interpretation reflected in political liberalism à la Rawls and Habermas and the philosophy of Kant and the Enlightenment or Popper's open society. In the holistic version, 'a people' is an organic whole, a unity, oneness. In the liberal and democratic tradition, 'the people' are a set of individuals, who arc autonomous and equal. I refer here to the distinction made by Popper (1995:80 and 100) and Dumont (1985:12), whereby *holism* describes an ideology,[67] which subordinates the individual under the whole (serving the community)[68] and primarily emphasises 'order' and hierarchy, i.e. the conformity of each element to its role in a whole. By contrast, *individualism* values first of all the human individual and sees society (the whole) as serving individual self-fulfilment. These political values are also reflected in the constitutive rules of economic systems. Under the holistic conception the needs of men (and women) are subordinated to mankind and the principle of hierarchy dominates traditional holistic economies (Collignon 1999). In the modern world, individual needs come before the collective. Contractual relationships structure the ground-rules of the modern economy.[69] Autonomous individuals are kept together by contracts, which are based on the norms of freedom and equality and also on rights; individuals recognise their collective interests in the social contract, rather than in a hierarchically structured whole. Hence, individualism is the normative foundation of modernity. Of course, as Dumont always insists, in every society both principles, holism and individualism coexist, but what matters is their mutual articulation, which makes one principle dominate whilst containing the other (Dumont 1991:11-22).

Even in the 16th and 17th century, long before the French Revolution, political philosophers referred to the 'sovereignty of the people', although it was 'exercised by only one', i.e. the monarch (Rosanvallon, 1992:30). But this traditional, medieval concept of people as an organic unit with one representative must be clearly distinguished from the modern concept of *demos*, which has individuals as its foundation.[70] In the old perception 'a people' (*ein Volk*) was an organic whole (*le peuple-corps social*), defined by the shared identity of language, descent and locality i.e. by their context. Those who did not share these cultural values were foreigners, aliens or traitors and remained excluded. In this context, the political role of the people was to provide public approval as an expression of consensus.[71] But from the modern view, the people *are* an aggregation of individuals, capable of reflection and rational choice. This principle of republican autonomy (Habermas 2001b:60) logically leads to the right to vote on collective decisions and creates the perspective of self-government (Rosanvallon, 1992:24-48). The French Revolution 1789 emancipated the individual from its communitarian subjection by proclaiming free and equal citizens as the sovereign. Policy-making became the expression of a general consensus to which *every individual citizen had a right to concur*.[72] The modern democratic ideal of the sovereign people is inclusive and individualistic; the traditional is exclusive and communitarian.[73]

The confusion between these two concepts of people shows up in the European debate when sovereignists claim that there can be no European democracy because 'there is no European people'. However, this view overlooks the fact that sovereignty, as any institution, is an epistemic concept, which only exists in the minds of those who accept it as their belief (Searle, 1998). This means that sovereignty can indeed draw its legitimacy from a cultural context, as sovereignists claim. But sovereignty also becomes legitimised through collective deliberation when individual citizens accept the constitutive rules by which policies are made. There is no reason why European citizens (i.e. individuals) could or should not agree on a constitution for the administration of their common affairs.

In Collignon and Schwarzer (2003) we have shown that deliberative processes have significantly contributed to the creation of European Monetary Union. Cowles (1995) and Sandholtz and Zysman (1989) have also noticed evidence for business mobilisation pushing for further integration. However, public deliberation on European policies still remains confined to ad-hoc and temporary initiatives. So-called policy deliberation in the Council has very little to do with an open democracy (Gargarella, 2000). The arguments are rarely made public and in any case they are prefabricated by national administrations and leave little space for the rational exchange of the best arguments. What is missing in Europe is a structured public sphere where European citizens, rather than governments as the proprietors of national subjects, contribute to the definition of collective policy preferences. The modern vision of autonomous citizens, *who have a right to participate* in the choice process of collective decisions, requires more democratic legitimacy than simply democratically elected governments negotiating on their behalf.[74] Europe's multilevel governance, contrary to republican federalism,[75] is a mechanism to *exclude* citizens at the European policy making level. What creates 'a European people,' a *demos*, is European-wide deliberation about the adequacy of policy choices and this requires an integrated polity, committed to and by constitutional consensus. Such a European polity needs to be *constructed*. It does not emerge 'naturally,' although our model of stochastic consensus explains this 'construction' as the endogenous creation resulting from communicative practices, rather than from the exogenous imposition of a European super-state. A European Constitution must therefore focus on setting up structures for European-wide policy deliberation.

Constitutions and Justice

Our discussion so far has yielded the result that human volitions, choices and actions depend on values and norms and are structured by rules. Constitutions are sets of 'ultimate rules', or rules of last resort that have normative content. Normativity gives purpose and direction to individual and collective actions. It stipulates, how persons *ought to* act. But in any society individual actions only become consistent, if they follow rules, which are recognised as *valid*. The validity of rules implies that they are legitimate. Therefore the question of how rules become acceptable is crucial for their factual existence.

Our definition of sovereignty as the power to set rules helps to clarify the close link between sovereignty and legitimacy. Day-to-day policy-making is mainly about regulative rules. The laws, directives and regulations issued by governments have a distributive impact. They create winners and losers, and determining who gets what is the genuine domain of markets and politics. However, in order to be acceptable to both, winning and losing parties, regulative rules need to be founded on legitimacy. In fact, legitimacy implies their acceptance and this is, as we have seen, intimately linked to the general background of values and norms. For early modern political philosophers legitimacy was derived from natural law,[76] constructed as the normative foundation of the legal system of state power. Thus, natural law was prior to the State (and to positive law) and rooted in religion and morality,[77] i.e. in the background of European day-to-day life. It acted as a constraint on the ruler. But even for contemporary thinkers, like Rawls and Habermas, constitutions need a moral foundation, which is different from the procedural justification of law. For otherwise positive law would become purely arbitrary.

If regulative rules, i.e. law, depend for their legitimacy on constitutions, what are the principles that give validity to these rules of last resort? They cannot be based on substantive or distributive justice, because constitutive rules are prior to the creation of the social facts, which are the object of regulation. Hence, constitutions require procedural justice, or fairness, for the foundation of their legitimacy.[78] Fair procedures imply that those who recognise them expect that they will yield outcomes consistent with distributive justice. Because the outcomes themselves are uncertain, agreement is possible on rules that realise potentially just distributions. Procedures that would not yield such outcomes would be rejected. Hence, only fair constitutions can be acceptable for everyone. The principle of fairness is a necessary, although not sufficient condition for the general acceptability of a constitution and for the construction of a European polity.

In modern Western societies fair procedures are understood to ensure individuals' equal rights and the protection of their freedom, although traditional holistic ideas of hierarchy, status and need are never totally absent and survive in subordinated forms. Dumont has insisted in all his writings on the fact that it is the articulation of both principles, the individualistic and the hierarchical, which structure a society and give it its particular character. The articulation of these principles is part of the cultural context through which individuals gain their identity. But in the European framework this means that individuals' sense of freedom and autonomy is simultaneously defined by a set of common European values, which partly refer to the modern universalist project of freedom and equality, and partly to their cultural particularities, which are rooted in the traditions of their communities. Hence, a fair constitution for Europe must permit policy realisations that are respectful to both – freedom and political equality, but also giving a voice for particularism and respect for pluralism.[79]

These different normative articulations are also reflected in conceptions of justice. John Rawls (1971) has analysed the structure whereby modern and traditional principles of fairness are both integrated and articulated in the modern conception of justice. His first principle of justice (liberty and equal rights of individuals) contains[80] the second principle (the needs of the least advantaged). The first principles of fairness or justice apply to constitutive rules and procedures. They must be clearly distinguished from the second principles, which give content to regulative rules and are guided by considerations of distributive justice. A legitimate constitution therefore only sets the framework, within which the consensus on the substance of policy decisions can emerge. It must specify just and workable i.e. fair and efficient political procedures without any constitutional restrictions on legislative outcomes:

'It is important to keep in mind that (...) the first principle of justice is to be applied at the stage of constitutional convention. This means that the political liberties of freedom of thought enter essentially into the specification of a just political procedure. Delegates to such a convention (still regarded as representatives of citizens of free and equal persons...) are to adopt, from among the just constitutions that are both just and workable the one that seems most likely to lead to just and effective legislation... This adoption of a constitution is guided by the general knowledge of how political and social institutions work, together with the general facts about existing social circumstances. In the first instance, then, *the constitution is seen as a just political procedure, which incorporates the equal political liberties* and seeks to assure their fair value so that the processes of political decision are open to all on a roughly equal basis. The constitution must also guarantee freedom of thought if the exercise of these liberties is to be free and informed. The emphasis is first on the constitution as specifying a just and workable political procedure so far without any explicit constitutional restrictions on what the legislative outcome may be. Although delegates have a notion of just and effective legislation, the second principle of justice, which is part of the *content of this notion, is not incorporated into the constitution itself.* Indeed, the history of successful constitutions suggests that principles to regulate economic and social inequalities, and other distributive principles, are generally not suitable as constitutional restrictions. Rather, just legislation seems to be best achieved by assuring fairness in representation and by other constitutional devices.' (Rawls 1996:336-337)

This can be understood to mean, that the discussion of the economic rules of European policy-making must focus more on the question of effectiveness and legitimacy than on the normative content of Europe's economic constitution. Such an interpretation has paralysed the Convention's working group on the economic aspects, because the left wanted to go further in defining normative content. This is an important debate. Habermas (2001a:85-103), among others, has raised the issue as to whether European integration can serve as a model for solving the challenges for policy-making resulting from globalisation and saving the welfare state. For many observers this implies making choices about Europe's social model.[81] They therefore suggest that a European Constitution should spell out social and economic norms and define a 'mobilising project'. But, these are questions of distributive justice that must be decided by political process. They are not related to the procedural character of fair constitutive rules. The idea of defining the European social model in a constitution is related to a model of legitimacy, which is different from Rawls liberal-democratic constitutionalising. It is not built on normative self-reflection but on cultural background. This approach belongs to the communitarian shadow-world of modernity. Walzer (1983) provides an account for deriving justice from the particularities of shared history, culture and membership. In the debate on European integration, sovereignists have developed similar arguments (Ferry, 2000:22). For example, Jean-Pierre Chévènement simultaneously called to defend the French Republic against cosmopolitan integrationists and appealed to European values (!) in his crusade against globalisation and the USA.[82] Curiously, as we shall see in the next chapter, this approach is more in line with the anarcho-communitarian tradition of German federalism, than with the modern concept of the Republic as a polity of autonomous, rational citizens as it emerged from the French Revolution. I will now turn to the normative background against which a European Constitution is drafted.

Chapter Four.
Federalism and Subsidiarity

Federalism seems to be the dominating concept of European integration. Both integrationists and sovereignists refer to it – positively or negatively.[83] For some it is a method for efficient governance in a regime of pluralism, for others it is the incarnation of an oppressive super-state. For some it leads to uniformation and the elimination of all peculiarities, for others it is a guarantee to preserve pluralism and differences. I will argue that these different views are not wrong, but simply confused. The confusion stems partially from incoherent norms for policy-making, partly from an ignorance of the ideological origins of federalism and their transformation in the course of history. However, any agreement on a European Constitution that is not simply a fudge requires a clarification of the principles involved. I will therefore discuss in this chapter the normative foundations of federalism. In the next chapter I can then focus on the issue of effective governance.

Federalism is about defining the 'sovereign', or more precisely about defining the group of citizens who bear responsibility for policy-making and establishing its size and range. Who should set the ground-rules for making certain policy decisions? Those who are affected by the consequences (the policy output) or those who share the normative context for making the decision (the policy input)? In the first case, the polity must be extensive to cover the whole range of the policy domain, but not more; in the second it must not be larger than a homogenous epistemic constituency. I will argue that the first case is described by the *principle of regional decentralization*, the second by *subsidiarity*.

Our discussion of sovereignty has made clear that constitutive 'rules of last resort' set up the game by which regulative rules distribute the outcome of policy decisions. The context in which their legitimacy emerges is the polity, i.e. the accepted institutional structures within which individuals aim to determine their own affairs. This legitimacy has two dimensions. As far as the policy output is concerned, these rules should be accepted by all those who are affected by them, i.e. by the policy domain. But this acceptance is the result of deliberative processes in the epistemic constituency, which legitimises the polity. This is the policy input dimension. Ideally, there is a polity for every specific policy issue that covers the entire policy domain and reflects the preferences of an epistemic constituency. In reality, such functional assignment is not practicable and responsibilities for policy choices are bundled.[84] A European Constitution is an attempt to tie different policy functions together. In most modern federal states, the federal government is charged with providing 'big' collective goods, such as national defence, foreign affairs and macroeconomic policy, while the states are responsible for intermediary goods and services such as highways, higher education and public welfare, and local authorities provide local goods and services like fire brigades, primary (sometimes also secondary) education, housing and zoning. Hence, these different jurisdictions (polities) reflect different policy domains and policy-making functions are decentralised when they respond to the limited reach of collective goods. The legitimacy of the policy decision is then derived essentially from those who are concerned and affected by their consequences. Building a road depends on the approval of those who use it and those who live close to it. If the decision to build it raises objections and creates conflict, legitimate public choices are still possible, provided the decision-making (e.g. voting) rules are approved by all members of the relevant polity.

However, it is also clear, that not all polities cover the entire policy domain. Some policy decisions affect individuals outside the polity, others only a small sub-group within. In the later case regional decentralisation is the appropriate response, in the former delegation and centralisation of sovereignty at a 'higher' level. While the noise of a highway may affect even individuals who do not drive, the road linking houses in a new settlement only affects a small subset of all those who may pass by on a long-distance road. The construction of a local school requires the approval of a local and not the national policy domain, while the content taught in the school may affect society as a whole. Hence polities providing local goods also require only local constituencies.

One would expect a modern theory of federalism to define decision-making institutions, i.e. jurisdictions, by drawing on their legitimacy from epistemic constituencies, which are (reasonably) congruous with the policy domain. In this case, different levels of government jurisdiction are defined by their output to the policy domain, i.e. decisions are made for those affected by them, and they are legitimised by a polity that reflects the views of these individuals as their input. Oates has called this the case of 'perfect correspondence' (1972:34) and has defined a federal government as:

> 'A public sector with both centralised and decentralised levels of decision-making in which choices made at each level concerning the provision of public services are determined largely by the demands for the services of the residents of (and perhaps others who carry on activities in) the respective jurisdictions.' (1972:17)

This definition contains both an 'economic' dimension with respect to the allocation of collective goods and a 'political' dimension that defines their utility. Because public goods are defined by their externalities, an efficient jurisdiction should cover precisely the entire policy domain. This is the economic argument to which I will return in the next chapter. But the demand for collective goods arises from political evaluations by epistemic constituencies and choices made in the polity. I will first deal with these political aspects of federalism in this chapter.

Manifestations of Federalism

The federalist project stood at the core of the European integration process over the last 50 years. Jean Monnet created the *Committee for the United States of Europe*, and Altiero Spinelli inspired the European federalist movement. But from the beginning, 'sovereignism' was federalism's shadow. De Gaulle declared '*L'Europe des patries*' and practiced the politics of 'empty chair' when his partners did not agree with him. In line with Monnet's gradual step-by-step approach the precise form of the European federal model always remained in a *flou artistique*. Partly, this ambiguity has helped to overcome opposition to European integration. But in order to create acceptance and a commitment to a European Constitution it is necessary to clarify the concept.

What does federalism actually mean? Why is it such a persistent issue? In recent years, federalist ideas have found renewed interest in the world. They have not only stimulated the debate on the European Union's governance, but even within member states like Italy, Spain and Belgium they have remained on the agenda. Federalism has even made an impact in traditionally unitary states like the United Kingdom, where regional governments in Scotland and Wales were created, or in France, who had to deal with Corsican separatists.

Political scientists distinguish between *federations* i.e. social institutions and organisations, and *federalism*, an ideology (King, 1982; Burgess and Gagnon, 1993; Burgess, 2000). Federations are often considered to be sovereign states, although the term may also be applied to other forms of associations of separate groups, such as industrial or workers' federations. According to King (1982:20) a federation is defined as:

> 'An institutional arrangement, taking the form of a sovereign state, and distinguished from other such states solely by the fact that its central government incorporates regional units in its decision procedure on some constitutionally entrenched basis.'

This is the modern, *republican*[85] concept of a federation as realised archetypically in the US constitution. It is usually associated with centralising federalism. An alternative concept of federation is 'self-rule plus shared rule' (Elazar, 1987:12). As we will see, this reflects the 'traditional' or holistic view of decentralising federalism.

Federalism is an epistemic or value concept that describes a normative structure for the state (Burgess, 1993; 2000:27; McKay 1999:25). It translates into a range of different ideologies[86] and has a long and complex history, which dates back to the beginning of the modern epoch as a 'counter-tradition' to the liberal ideas of Western state and society (Hueglin, 1999:3).

Federalist ideas are not uncontested. In the European context, criticism is particularly linked to the issue of sovereignty. The modern doctrine of sovereignty since Bodin and Hobbes argues for the concentration of power at the centre of the state, claiming that this power must be absolute, total, illimitable and *indivisible*. The above-mentioned definition of federations by King reflects this view of a federation as a state, but considers that sovereignty can be divided and decentralised according to the functions of policy making. Citizens are simultaneously the sovereign of the local state and the federation. It would seem that the monist axiom of Republicans à la Bodin would violate such pluralist federalism: who will exert the ultimate power in the state if there are several authorities? How can power and authority be shared? But this is the wrong question. What matters are the functions which relate policy-making rules to their policy domains. For example, because the constitution of the United States of America considers 'the people' as the ultimate source of power, it was able to simultaneously invest the federal government and state governments with powers of policy-making, although these levels covered different functions and the constitution provided plenty of institutional restrictions (checks and balances) to ensure the separation of responsibilities and policy domains. This reasoning is contested by European opponents of federalism, especially in unitary states. If a centralised European government could overrule nation-states, what would that mean for the democratic legitimacy of national governments?[87] I will return to this question below.

The alternative interpretation of federations, as given by Elazar goes back to Bullinger and Althusius in the 16th century and assumes that *sovereignty can be shared* between autonomous public entities. Hence the distinction is between policy-making input, and not along functional lines of output. Here, federalism is seen as a political system constructed from collectives that are generally alike and equal (Hueglin, 1999:222). According to whether more weight is given to the 'alikeness' or the 'equality', this interpretation of federalism is either more 'communitarian' or 'anarchist', but they actually belong both to the holistic tradition of political thought. As Michael Taylor (1982) has shown, anarchy ('doing without the state') is only viable if relations between people are those characteristic of 'community'. Hence, the pluralism of voluntarily co-operating authorities must be contained in an *organic order* where the parts conform to the whole because the association is based on trust and consent, built from below. One easily detects the holistic connotations in these formulations.

The coexistence of the modern republican and the holistic anarcho-communitarian traditions under the label of federalism has intrigued many scholars. King (1982) has distinguished between federalist centralism, decentralism and balanced centralism. Burgess (2000) sees centralising federalism as an 'Anglo-American' *intra*-state relation and decentralisation as a 'Continental European' *inter*-state tradition. From my point of view, intra-state relations describe the policy functions with respect to policy domains, inter-state relations concern different epistemic constituencies. Elazar (1987:34) has rejected the notion of 'decentralisation' in favour of 'non-centralised' political systems where 'power is so diffused that it cannot be legitimately centralised or concentrated without breaking the structure and spirit of the constitution.' Sometimes centralising federalism is assimilated to a 'federalist state' and distinguished from more decentralised 'confederations'. In recent years decentralising federalism has been promoted by European political leaders under the label of *subsidiarity* and as *New Federalism* in the USA. For our purposes, King's distinction is still useful, for it addresses some of the major argument for and against federalism in Europe. In a subsequent section I will show that these two interpretations of federalism go back a long way in European history.

Centralising Federalism

The centralisation of power implies a hierarchical relationship between a federal centre and subordinate member states. Some decisions are reserved to central agents who have displaced earlier, more multiform and disparate decision-makers, like the confederal states in America. There is a binding effect of policy decisions because, the constitutional consensus accepts the entire hierarchy as one polity. The approach emphasises the coherence of policy-making as a 'top down' exercise of power. In the context of European integration, this centralisation is called the *delegation* of national sovereignty to a European institution. The creation of the European Central Bank, the assignment of competition and trade policy to the Commission, were centralisation of this kind. Yet, while the 'Community method' of European integration built on the delegation of government functions to a supra-national authority, the issue of the relevant polity was never clearly addressed. The constitutional consensus therefore remained fragmented within national polities, while multilevel governance 'aggregated' national preferences through intergovernmental negotiations. Instead of creating an integrated European polity where matters of common concern are publicly deliberated, the European Union maintains a high degree of political dissent by keeping policy deliberations exclusively to the Council. As a consequence, today's EU institutions reflect neither centralising nor decentralising federalism.

Regional decentralisation of power implies that the number of agents taking decisions is increased rather than restricted. Decisions are then supposed to be taken by the agents themselves in a 'bottom up' approach rather than *for* them by a delegated authority (King 1982:45). The range of decision-making is then logically the policy range, and citizens can express their preferences on different functional levels. This is an efficient criterion because the level of decentralisation depends on the policy range, i.e. the limited nature of externalities.

However, in Europe, decentralisation is not understood in this sense. Under the intergovernmental approach to European integration decisions are not taken *by European citizens for themselves*, but by member states governments *on behalf* of their citizens. This is an important distinction between European practices and the modern democratic republican concept of policy-making. Because the European polity is splintered into different epistemic constituencies, coherence between the political domain and the European polity is prevented. Policy decisions *cannot reflect the preferences of those who are affected by them*.[88] Hence the *flou artistique* of European integration tried to combine simultaneously bottom-up and top-down approaches.[89]

Centralist federalists are concerned that multiple governments are inefficient, and carry the danger of conflict, even war, when divergent interests clash and no overriding authority exists. They want a 'strong constitution'. For example the authors of the *Federalist Papers*, a subgroup of the Founding Fathers of the US Constitution in Philadelphia, shared the ideology of centralising federalism. Their intention was to create an efficient centralised government, not to retain local state identities. They promoted a federal government legitimated by popular consent in the Union, not by the delegated authority conceded by member states and reflecting the preferences arising from local backgrounds. In the next chapter I will show that their approach followed impeccably the logic of collective action.

Interestingly, the arguments advanced in 1787-1788 for increased centralisation in the US constitution were related to the preservation of peace. The effects of a closer union were expected to secure a better defence against external threats, against war between the member states and against domestic factions and insurrection, thereby simultaneously providing a solid base for external trade and private prosperity. These arguments have a strong echo in the debate on European integration. However, in order to prevent the misuse of increased power by the centre, the US constitution relied less on the veto by states, and more on a system of protections for the defence of *individuals* against the centralising state.[90] First of all, the constitution derived its powers from all citizens and not only from the Union's member states. Secondly, it aimed at dividing and balancing the power of the centre itself. Thirdly, the constitution assigned popularly sanctioned governments territorially between the national centre and various state localities. Finally, it divided up the interests of various sections of the population so that no one of these could automatically and unjustly prevail (King 1982:28). I call this the *republican model of federalism*.

The concern for the protection of individual rights against the state has also emerged in Europe, although only in a weak form. It has been bundled into the Charter of Fundamental Rights, which was 'declared' at the European Council in Nice in December 2000 (Bossi, 2001). However, the Charter was not integrated into EU law and does not give the same degree of protection to individual liberties as, say, the US Constitution. Furthermore, the European Union provides few institutional 'checks and balances' other then intergovernmental 'hold-ups'.[91] The reason for *this weakness of individual rights is partly related to the fact that centralising federalism has remained weak, because individual rights are hijacked by the communitarian values of governments*. Europe still seems to be dominated by the holistic vision that individuals are 'subjects' of their states or governments.

An early centralising federalist in Europe was Saint-Simon, a contemporary to the American Federalists, who argued two hundred years ago for a distinctly European parliamentary federation. He thought that only a political union of the continent, starting with England and France, could inhibit the recurrence of war (Saint-Simon, 1814). In a visionary passage he wrote:

'Europe is a violent state, everyone knows it and says as much. (...) In any coming together of peoples, as of individuals, common institutions are obligatory. Without them, only might decides. To expect to create peace in Europe by treaties and congresses is as much as imagining that social systems may survive on the mere basis of convention and agreement. What is required is a compelling force to unite divergent wills, to concert their activity, to render their interests common and their commitments firm'. (Quoted in King, 1982:31)

It is not difficult to detect that the Founding Fathers of European unification, Monnet, Schuman, Adenauer, but also Schmidt, Giscard d'Estaing or Kohl, Delors and Mitterrand shared similar views,[92] even if they did not necessarily call themselves 'federalists'.

Decentralising Federalism

The centralising approach is often contrasted with federalism as a decentralising ideology. Here, the *multitude of decision-making units agree voluntarily on a covenant to share the exercise of power equally.* The federation is seen as a composition of states, hence the opposite of the 'unitary state'.[93]

Although centralising and decentralising federalism seem to have diametrically opposed intentions, they both perceive the organising principle of society representing a balance or equilibrium between opposed forces. Decentralising federalism is more strongly associated with the idea of 'give and take', reciprocity and notions of compromise, while centralising federalism gives more weight to constitutional rights and the function of statehood, emphasising contractual agreements. Both approaches are building on the concept of compact or contract, but decentralising federalism has integrated them into a holistic articulation of society that resembles communitarian ideals. It regards the federation as a *foedus*, a pact deriving from *fides* or trust. The emphasis on trust is the basis for strong consensual attitudes in policy-making, but also for a relatively high degree of cultural homogeneity, linked to exclusiveness, and bordering sometimes on xenophobia.[94]

The holistic character of decentralising federalism implies a collective agreement that is freely and mutually consented to, each party surrendering a degree of autonomy in exchange for some compensating *advantage* (King 1982:56) although not for some *rights*. Hence trust is required and seems most easily to emerge when communities share similar backgrounds. This is the communitarian dimension of decentralising federalism. It describes consequently a set of political groupings, which coexist and interact as autonomous entities united in a common order (Friedrich, 1974). The emphasis on a community with a structured order, on a hierarchy based on authority and status (competences) rather than on fundamental rights by individual citizens, and the idea that sub-units must serve the common interest of the whole, characterises decentralising federalism as a holistic ideology.

Because decision-making here is essentially 'bottom up', some observers see in decentralising federalism a fundamental democratic quality. Especially in Germany, where federalism was reintroduced after the Nazi-era by the Allied forces seeking to prevent a 'strong' unitary German state, federalism is often considered a pillar of democracy. However, this view mixes the republican i.e. state-like and federalist i.e. intergovernmental dimensions, which are both realised in the constitution of the Federal Republic of Germany. It is usually forgotten that, although Bismarck's Reich created a weak central government with strong states and decentralising federalist principles, the German Reich can hardly be called a democratic state. There is nothing intrinsically democratic in federalism.

The apparent autonomy of communities in holistic tradition made decentralising federalism appealing to anarchists like Kropotkin, Bakunin and Proudhon (Woodcock, 1975). Many early anarchists believed that once the existing, repressive state was overthrown, a new, voluntary, natural unit would emerge to take its place. Bakunin expected that 'when the states have disappeared a living fertile, beneficent unity of regions as well as nations ... by way of free federation from below upward - will unfold itself in all its majesty.' (quoted in Olson, 1971:130). These writers hoped to overcome power by structuring society around the associative principle of mutual aid, which they contrasted with the functions of the modern state.[95] Proudhon claimed that 'every state is by nature expansionist' with the exception of federations. He thought that Europe was much too large for any single federation and therefore needed to be built as a federation of federations. Hierarchy always creeps in when individualism is rejected. Kropotkin clearly emphasised the self-identity feeling over reason: 'The sophism of the brain cannot resist the mutual-aid feeling.' Thus, decentralising federalism, anarchism and communitarianism share the common logic of naturalistic preferences.

Even if decentralising federalism attaches great weight to the notion of compact and voluntary agreement, its holistic ideology poses a problem. For modern contract theory requires the notion of *individuals* as contracting partners, while federal forms of government imply arrangements between *groups* in which individuals disappear as autonomous actors. It is this fact, which makes decentralising federalism an ideology that sits uneasily between the traditional view of hierarchical communities and the modern liberal state where free individuals assume responsibility for the collective because they respect and defend the fundamental equality of their rights. To understand this dilemma correctly, we must dig for the historic roots of federalism in European history. Without this knowledge one cannot appreciate the difficulty that republican France or the unitary UK have with federalism, while it seems so 'natural' for communitarian Germans and ambivalent in Italy or Spain. The forward-looking hurried reader may jump to the next section.

Federalism and the Origins of Sovereignty

Both federalism and sovereignty are 'modern' phenomena in the sense that they emerged in the 15th and 16th century with the expansion of the monetary market economy, contracts and individualism. Both were an attempt to overcome the tensions, anarchy and conflict which the new economic system produced and an answer to the need to integrate autonomous individuals into a state. However, the forms of this integration were rather different. International relations theory links sovereignty to the modern state as it emerged after the Thirty Years War at the Peace of Westphalia in 1648.[96] However, by that time the concept had already grown up. Originally, sovereignty with federalism as its twin were conceived by rape. Even though Protestant Swiss theologians like Heinrich Bullinger, the successor of Zwingli, had already published some ideas on federations earlier[97], and Machiavelli had already developed the vision of the autonomous prince, the defining event from which the ideologies of sovereignty and federalism developed was the St Bartholomew's Day Massacre of 1572. It has to be seen against the background of the emerging modernity in Europe.[98]

The Middle Ages had come to an end, when the traditional community subsistence economies (*Naturalwirtschaft*), with hierarchy as the dominant principle of regulation, were increasingly replaced and complemented by individual contract relations in monetary economies. The development of market transactions in the 15th and first half of the 16th century simultaneously undermined traditional habits, customs and cultures and ushered in an era of social change, upheaval and conflict. Gold and silver were the settlement assets in these commercial transactions. As the amount of buying and selling increased, market structures became more complex. With only limited amounts of gold and silver in circulation the economic expansion was based on the increasing use of credit (Muldrew 1998:3)[99] and the need for increasing the supply of gold and silver. This had three consequences. The first two changed political ideologies, the third the political economic structure of Europe, the consequences of which affect us to this day. Firstly, the hierarchical principle of the subsistence economy, where the allocation of wealth takes place according to status and rank, was increasingly replaced by the contractual principle[100], which implied *equality* between contracting partners and the *freedom* to accept or refuse the terms. Thus, freedom and equality became the normative foundation for the project of modernity with the political right and left giving greater weight to one or the other of these two values. Secondly, the monetary economy developed a *culture of credit* whereby the creation of wealth was based on the reputation and trustworthiness of individuals. Thus, individualism developed in a context, where credit was a public means for social communication and the circulating of judgements about the value of other members of community (Muldrew 1998:2). Trust became the link, which made contracts possible and kept autonomous individuals together. This is well expressed by the famous slogan among London's City: 'My word is my bond'. These two dimensions - contract and credit - have formed the economic backbone of modern individualism.[101]

Third, Spain had become the dominant power in Europe partly thriving on the import of gold and silver from the newly discovered colonies in the West Indies and America. However, the influx of precious metals and other goods undermined the Castilian economy by what is now called 'Dutch disease'. The Spanish economy became overvalued, leading to an increasing share of imports, but hampering local production (Elliot, 2002:193-199). This undermined the Empire's tax base and finance. Public debt had to close the gap, fostering a prosperous rentier class but preventing the emergence of the private credit culture, which was so dynamic in Central Europe.[102] The Spanish Empire also sought revenue by a vigorous system of imperialism. But while it ultimately lost control of Spanish Flanders, the grip on the Italian peninsula was strong. As a consequence, the emerging modern individualism of Italy's *renaissance* and monetary economy was repressed and the traditional economic structures of oligarchical estates, property rents and public debt caused the 'delay' in Italy's transition to modernity (Galli della Loggia, 1998). But the economic weaknesses of Spain also provided opportunities for the new emerging bourgeois classes in Central and Western Europe, that were to transform the world. This provided the background to new ways of thinking about the economy, politics and power.

Economic developments are the key to understanding the change in political ideologies. As chains of credit among merchants grew longer and more complex, defaults became more common. Disputes and litigation about unpaid debts and the risk of downward social mobility created a general climate of economic insecurity. Thus the downside risk of modernity was mistrust, fear and the war 'of every man, against every man' as Hobbes described it.[103] Consequently, limiting agreements or covenants to those one could trust was a way of reducing uncertainty and making the future more predictable.

There were two approaches to deal with these problems: morality and segregation. In the medieval context, a model for how the world ought to be was provided by God's covenant with man. But while the Catholic Church emphasised man's traditional *duty* to God, and the *quid pro quo* in the restitution of damage for those who failed in their duty, Protestants turned to the *individual faith* in God which mirrored the increasing emphasis on *trust* within the everyday social relations of the time (Muldrew, 1998:131-132). Moralism and Puritanism were attempts to reduce insecurity and to restore reliability and trustworthiness. In modern parlance, Protestantism used religion as a commitment device. It therefore became the ideology of the emerging class of modernisers, representing a growing prosperity that distinguished them from the traditional economy.[104]

Secondly, it is easier to trust someone whose background we (!) share, than those who live in less familiar cultures and contexts. Therefore the 'belonging' to a community increased the trustworthiness between individuals. But simultaneously it also reinforced *segregation and exclusion* of individuals from other cultures. The higher the degree of mutual respect within communities, the lower is automatically the respect for outsiders.[105] Hence, the protestant ethics in the emergent monetary economy also increased the potential for disrespect, conflict and ultimately the physical elimination of others. Hence, the thicker matrix of trust and communication within local communities strengthened the particularistic, local and provincial character of values, rather than the universalistic dimension of ethical norms. Intra-communitarian consensus (and conformism) increased inter-community conflicts.

The material and ideological upheavals in the 16th century gave rise to defensive reactions by the traditional sectors of society. Often a return to old values and the elimination of those who were different seemed to be an obvious solution. The development of anti-semitism, especially in Spain where religion was linked to the 'purity of blood', was an early model. It was soon extended to protestants. In this respect, the War of Religions was a precursor of 20th century totalitarianism such as fascism and communism, or more recently Islamic fundamentalism.[106] When on 24 August 1572 20,000 Huguenots, the elite of French protestants, were murdered all over France by order of King Charles IX and his mother Catherine de Medici, this was the first genocide of modern times, eliminating 2 per cent of all French protestants, and more than 1 per cent of the total population of Paris (Ladurie 1987: 310; Hueglin, 1999: 30)[107]. The shock of this massacre led to a massive exodus of Protestant asylum seekers into neighbouring Geneva, Germany, Netherlands and England, with far reaching effects for France's road to modernity and a transfer of political cultures into other parts of Europe that marked subsequent centuries. It also galvanised political thinking into two opposite schools: Jean Bodin laid the foundations for the modern concept of sovereignty in his *Six Livres de la République* (1576). After the English revolution, he was followed in this tradition by Hobbes who published the *Leviathan* in 1651. On the other side Johannes Althusius became the first systematic thinker of federalism, the principles of which were exposed in his *Politica* (1603).

These three early political philosophers had in common the search for a unifying principle, which would allow to overcome the diverging interests, competition, conflicts and wars that seemed to have followed the emerging individualism of their time. They all found this principle in the notion of *sovereignty*. For Bodin, who although not a Huguenot himself, had narrowly escaped the St Bartholomew's Day massacres, the answer consisted in centralising power in the sovereign ruler who was, however, restrained by 'divine and natural law'. Bodin certainly did not want his ruler to be an arbitrary despot, but he also did not want him to be exposed to the control of any other competing power (Hueglin, 1999:46). By centralising power, conflict between competing interests could be avoided. Similarly, two generations later, Thomas Hobbes, whose life had come under threat during the civil war and the turmoil of England's transition to modernity, rejected any notion of mixed sovereignty.[108] Because Hobbes conceived his Commonwealth as a *unanimous* agreement between all individuals,[109] there could be 'no breach of covenant on the part of the sovereign' (Hobbes, 1973:91). Hence, we find here first traces that sovereignty is based on consensus. What makes Hobbes a 'modern' thinker is that he constructed sovereignty from a covenant between individuals[110] about public goods (Kavka, 1986), while 'civil society' reflected the space of norm-regulated competition in a market society. For both Bodin and Hobbes, sovereignty had to be 'indivisible' because it reflected the ultimate authority to settle conflicts.[111]

For Althusius, matters were different. Although he grew up and lived all his life in Protestant environments (mainly in the Low Countries, but also in Geneva and Basle), his political theory remained deeply rooted in the holistic ideologies of traditional societies. Althusius built his political theory on a vision of society that he had inherited from Aristotle, Germanic communitarianism and Calvinism (Hueglin, 1999). This is clearly expressed in the definition of sovereignty:

> 'The (...) right of sovereignty does not belong to individual members, but to all members joined together and to the entire associated body of the realm. For as universal association can be constituted not by one member, but by all the members together, so the right is said to be the property not of individual members, but of the members jointly. Therefore, 'what is owed to the whole (*universitas*) is not owed to individuals, and what the whole owes, individuals do not owe.' (...) By their common consent [the members of the realm, note by the author] are able to establish and set in order matters pertaining to it. And what they have once set in order is to be maintained and followed unless something else pleases the common will. For as the whole body is related to the individual citizens, and can rule, restrain, and direct each member, so the people rules each citizen.' (Althusius, 1964: 65).

The holistic ideology in Althusius' thinking is also manifest in the role of association in guilds, colleges and estates, which had been one of the most important elements of medieval social life (Hueglin, 1999:63). While Bodin sought to eliminate them as autonomous units of political authority, Althusius considered them as 'created by their members' common consent' (Althusius, 1964:28). They were the constituent element of higher authority in the context of an organic social order.

Despite this traditional holism, Althusius as a Protestant thinker had to articulate the logic of the emerging modern economy. He did this through the concept of covenant. In the aftermath of the St. Bartholomew's Day Massacre, many Calvinist-Huguenot publicists developed the idea of a 'double covenant' referring to the Old Testament whereby God had entered a covenant not only with Israel's rulers, but also with his people.[112] They thereby transformed the covenant idea into a principle of contractual mutuality between people and ruler, which gave them also implicitly the right to remove tyrants. The 'people' became thereby equal subjects under God's authority, while the kings were partners only on the condition that they upheld their obligations (Hueglin, 1999:57-58). However, given the fundamental equality before God and his natural law, Protestant ideology was also open to absorb Aristotelian ideals about the virtue of citizens' participation in public affairs. Nevertheless, Althusius did not anticipate modern democracy where citizens act as autonomous individuals. Instead he saw every person as a 'member' of a community, which assigned positions, status and rank to them in the normative context of conventional hierarchy. The 'freedom of the Jewish Covenant' consisted in the escape from Egypt, in the liberty to live and practice one's cultural identity, not in the freedom of the individual.

Like Bodin and Hobbes, Althusius sought to overcome the anarchy and conflict resulting from the monetary market economy and the correlated individualism. But while the French and English traditions gave predominance to contractual agreements between individuals and therefore to rights and ultimately the state, the German, Swiss and Dutch traditions developed a corporatist view of society, where *conflict was eliminated by trust and consensus, which required maintaining cultural homogeneity and purity.*[113] In that respect Protestant holism was no better than its Catholic equivalent, the Counter-Reformation. The context of a shared cultural context facilitated the emergence of social consensus within the community, but also conflict between them. Amongst people who thought the same, trustworthiness was by definition high but outsiders deserved little credit, Althusius (1965:62) was perfectly clear:

'The bond of this body and association is consensus, together with trust extended and accepted among the members of the Commonwealth. The bond is, in other words, a tacit or expressed promise to communicate things, mutual services, aid, counsel, and the same common laws *(jura)* to the extent that utility and necessity of universal social life in a realm shall require. Even the reluctant are compelled to comply with this communication.'

Hence what keeps the community together is the constituency and not the constitutive ruler of the polity. Controlling the epistemic constituency, or rather keeping the polity to remain congruous with the epistemic constituency, was necessary to maintain the bonds of trust. As pointed out above, the imperative of cultural homogeneity would be translated into the rigid imposition of moral behaviour on the members of the community. Puritanical Protestant morality, bordering at times on religious fanaticism, was doubled by intolerance for those outside the community.[114]

The diverging logical perspectives implicit in Althusius' holistic federalism and Bodin's individualist Republic with an absolute ruler are still underlying the interpretation of politics and the state today. Bodin and Hobbes' response to the anarchy of unconstrained individualism was to limit it by the higher authority of natural law, i.e. by norms and reason and ultimately by human rights. They opened the way to absolutist monarchy in France and to the absolute rule of parliament in England. But the absolute reign of constitutive rules also helped to develop the constitutional state *(Rechtsstaat)* as a means to solve conflict between individuals who possessed rights. Only when the regime of the absolute ruler became incoherent with its own norms, because it lived by ever increasing privileges for the aristocracy, the French Revolution re-defined 'the people' as the ultimate sovereign (Rosanvallon, 1992). Bodin's Republic became the nation-state. In contrast to the holistic communitarianism of the Germanic world, the French Revolution firmly established the principle of modern individualism and democratic equality as the dominant ideology of modernity by setting the order of values as: *liberté, égalité, fraternité*.[115] It did, however, maintain the role of a centralised, indivisible state as the highest authority. In the United Kingdom this process was more gradual because the sovereign parliament was able to integrate the Protestant informalism of trust into the growing demands for the rights of freedom and equality. The end result was similar: a unitary democratic state with centralised power.

In an important side effect, the universally applicable rules and rights developed by a centralised government contributed to the harmonisation of cultural contexts, in particular through unified models of education (Oxford and Cambridge in Britain, later Jules Ferry's *éducation nationale* in France). They structured the background against which individuals defined their collective identity. This coincidence helped to transform local communities into the nation-state, while the communitarian model of homogenous cultures concluded holistic 'compacts', which preserved the ethnic separateness of local communities in the Netherlands, Germany and Switzerland.[116] The great synthesis between the two ideological approaches was only achieved by the American revolution.[117] Rather than basing federalism on a covenant of autonomous communities, Madison and his Federalist colleagues established the individual citizen as the sovereign of both, States as well as the Federal Union (Chopin, 2002). They thereby created the modern conception of republican federalism. It is based on the principle of the *division of powers* between centre and regions, i.e. of the separation of policy functions, and it established constitutionally that *citizens hold identity on both levels* (McKay, 1999:160). These historic developments can be traced in the different interpretations given to the ideology of federalism in political debates today. Different versions of federalist ideology therefore recommend very different rules for structuring society and the state.

We may summarise that Bodin's answer to the emerging individualism in monetary economies was the holistic articulation of the state, while Althusius' was the community. However, once individualism became the dominant norm in the late 18th century, it was expressed in the concept of the sovereign citizen, while Althusius' tradition disappeared into the shadow of anarcho-communitarianism.

Subsidiarity

Holistic ideologies violate the normative claims of modern individualism and a monetary market economy. This may explain, why Althusius has remained a political philosopher of the shadow world. One should expect that decentralising holistic federalism has lost its relevance in the modern world, while Bodin and certainly Hobbes are still in the limelight. However, as mentioned above, all societies contain both, individualistic and holistic ideological elements, which they articulate in different forms. In recent years, holistic federalism has found a new lease of life as the 'principle of subsidiarity'. It first appeared in the Maastricht Treaty and in 1997, a new 'Protocol on the Application of the Principles of Subsidiarity and Proportionality' was inserted into the new Amsterdam Treaty. Article 5 of the Amsterdam Treaty and its successor, the Nice Treaty, states:

> 'The Community shall act within the limits of the powers conferred upon it by this Treaty and of objectives assigned to it herein (...). In areas which do not fall within its exclusive competence, the Community shall take action in accordance with the principle of subsidiarity, only if and insofar as the objectives of proposed action, be better achieved by the community. Any action by the Community shall not go beyond what is necessary to achieve the objectives of the Treaty.'

Not by coincidence does this formulation resemble a resolution passed in 1571 by the Church Synod of Emden where Althusius became city syndic in 1603. It declared that:

> 'No parish should predominate over another' and that the provincial or general synody must not deliberate on matters already decided [at the regional level, note by the author] but should instead deal with those matters only upon which previous agreement 'could not be reached' or 'with matters pertaining to all parishes of the province'.'[118]

The principle of subsidiarity is commonly understood to mean that policy-making functions should always be exercised at the lowest possible level, and only 'if necessary' should they be delegated to a higher level. The ambiguity of what is necessary results from the fact that the policy functions are not specified clearly, so that the communitarian principle of input legitimisation by homogenous preference groups interferes with output efficiency of decision-making. The Amsterdam Protocol attempted a clarification by setting a long list of procedures on how to determine the application of the principle, but rather compounded the ambiguity, complementing subsidiarity by the principle of proportionality. Burgess (2000) gives an excellent overview of the difficulties and ambivalences of the subsidiarity principle in the EU Treaties and the 'somewhat confused and confusing context' in which it was developed. I would like to focus here on the holistic roots of subsidiarity that contradict the norms of a modern monetary market economy and liberal individualism.

Subsidiarity derives from a particularly Catholic view of organic society as it was developed in three papal encyclicals, *Rerum Novarum* (1891), *Quadragesimo Anno* (1931) and *Pacem in Terris* (1963). The emergent 'Social Catholicism' of the late 19th century rejected both economic and political liberalism and socialism. The first document was an instrument in the Catholic Church's warfare against the recently united Italian state and its liberal governments.[119] The rapid economic change, especially after the agricultural crisis in the mid 1870's and the return to currency convertibility in 1882 which caused the following boom (De Cecco, 2002), opened the gap between North and South, increased the difficulties of the agricultural sector and led to massive migration of labourers. New policies to combat poverty were needed and the 1890 reforms by Prime Minister Francesco Crispi placed all benevolent institutions under state control. The Pope replied with the encyclica *Rerum Novarum,* which spoke of rights and justice, beseeched the faithful not only to commune (!) with the less fortunate but also to supplement conventional religiosity with social responsibility (Kelikian, 2002:48). Effectively, the church exhorted communitarianism against the modern state:

'It is a fundamental principle of social philosophy, fixed and unchangeable, that one should not withdraw from individuals and commit to the community what they can accomplish by their own enterprise and industry. So, too, it is an injustice and at the same time a grave evil and a disturbance of right order to transfer to the larger and higher collectivity functions which can be performed and provided for by lesser and subordinate bodies. In as much as every social activity should, by its very nature, prove a help to members of the body social, it should never destroy or absorb them.' *(Rerum Novarum* quoted by Burgess, 2000:227)

While the first papal text still idealised the organic society of the feudal age with guilds and professional associations and religion as the social bond, the 20th century experience of communism and fascism led the Church to re-value individuals although still attacking the 'pagan worship of the state' (Kelikian, 2002:59) and insisting on the 'social responsibility' of markets and individuals. This ideology later became one of the explicit foundations of the social market economy in West Germany, but it was effectively accepted by all Christian Democratic parties in Europe after the Second World War. It re-articulated holistic values in a liberal society by accepting individual freedom as the dominant norm, although linking it with the organic principle of socialisation, i.e. family and church, and rejecting the Socialist demands for freedom through equality based on rights and the support of the state.

The 1931 encyclical has been seen as a 'practical compromise between liberalism and socialism' (Hueglin, 1999:155). But, in effect it cut this axis of modernity, which is defined by the contractual norms of *liberté* and *égalité* by re-introducing communitarian *fraternité* (rather than *solidarity*, which is based on the idea of voluntary co-operation of equals) in the form of structured holistic entities. The EU Treaty's subsidiarity principle stands in this tradition, although it replaces Catholic corporatism by intergovernmentalism. The basic actors in the European polity are not individuals, that is to say autonomous citizens, but national governments representing 'member states'. In the words of Hueglin (1999:158):

'Significant actors in the policy fields appear deliberately excluded. Instead, European subsidiarity must be essentially understood as a general clause providing each member state with a veto in the name of national interests as defined by national governments. (...) As a consequence it has been pointed out what the future of the European Union might look like: each member state decides for itself - but the consequences are then to be carried by all.'

It is probably true that the reference to subsidiarity in the Treaties reflected an ingenious political compromise that assuaged the fears of those who felt European Political Union went too far in eroding national sovereignty (e.g. in the UK), or not far enough in establishing common policy standards especially in the social and environmental (e.g. Denmark) (Hueglin, 1999:156). Yet, its ambivalent character translates into legal ambiguity. The principle of subsidiarity has been complemented by the 'principle of proportionality' (article 1 of the Amsterdam Protocol) and the Treaty has reconfirmed the commitment to former article 235 of the Treaty of Rome (now article 308 in the Treaty of Nice), which empowers the Council of Ministers to take on new competencies. Furthermore, the principle of subsidiarity does not seem to be, in practice, justifiable by the European Court of Justice. Hence, this principle does not seem to be suitable to assign policy-making functions to different jurisdictions. What is needed are logical criteria, which take into account the efficiency of policy decisions, i.e. the impact on the policy domain, and the legitimacy of these decisions, based on a large European epistemic constituency. By definition, national governments cannot fulfil this function. Their polity is too narrow with respect to the policy domain and their epistemic constituencies are often even more restricted. The answer must come from republican federalism. In the last chapter I propose the creation of a European Congress as the solution.

Implications for Europe's Constitution

Which conclusions can we draw from this short overview of European political thought on federalism? First of all, at a time when globalisation is carrying the market economy into the last corners of the globe, it is useful to remember the origins and factors that created the cultural innovation of monetary market economies and liberal individualistic ideologies. The enormous economic development that has taken place over the last few centuries would not have been possible without it. However, with the advancement of the monetary economy a process of creative destruction with respect to traditional cultures and economies has taken place. It is not surprising that some of the tensions and conflicts that shook up Europe's history over several centuries are presently re-emerging on a world scale. The destruction of traditional cultural context is creating an environment of uncertainty, mistrust, conflict and defensive reactions in the form of a forced return to traditional and well-established identities and conventions. Even within Europe, globalisation has brought back some of these phenomena in the mild form of populism. Outside Europe, where the destabilisation goes much deeper, the temptation of totalitarian (i.e. eliminative) solutions is strong.

While Europe's history allows us to study many of these problems, it has also produced some solutions. The most dominant is the creation of the modern democratic state as a stabilising framework for the anarchical culture of individualistic markets and the individual citizen as the ultimate sovereign.

Yet, with the globalisation of the monetary market economy, the traditional nation-state has lost its capacity to regulate global markets. With the increasing degree of integration in Europe and beyond, individual actions and government policies are causing externalities, which transcend the territorial framework of nation-states. Thus the creation of a larger regulatory framework becomes imperative, although such a framework can no longer be the traditional nation-state.

Originally, federalism has been a communitarian ideology seeking to create a higher unity out of smaller collective units by voluntary co-operation. However, in its holistic form federalism is incoherent with the larger economic framework in which European integration is taking place. With the creation of the single currency European integration has clearly opted for a monetary market economy as its normative framework. This economic constitution is also the normative foundation for Europe's political system as a liberal democracy (see also Friedrich, 2002a).

This has several implications for a European Constitution. First, it means that such a constitution *must remain neutral with respect to distributional issues* and the normative emphasis between freedom and equality. Political preference formulation must be left to the ongoing public debate between right and left, between liberal centre-right parties and social democrats. Both, freedom and equality are the essence of political modernity. However, a modern constitution *cannot remain neutral with respect to the cleavages between holism and individualism*. A European Constitution must confirm its commitment to modern republican and democratic norms, but also to their precedence over holistic and ethnic values. *Fraternité* can be contained in a republic, which is based on *liberté* and *égalité*; it must not dominate it.[120]

These ideological structures are embedded in the normative content of monetary market economies. They are clearly expressed in article 2 of the Treaty on the European Union. However, taking this article seriously implies also that *individualism* needs to be acknowledged as a constitutive rule for policy-making in Europe. This means the foundation of the European polity must be European *citizens, not governments*. The sovereign behind regulative rules is individuals, not their agent. There exists a fundamental contradiction in norms between the intergovernmental approach to European integration that has its roots in the holistic anarcho-communitarian forms of federalism, and the principles of a modern market economy and liberal democracy to which any nation-state is committed domestically.[121] Hence, the proposition that national governments remain the primary source of political legitimacy or that Europe should develop as a 'union of sovereign states' as recently proclaimed by the

British government, is utterly inconsistent with a modern liberal view of politics and economics. It may have been acceptable for a semi-democratic state like Bismarck's Reich[122], but more than 130 years later Europe should have learned the lesson. It may be surprising that the government of one of the most liberal-minded countries in Europe is one of the strongest defenders of this inconsistency, but British anarcho-communitarianism has even prevented it from joining the single currency. For those who share the same money, individual freedom and democracy imply political equality, not communal segregation. They must address the question of state and democracy in Europe. If citizens are the principal, only governments as their agent may fear the outcome.

How can this contradiction of political norms be overcome? Part of the answer consists in focussing on policy-making as rule setting and looking at its functions. At the heart is the question of legitimacy. If constitutive rules are determining the games to be played, then the question is which games need to be played at the European level? *This question emphasises the outcomes of policy-making, hence, the size of the policy domain.* The assignment of technical competencies is a matter of regional decentralisation, not of subsidiarity. Yet, the legitimacy of policy-making in Europe cannot be derived only from the functional efficiency of policy arrangements or the optimality of their outcomes. Rather, *it requires input legitimacy as well, i.e. the deliberative evaluation of collective preferences through the participation of the free and equal political citizen.* This is the republican approach. It is coherent with the contractual foundation of liberal individualism. It does not mean that the republic is necessarily a nation-state; state and nation, polity and cultural community can be separate. It is simply required that all those who are concerned and affected by policy decisions have a right to participate in making collective policy choices.

A European Constitution therefore needs two mechanisms. On the one side, a vertical delimitation of policy domains is necessary for efficient policy outcomes. This requires criteria for assigning policy decisions to the European and the national or regional level. On the other side, once it is clear which policies are dealt with at which level, proper democratic structures for policy decisions at the European level must be set up in order to sustain the legitimacy of these decisions. In the next chapter I will discuss criteria on how such an assignment could be undertaken. In the last chapter I will make some practical suggestions as to how these general principles can be applied to a European Constitution.

Chapter Five.
Collective Action and Economic Federalism

Our discussion has so far dealt with the political aspects of federalism. We will now focus on economic implications. The basic issue is how to align policy responsibilities and appropriate means with proper levels of government (Oates, 1999). In this context we will interpret specific policies as decision rules providing collective goods. In economic theory, a good is something from which some utility or benefit is derived, whatever that may be. The production of goods requires resources and causes costs. The value of the good is its net benefit. Similarly, we can consider the value of a policy as the value of the reward sequence resulting from certain policy decisions, i.e. as a stream of net benefits discounted over time. An optimal policy would maximise the value subject to some constraints. Policy decisions are about making resources available to obtain these rewards and we will now discuss under what conditions European policies can be optimised. First, we need to clarify the notion of collective or public goods and will then discuss efficiency criteria for the assignment of competencies to government levels. We can then analyse the required forms of governance. In this context we can make use of the theory of fiscal federalism and the logic of collective action.[123]

Collective Goods and Externalities

Economic theory distinguishes between private and collective goods. Private goods are restricted to individual users. Collective goods, once produced, are there for everyone. Hence, they are related to groups. Collective goods are defined by two properties: indivisibility or jointness of supply and impossibility of exclusion from consumption. If a good is joint (or non-rival) in supply, one person's consumption of it does not reduce the amount made available to anyone else. For example the beauty of Mona Lisa's smile will not lose its effect if the number of visitors in the Louvre changes. Price stability is also a collective good that is non-rival in supply: a low rate of inflation for me is the same for you. On the other hand, if a good is characterised by the impossibility of exclusion, it is not possible to prevent anyone from consuming it (Hardin, 1982:17). Thus, if a factory pollutes the air, everyone in the neighbourhood has to breathe it. Similarly, when the central bank raises interest rates, no one can be excluded from the effects of this new monetary environment. Samuelson (1955) has called collective goods that fulfil both conditions non rivalness in supply and non-excludable consumption 'pure public goods', but Figure 5.1 shows that the notion of collective goods is broader.

Figure 5.1 Typology of Collective Goods

		Consumption (Benefits)	
		Excludable/rival	Non-Excludable/ non-rival
Supply (Costs)	*non-joint/rival*	*I. Pure Private Goods* (exclusive goods) Apple, Pears	*II. Common property resources* (exclusive collective goods) Oil wells, fisheries, Central bank liquidity
	Joint/non-rival	*III. Club goods* (inclusive goods) Swimming pool, toll highways, joint ventures, EMU	*IV. Pure public goods* (non-exclusive goods) Defence, lighthouses, streetlights

Boxes I and IV are two extreme polar cases. Pure private goods, in box I, are items like apples and pears where consumption is excludable or rival, and production non-joint. It means that if I eat an apple, you cannot consume it; and, if the apple grows on my tree, it does not grow on yours. In this context a 'private policy' would be a commercial strategy by a firm that appropriates benefits from private goods. At the opposite end (box IV) we have pure public goods where consumption is not excludable and production is such that if it is supplied by one, it is available to all.[124] These goods are non-exclusive or public in the sense that the benefit of no consumer is affected by any other consumer and therefore they are made freely available. For example, if a policy produces clean air, this good is available for everyone and none can be excluded from breathing it. Other standard examples are national defence, lighthouses, flood control projects.

Box III is known as club goods where access to consumption can be restricted by imposing an entrance fee or toll; but once a member has joined the club, the use of the good is available to all club members because its supply is joint and not divisible. Such goods are also called inclusive, because below a given capacity limit (when the swimming pool is full, etc.) there are advantages from admitting more members, either because average costs per member fall or because benefits increase. For example, the benefit I derive from being members of a club may increase, if I can bring my friend as well, provided the marginal cost of membership do not exceed the additional collective benefits.[125] Thus, collective benefit levels need to be regulated by excludability while individual benefits create incentives to open the group to additional members. For example the benefits of a single market, or a currency that provides monetary stability is available to all members, although it is important to keep costs low and exclude those who may not play by the rules of the *acquis communautaire*. European integration can be interpreted as a club good. The benefits from belonging to the Union are great until capacity limits are reached. This is one reason why enlargement now requires new forms of governance.

Finally, common property resources (box II) are rival in production but non-excludable in their consumption. Usually their benefits are fixed, because consumption is the same for every individual. This applies for example to exhaustible common resources such as fisheries or interconnected oil wells. In the next chapter I will show that public debt in EMU can be interpreted as such a common property resource. The benefits are available to all although fixed by the quantity of the resource, and supply is rival because if one is fishing, drilling or borrowing more, others will be getting less. Many macroeconomic policy variables share the characteristics of common property resources. For example, no one can be excluded from 'consuming' a given rate of inflation or exchange rate or from having access to the integrated financial market, although there may be 'rivalness' between the 'suppliers' of inflation, foreign reserves or borrowers.

The goods in box II are called *exclusive* collective goods (Olson, 1971:38), because the limited or fixed amount of (non-excludable) benefits implies falling average benefits for each group members if the size of the group increases. This fact is an incentive to keep rival suppliers out, i.e. to be exclusive. By contrast, within capacity limits club goods, and possibly also pure public goods are *inclusive*, i.e. open to additional group members, as the collective can enjoy the good without any reduction in the consumption of the old members. Therefore groups, which supply inclusive collective goods usually accept new members, especially if benefits expand, when the group expands. Such inclusive goods may then be provided on a voluntary and co-operative basis, as the creation of joint ventures and stock companies prove.

Some of the borders between our four groups are blurred. For example, pure public goods may become excludable and therefore move into the realm of club goods, if property rights can be assigned. Similarly, if the costs of supply and exclusion can be lowered, by making them divisible and assigning efficient property rights, club goods and common property resources may effectively become private goods. For example, the cost reductions resulting from technological progress especially in information and communication technologies has opened the possibility to privatise many goods and services that were previously public.

Because of their non-rival character, collective goods may be regarded as reflecting a special type of *externality*. An externality, sometimes also called spillover, is said to be present when the utility of an individual A is affected not only by the goods and services that A purchases and consumes, but also by the activity of some other individual, B.[126] If B's activity increases A's welfare, we say a positive externality is present, if it lowers it, the externality is negative.[127] Externalities are a major cause for trouble in the interaction of human beings. Without them, competitive markets would always produce an efficient allocation of goods and services. But in the presence of externalities, the price mechanism breaks down. Prices may no longer reflect marginal costs or marginal benefits. This market failure requires alternative modes of allocating goods and services. The internalisation of externalities is the essence of collective action arrangements, where governments play a central role. It is generally accepted that solutions for externality problems can be obtained by direct government intervention, policy regulation[128] or by 'unitisation' and centralisation where actors and beneficiaries are brought together into one decision-making body (Cullis and Jones, 1998:36). Public finance theory is based on the idea that governments must step in when the link between producer (actor) and consumer (beneficiary) is broken (Musgrave and Musgrave, 1973:7). However, this model for solving problems of externalities is also not always efficient. If government intervenes and regulates, it becomes itself an actor who may produce externalities. For example the creation of a customs union, or the single market had significant regulatory externalities, which affected producers within member states, the EU and outside trading partners on the world market. Sometimes these government interventions can lead to 'government failure': who is to deal with these externalities? From a theoretical point, market failure can be remedied by governments as a partial equilibrium solution, but government failure requires a general equilibrium solution, where the preferences of all individuals may have to change.[129] I will argue that at least some short-comings will be overcome by delegating policy-making from the national to the European level.

The provision of collective goods raises questions of collective action that are at the core of public policy choices. Efficient markets are able to provide an optimal amount of private goods to satisfy consumer preferences when the pricing mechanism equalises marginal costs and marginal benefits because this is where total net benefits are maximised. However, this mechanism does not work with pure public goods, as Samuelson (1955) has shown. Because of the non-rivalness of pure public goods, their optimal supply requires that the *sum* of marginal benefits equals the marginal costs of the public good.[130] Under these conditions markets fail to provide the optimal amount of collective goods because the revelation of consumer preferences through the pricing mechanism is no longer assured. If I can use the public goods provided by you (and someone else) why should I contribute to the costs and reveal my preference? There is a problem of *free-riding*. If the contribution to the provision of a collective good required by individuals is positively related to their demand, they have an incentive to understate their demand as long as they know that it will be supplied by the collective anyhow. This free-rider problem may cause the supply of collective goods to be sub-optimal. The logic is the prisoners' dilemma: all individuals together would find it preferable to provide the collective good, but each single one has an incentive not to contribute to it. As a consequence, other mechanisms than the market are required to decide the desired level of collective goods. The same argument applies to public policies. The sequence of rewards or benefits requires the allocation of resources and policy decisions must reflect preferences. The question is then, who takes these decisions and whose preferences do they reflect? This leads us to the question of how collective goods can be supplied efficiently.

Two Types of Efficiencies

The purpose of economic or fiscal federalism is to determine which collective goods should be provided by which level of government (Oates, 1972). In recent years it has become customary to discuss European constitutional issues in the context of assigning *competences*, not goods, to different jurisdictional levels of administrations and governments. How should *powers* be divided between the European or central level and the national or regional level? However, this is an ungratifying question because, first of all, in practice, the division invites strategic bargaining among intergovernmental negotiators who have much to lose and little to gain from giving powers away and this fact may distort an efficient assignment. Secondly, I have pointed out earlier that power is not exogenously given, but dependant on legitimacy. If we understand power as the capacity to make legitimate policy decisions which provide collective goods, then the assignment should follow the logic of the externalities resultant from these goods. In Chapter Four I have called this approach 'the principle of regional decentralisation.' I will now show that the *level* of government should be determined by the policy domain of collective goods, but that the *form* of policy-making must depend on the different characteristics (i.e. externalities) of public goods. Once the adequate institutional level of government responsibility for providing collective goods is established (a technical issue) the question of centralisation or decentralisation is about who should exercise power in making decisions about the provision of these collective goods: a Union government as centralising federalism postulates or national governments by voluntary co-operation as decentralising federalism claims? I propose an articulation of centralising and decentralising federalism that derives its logic from the nature of externalities of collective goods and responds to the specificities of European policy-making. This implies also that the policy assignment must focus on how the polity operates and how legitimating procedures cover the policy domain. The literature has formulated two principles, fiscal equivalence and jurisdictional congruence that need to be fulfilled.

The question of economic federalism may also be put differently: can a constitution establish a coherent system of policy-making rules to maximise the social welfare derived from these policies? Coherence implies here that the consequences (rewards) of policy choices by one jurisdiction do not interfere with those of another, i.e. *they do not cause unaccounted externalities*. This is the essence of the *principle of 'fiscal equivalence'* (Olson, 1969), which requires that the incidence of benefits derived from the collective goods should coincide with the jurisdiction of governments. Thus, the optimal jurisdiction would maximise the welfare of its citizens or, to use our previous notation, the optimal government should reflect the policy preferences over the whole policy domain. However, this is not always the case. A problem arises when policy decisions are taken in the context of a given polity but the polity is smaller (in terms of its competences) than the policy domain. Certain policies will then have consequences for individuals outside the jurisdiction (spillovers). This may lead to the sub-efficient provision of public goods because of the failure to take into account the costs and benefits conferred on residents of other jurisdictions (Oates, 1972:37). In this case, the policy domain contains a disenfranchised sub-domain whose evaluation of the policy choices does not enter the decision-making process. I will call this *type-I-inefficiency*. It constitutes a violation of the *'equivalence principle'* formulated by fiscal federalism. This inefficiency is eliminated, i.e. the structure of governance is optimal, when the jurisdiction determining the level of provision for each public good includes precisely the set of individuals who consume the good. We have then the case of 'perfect correspondence', postulated by Oates (1972:34).

Type-I-inefficiency is a typical problem of policy output externalities (spillovers). It implies, that the policy decisions of any given jurisdiction affect the utility of the members of another jurisdiction and thereby creates a disenfranchised sub-domain. For example the decision by one government to build a nuclear reactor close to the border of its territory affects the security of citizens across the border who have no vote in this decision nor are their opinions necessarily part of the policy deliberation. Or the security provided by a strong military alliance may also protect small neutralist states in its vicinity. Monetary policy in the European Monetary System during the 1980s and 1990s was a prime example of type-I-inefficiency. Any monetary policy decision by the Bundesbank affected all members in the exchange rate mechanism, but the decision itself was taken only with respect to the German constituency of the Bundesbank. Hence, the policy domain consisted of all members of the Exchange Rate Mechanism (ERM), but the monetary jurisdiction was restricted to Germany. This type-I-inefficiency in monetary policy has been eliminated by the creation of the European Central Bank, whose jurisdiction corresponds nearly perfectly[131] to the policy domain.

In Europe, the problem of type-I-inefficiency has become endemic, but globalisation is pushing it also beyond regional limits. After the creation of the customs union policy spillovers justified the delegation of trade and competition policies to the European Commission. Other policy domains followed. With the start of EMU, the economies of the participating member states have effectively become one single unit. The benefits from these new collective European goods, such as price stability, the exchange rate, money market interest rates etc., affect all individuals living in Euroland. But economic policy-making remains fragmentised between different member states who rely for the formulation of policy preferences on the policy consensus as it emerges from their domestic epistemic constituencies. Hence, the 'deepening' of European economic integration has enlarged the policy domain, while the lack of progress in political integration prevents the creation of the corresponding European polity and produces new problems due to preference heterogeneity.

However, respect of the principle of fiscal equivalence is not sufficient to eliminate all inefficiencies in the provision of collective goods. As discussed in Chapter One, the efficiency and legitimacy of policy-making require that the principle of *jurisdictional congruence of political action* is also respected (Fischer and Schley, 1999). This principle demands that the polity coincide not only with the policy domain (the equivalence principle), but also with the decision-making domain. If fiscal equivalence and jurisdictional congruence are given, those who are affected by a particular measure can determine the influence of their actions on themselves. Habermas (2001b:65) has formulated this as follows:

'The democratic constitutional state, by its own definition is a political order created by the people themselves and legitimated by their opinion and will-formation, which allows the addressees of law to regard themselves at the same time as the authors of the law.'

Ideally, this condition has been realised in the modern democratic nation-state. But the nation-state is no longer capable of internalising all the externalities resulting from globalisation and Europeanisation. In the age of globalisation the policy domain has outgrown the nation-state. This causes a second type of inefficiency: preference frustration. If policy preferences are formed in the context of national polities, rather than a European polity, the heterogeneity of local preferences will dominate policy decisions. Imposing a centralised decision would cause costs in welfare terms. I call this type-II-inefficiency. This inefficiency is the main reason for Europe's presumed lack of legitimacy. People are expected to obey laws they themselves or their representatives have not authorised (Eriksen, 2000:43). The problem in writing a European Constitution lies in finding mechanisms to internalise these externalities and to reduce *both* forms of inefficiency. The appropriate answer is to expand the polity *by creating and expanding a constitutional epistemic constituency that covers the whole European policy domain*. This requires the creation of a democratic government at the European level, as a framework within which a stochastic consensus on policy preferences becomes possible. *The constitutional set-up must create the conditions for European-wide policy deliberations which make heterogeneous policy preferences converge.*

The recent literature on fiscal federalism has postulated a trade-off between the benefits of centralising policies (a larger polity), which internalise the externalities from spillovers, and benefits of decentralising policies responding to the heterogeneousness of preferences, which grow as unions become larger and more diverse (Oates, 1999; Alesina, Angeloni and Schuknecht, 2002; von Hagen and Pisani-Ferry 2002). From the point of view put forward in this book, that analysis suffers from an exogenous notion of preferences. First of all, because preferences are assumed to be given, these authors do not provide a theory for explaining their formation. Therefore, 'countries' remain in a natural state of conflict. Secondly, collective preferences reflect deterministic consensus. They do not allow for the possibility of dissent held together by constitutional consensus on policy-making procedures. As a consequence, they assign competences along a given trade-off curve, while our theory of stochastic consensus allows us to explain the factors which shift the curve. If these conditions are incorporated, expanding the polity reduces type-I-inefficiencies without rising costs from preference heterogeneity, as I will show in the next section.

One further reason for enlarging the polity to the size of the policy domain is that a single European government would overcome informational asymmetries by expanding the epistemic constituency. For it is the nature of political 'externalities' that the effects outside the polity are often also outside its own information range. For example, if one European government wishes to unilaterally subsidise a steel factory to keep jobs, thereby reflecting the preferences of its limited epistemic constituency, it would prevent the market adjustment of European supply. But this consequence may not be highly visible for those who take the decision of paying the subsidy, although it has negative consequences for efficient companies operating in the single market. Thus institutions are necessary to overcome the informational asymmetries.

In the European Union, the Commission has been charged with this task, although traditionally the nation-state was the institution to create transparencies by giving every citizen a voice to express concern and an equal right to vote, hence, to deliberate and decide. The problem with the European Union is that although the Commission may increase transparency across the EU, and thereby influence the public debate, it does not draw legitimacy from a European polity and constituency of its own and is therefore limited in power and decision-making capacity. As I will show below, the Commission's role is adequate when better information induces governments to improve their policies. This is the case for inclusive public goods. But it is not suitable when unified action is required, because under the European multi-level governance the epistemic constituencies from which policy preferences emerge remain largely segregated. Hence the legitimacy - and power - of European policy decisions are not only low, they are also likely to be inefficient from a welfare point of view. With the growing interdependence of global and European economic and political actions, governments are less and less capable of respecting the principle of jurisdictional congruence. In Chapter Two, I have indicated some of the externalities which will dominate the next half-century - population growth, resource scarcity, globalisation, military conflicts etc. But in addition, European economic integration, which is partly a response to those global challenges, is creating new externalities. In what has been called the 'post-national' age (Habermas, 2001b), the principle of equivalence and Oates' perfect correspondence does no longer apply.

Shifting the Inefficiency Trade-off curve

The economic concept of 'efficiency' refers to the allocation of scarce, or costly, resources to achieve certain benefits. With respect to collective goods it implies that the sum of marginal benefits from collective goods *supplied to a policy domain* equals marginal costs. Hence, this is the criteria for determining the efficient governance level of specific collective goods. If the benefits only affect a local or regional group of individuals, they need a local government. If they extend to the whole Union, they need a European government.

However, things are not that easy. Because neoclassical economics usually assumes benefits or utilities as exogenously given (*de gustibus non est disputandum*), it focuses on the optimal allocation of factor inputs. But what matters for public policies is the realisation of collective benefits. As we have seen in Chapter One, their definition depends on the collective evaluation by an epistemic constituency. Now assume that the polity and the epistemic constituency are identical. In other words, there is consensus, if not on policy issues, at least on constitutional procedures. In this case the government of a jurisdiction can maximise the welfare of its constituency in a Pareto-efficient manner.[132] Preferences are clearly and coherently defined and the government can allocate the resources required for their realisation at minimal cost.[133] Difficulties arise when the polity is split into several epistemic constituencies. Let us assume for the moment that a jurisdiction contains two such separate epistemic groups and the government serves the interests of the larger one. A chosen policy may imply that the smaller group gets to consume less of the public good than it would wish. This reduces its welfare.[134] This is less an argument about distribution than about constitutional arrangements, because as we saw in Chapter One, conflict about distributional outcomes can be overcome by procedural rules. Therefore the lack of consensus in the polity causes welfare losses, which I called *type-II-inefficiencies*. The larger the degree of dissent and conflict in a jurisdiction, the higher are the type-II-inefficiencies.

Figure 5.2 illustrates our argument. If the range of the policy domain is larger than the polity, i.e. the number of individuals affected by a policy is larger than the number of people who have a constitutional say in formulating the policy, the size of the disenfranchised group, which is subject to a policy externality, reflects type-I-inefficiency. If the policy decision reflects the evaluation of an epistemic subgroup in the polity, the frustration of the disenfranchised constituency is represented by type-II-inefficiency. For example, if the European policy decisions are taken intergovernmentally by, say, a majority of member state *governments*, the *citizens* of the minority states are the disenfranchised constituency. An optimal European Constitution should aim to minimise both inefficiencies.[135]

Figure 5.2 Policy-making Inefficiencies

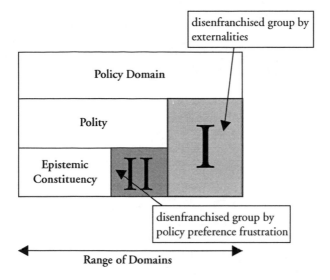

Range of Domains

Oates (1972) has built a model for determining the optimal size of jurisdictions by taking welfare-losses from lack of consensus into account. It starts with the plausible assumption that the larger a group, the higher the degree of dissent due to preference heterogeneity, although our model of stochastic consensus would qualify this assumption. We know that the degree of consensus in a given group depends on the degree of mutual respect and the connectedness condition. Oates' assumption is valid, if a larger group narrows the degree of respect and lengthens the chain of connectedness, because more iterations are required to achieve consensus and spread information. It may also be the case that in larger groups, individuals give others zero weight to avoid being driven to consensus that co-opts their interests.[136] In any case, if dissent increases with the size of a group, one would expect greater welfare losses for larger groups. Hence, policy decisions by smaller jurisdictions, representing more homogenous constituencies, would improve policy outcomes by reducing or eliminating type-II-inefficiencies.

Oates (1972:35) has formulated this insight in the Decentralisation Theorem, which is the economic equivalent of the subsidiary rule in political federalism. It states:

> 'For a public good (...) it will always be more efficient (or at least as efficient) for local government to provide the Pareto-efficient levels of output for their respective jurisdictions than for central governments to provide *any* specified and uniform level of output across a jurisdiction' (Oates, 1972:35).

The theorem effectively implies that policy-making should take place on the level of epistemic constituencies:

> 'The potential losses from an increased centralisation of decision-making depend primarily on the diversity in individual demands for the good and the extent of geographical groupings of consumers with similar tastes. If for example, there are wide divergences in individual preferences for the public good and in levels of income within a society that give rise to a wide dispersion of individual demands for that good, and if at the same time people with similar demands for the good tend to reside near to one another geographically, one can expect large differences in desired levels of consumption among various areas in the country. In such cases the potential losses from the collective consumption of the good on a highly centralised basis could be substantial. (...) If, on the other hand, all individuals possess quite similar preferences for the public good (...) there will be a much smaller loss in welfare from uniform levels of consumption over large groups of people.' (Oates, 1972:43)

However, by creating small jurisdictions the elimination of type-II-inefficiency is likely to come at the price of greater type-I-inefficiencies. For reducing the jurisdiction to the size of epistemic constituency does not eliminate the fact that the consequences of such policy decision affect other individuals in the policy domain. Instead, it rather increases the scope for policy externalities and this gives rise to type-I-inefficiencies. Figure 5.3 shows this effect: after the polity has been reduced to be closer to the epistemic constituency, the population affected by type-II-inefficiency has shrunk, but type-I externalities have increased.

Figure 5.3 The Inefficiency Trade-off

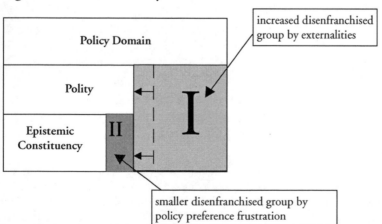

This trade-off between type I and type II inefficiencies is a frequent problem in pluralist societies. It has found very different solutions in history. Modern Enlightenment has been one[137], Fascism and Communism have been two others.

The dilemma reappears in force during the process of globalisation when technological progress multiplies the scope of externalities, while this disempowerment of the nation-state (Habermas, 2001b:69) undermines the legitimacy of decisions made by states. Political theorists have responded in two ways to these new challenges from growing externalities. Cosmopolitans request more global institutional capacity to govern worldwide relations. They seek effectively to enlarge the polity to cover domains of global governance. But unless they also provide mechanisms to enlarge the epistemic constituencies, their strategy simply increases type-II-inefficiency. This is the dilemma of the 'technocratic' approach to European integration. Nationalists and communitarians stress the principle of self-determination. They distrust projects of cosmopolitan governance out of fear of cultural homogenisation and domination. But by refusing to enlarge the polity to the size of the policy domain (small is beautiful), they fail to internalise externalities. This can prevent the emergence of economies of scale and thereby reduce welfare. These issues reappear in the European debate. Integrationalists reflect the cosmopolitan response, intergovernmentalists and sovereignists the nationalist-communitarian view.[138]

I will argue for a third way: *by creating a fully legitimised democratic government for Europe, both types of inefficiencies can be reduced or eliminated*. The debate between cosmopolitans and nationalists assumes the size of both policy domain and epistemic constituency to be fixed. The only variable to adjust is the dimension of the polity. However, from a theoretical point of view it is perfectly conceivable to shift the framework of the debate by focussing on how *to extend both, polity and epistemic constituency*. In my mind, this goes back to the very core of Jean Monnet's idea of European integration when he said: 'We do not create coalitions between states, we are uniting men'.

The purpose is then the creation of institutional arrangements to deal with externalities at the European level and to set up structures which allow for the convergence of policy preferences through deliberation. There is obviously a wide range of policy issues where polity and policy domain correspond quite perfectly. Public facilities are built by local authorities. National governments legislate on a wide range of issues that do not create spillovers and externalities at the European level. If they affect immediate neighbours, they may be dealt with quite effectively on a bilateral level. In these cases, the policy domain is the criterion to assign policy functions in such a way that type-I-inefficiencies are minimised. Fiscal federalism has provided some guidelines for such functionalist policy assignment, which I shall now review briefly. I will then address the question of how to reduce type-II-inefficiencies. This question poses the problem of Europe's governance for truly European collective goods, i.e. goods that affect all European citizens, for which the policy domain is the European Union. I will now discuss the assignment of policies and forms of government.

Fiscal Federalism and the Functions of Government

Our first question is which goods should be classified as European? The theory of fiscal federalism has discussed the assignment of economic functions to jurisdictions extensively, so we can be brief (see Musgrave and Musgrave, 1973; Oates, 1972). It has focussed on three functions of government, which are the allocation function, the distribution function and the stabilisation function.

The *allocation function* deals with the provision of social or collective goods and the process by which total resource use has to be divided between private and public goods. Regulatory policies and the underlying rules may also be considered as part of the allocation function. Government has to intervene when markets fail to provide the collective goods to an optimal amount. However, the benefits may have limited geographical reach, so that the allocation function of government covers a wide range of jurisdictions from small local municipalities up to European collective goods. If these different jurisdictions also have the sovereignty to raise the necessary resources by taxes and other contributions, the principle of perfect correspondence is achievable. All those who benefit from collective goods must contribute to their provision. The competencies of different jurisdictions should therefore reflect the policy domain. European collective goods are all those goods, services and policies that affect all citizens in the European Union, either through their benefits or through their costs.

The second function is the adjustment of the *distribution* of income and wealth. In the national context, redistribution should be assigned to central governments, in order to avoid that rich taxpayers try to evade paying their contribution by moving to low taxing regions. The distribution function would require centralising policies if the degree of factor mobility is high. Highly mobile capital will move rather quickly to jurisdictions where taxes and levies are low. This argument also concerns labour. Though taxpayers may move into low taxing jurisdictions, they may consume public goods elsewhere. This would lead to sub-optimal supply. In this case, as Tiebout (1956) has shown, the optimal size of a jurisdiction depends on voting by feet, or rather, in our terms, on the size of the epistemic constituency. However, the question is how mobile are the factors of production. In the European Union it seems that labour is rather immobile, while capital is perfectly mobile at least within the Monetary Union. This would mean a certain degree of harmonisation for taxes on capital, though less, if any, on labour. The benefits of distribution are non-rival as they apply to all the poor, but the resources of distribution are rival and we must classify income redistribution as an exclusive good. Hence the need for delegation to the central level.

However, the evaluation of benefits depends on the epistemic consensus. In a highly heterogeneous polity the distribution of income and resources may not reflect aggregate preferences, but local consensus on the value of solidarity. Oates' Decentralisation Theorem takes preferences as exogenously given. The issue of allocating resources effectively according to people's tastes depends whether there are genuine preferences across the whole polity. Only in this case should policies be decided at the European level. But if tastes are localised, maximising consumer preferences would require the decentralised provision of such goods. A similar argument for subsidiarity can be made by emphasising the cost of real resources that may be more correctly valued on a decentralised basis. Competing pressures on policy-makers (policy competition) may also lead to policy innovations that would not take place on a centralised level (Oates, 1972). Yet, in all these argument there is no role for the deliberative practices and the production of new evidence that will transform context-determined preferences as we have shown in our model of stochastic consensus. Hence, the subsidiarity approach is blind to the effects of creating a European constitutional consensus. The assignment of competences in Europe is more subtle than standard models would postulate. They chose, and only make sense if institutions exist to first deliberate, then formulate and finally implement European policy preferences.

In the European Union redistribution between individuals takes place within the context of national policies while redistribution between *national governments* takes largely place through regional cohesion policies and transfers through structural funds within the European Union. Tsoukalis (1997:187) has summarised this:

> 'Redistribution is one of the central elements of the European mixed economy at the national level; and this has become increasingly true of the EU as well, although there is still a large difference between the two. Redistribution can also be considered as an index of the political and social cohesion of a new system; large transfers of funds, as a very tangible expression of solidarity presuppose the existence of a developed sense of *Gemeinschaft* (a community based on common values) which is, of course, not a feature of international organisations.'

Thus, the European distribution model is holistic, while national models are largely individualistic. Hence, issues of European distribution are regularly addressed in terms of net contributions *by member states* to the European budget, or worse, in terms of 'I want my money back'. They do little to create trust and mutual respect across countries (except, maybe, satisfaction on the side of receivers), but perpetuate dissent and conflict with damaging consequences for Europe's legitimacy and power. In view of the normative coherence requirements in modern societies discussed in the last chapter, one should discuss whether it might not be a better solution to find more individualistic mechanisms for redistribution. Why should a poor German pay for a rich Portuguese? A modern, progressive re-distributive system would make the rich Portuguese and Germans pay for poor fellows in the Union. Some form of minimum social welfare program at the European level would be a device to individualise such redistribution. It is frequently argued that such Europeanisation of income redistribution is culturally unacceptable. Yet, there is a widespread feeling that the 'European model' of society is different from other societies, say the American. There is therefore a shared consensus on certain minimum social standards. If the policy responsibility for these essential functions of the welfare state were transferred to the European level, this could lead to both, a differentiated welfare state with European minimum standards and regional extras.

Finally, the *stabilisation function* deals with the instruments of macro-economic policy. The theory of fiscal federalism established that the stabilisation function is an issue that needs to be dealt with by a central government. Individual states in a larger union are generally unable to execute stabilisation efficiently. Inter-state trade and financial flows would cause the additional demand created by a fiscal or monetary expansion to dissipate into neighbouring states (von Hagen, 1993:269; Englander and Egebo, 1993). Oates (1972:21-30) presents a formal model to put this argument 'to rest on a firm foundation.' He also quotes Engerman (1965) with the conclusion:

> 'Thus, as long as stabilization measures are left to particular states, there can be no expectation of an optimal national policy, for there may be either smaller or larger changes in demand than would be considered desirable. (...) Given both financial constraints and interstate strategy, the presumption that stabilization measures will be insufficient if they are left to lower-level governments appears most reasonable.'

European monetary policy reflects this thinking by delegating policy-making responsibilities to the European Central Bank, but even with a fully independent central bank, fiscal policy may have an impact on price stability, external balance, economic growth and full employment. We will discuss these issues in Chapter Six.

The theory of fiscal federalism has derived policy assignments from the economic functions of a state. They by and large reflect republican federalism, mainly of the US or Canadian brand. In the European context it is useful to determine the policy domain of European collective goods. Macroeconomic policies must clearly be seen as European collective goods. Distributional issues such as transfers between national jurisdictions and structural funds also have a large European dimension. On the other hand, many issues related to the efficient allocation of resources may be in a grey area. Their assignment depends on the size of the policy domain. But the theory assumes what is not Europe's reality: a centralised state. In the context of anarcho-communitarian federalism, there is no central government. Hence economic policy-making is a matter of voluntary co-operation. Does this form of governance provide an efficient solution to policy making in Europe?

Voluntary Policy Co-ordination?

If the institutional arrangements for subsidiarity reduce the range of the polity to epistemic constituencies, policy externalities will increase. That is to say, the more jurisdictions take decisions independently from each other in a given policy domain, the greater is the likelihood that the outcome of their policies will conflict or create externalities for each other. In order to overcome this type-I-inefficiency the governments of these jurisdictions have to delegate part of their sovereignty to a central government or alternatively they must voluntarily co-ordinate their policies. I define voluntary policy co-ordination as the *maximisation of common net benefits derived from the autonomous policy decisions of separate jurisdictions belonging to the same policy domain*. These benefits can be seen as the utility or pay-off related to common goods. If all autonomous actors contribute to the achievement of this result, the policy outcome is Pareto-optimal. In game theory, a co-operative game is defined by the existence of an external mechanism through which agreements and obligations are made binding and can be enforced. In non-co-operative games, agreements between players only make sense if they are self-enforcing, that is to say when it is optimal for each player to keep to the agreement as long as the others also do so (van den Doel and van Velthoven, 1993: 187). Thus, voluntary policy co-ordination belongs to the class of non-co-operative games. Because in our model jurisdictions are autonomous and define their own separate policy preferences and objectives in response to their dominant epistemic constituencies, we will discuss voluntary policy co-ordination in the framework of intergovernmental policy-making. Hence we will reason within the logical context of the highly influential theory of liberal intergovernmentalism (see Moravcsik, 1998). The question that interests us is whether voluntary co-ordination of policies between national governments is likely to produce the optimal amount of European collective goods.

The success of a co-ordinating strategy depends crucially on the availability and the processing of information. Co-ordination failure is the consequence of incomplete information or a failure to react to this information leading to inefficient or sub-optimal outcomes. The provision of European collective goods can be seen as a problem of *collective action*. Collective action may be defined as the investment of resources by individual organisations in the pursuit of a common interest. Olson (1971) has explored if and under which conditions rational and self-interested individuals will participate voluntarily in actions to achieve their common or group interest. He found that it does not follow from the premise of rational self-interested human behaviour that *groups* will always act in their self-interest:

> 'indeed, unless the number of individuals in a group is quite small, or unless there is coercion or some other special device [...] rational, self-interested individuals will not act to achieve their common or group interests.' (Olson, 1971:2)

Since the publication of Olson's book a vast literature has developed, mainly focussing on the collective action of interest groups and the creation of special incentives. However, its logic can also provide the foundations for centralised government and the institution of the state. We can therefore use it to establish the necessary conditions for European Union member state governments to voluntarily co-operate in order to supply European collective goods. We would expect that (1) if the benefits for one government are less than the total cost of providing the European good, there is a rational incentive to this government *not* to participate in the EU's provision of the collective good and to 'free ride'. (2) The larger the number of EU member states, the less likely they are in providing the collective goods. I will now show the reasoning. A formal treatment is presented in Annexe 2.

Quite sensibly Olson argued that the provision of collective goods depends on the amount of their net benefits and the distribution between the members of the group. In our case the group can be interpreted as consisting of EU member state governments or in the case of stabilisation policy of the Euro-group.[139] In order for a collective good to be provided, the total costs related to its 'production' need to be covered. The problem of collective action consists in the fact that net benefits are not a sufficient condition for the collective good to be provided voluntarily by a group. What matters is that the *individual* marginal benefits exceed the *social* marginal costs. The total benefit to the group would depend on the rate or level at which the good is obtained and on the value assigned to it (Olson, 1971: 22-36).[140] For example, the benefit of a specified European policy such as the Common Agricultural Policy, the single market or EMU would depend on the size of the market in terms of euros, GDP etc.[141] Yet, the benefit to an individual member of the group would depend upon the fraction or share of the group gain he or she would be able to appropriate. How much of the collective good will be optimal depends on the calculation of marginal benefits and costs of individual group members with respect to quantity. Yet, whether such optimal amount of common goods is actually going to be supplied at all will depend on *whether at least one member of the group will* derive sufficient individual benefit to *provide the whole collective good.* Because we develop our argument in a non-co-operative game setting, sharing the costs between different group members or coalitions is not possible. I will lift this restriction below.

The answer to our question whether European collective goods will be provided by voluntary intergovernmental action depends on the net benefits for each EU member state, which are a function of group size. The European Union will be a *privileged group* if it contains members who derive sufficient net benefits from belonging to the Union so that they are willing to pay for the cost of the collective good. However, these net benefits vary with the size of the Union. An *enlarged European Union with sovereign members is likely to lower the benefits for each individual member, although the total benefits may increase.* The precise impact depends on the nature of the collective good and the costs of decision-making. We have discussed this nature above (see Figure 5.1 and Annexe 2). For exclusive collective and pure public goods, marginal (net) benefits from enlargement will fall. For inclusive club goods, they may increase. The implication is that *only inclusive club goods might be provided efficiently by voluntary intergovernmental policy co-ordination.* All other collective goods need to be provided through a decision mechanism that does not increase costs when new members join the group. This condition *requires the delegation of decision-making to a central European government.* Unless this happens, a larger Union will become a *latent group*, which will not provide collective goods to an optimal amount.

One can articulate this logic also in terms of *strategic interactions* between members of the group. If a group is large, it is unlikely to provide exclusive collective and pure goods, because the net benefits accruing to individual members will be low and they may therefore not be willing to provide the good. Hence individual behaviour will go into the opposite direction of what is needed to produce the productive good. The literature calls this phenomenon *strategic substitutability*. (Benassi et al., 1994. See also note 127). On the other hand, inclusive club goods contain the possibility that by having a larger group, some members may attain larger individual benefits and consequently they may be willing to provide the necessary resources for the provision of the collective good. Hence, individual and collective behaviour go in the same direction. This is called *strategic complementarity*. The literature has shown that strategic complementarities may have multiple equilibria, which may be improved by overcoming information asymmetries. Practically this means that intergovernmental policy co-ordination, with the European Commission acting as an 'honest broker' between member states, may be sufficient to improve European welfare for such club goods. But for all other European collective goods, only a proper European government will do.

Neofunctionalist theorists of European integration attributed the role of honest broker to supra-national institutions like the European Commission. They were supposed to be 'agents of integration' (Haas, 1958). Our analysis reveals that this role could only be successfully achieved in the case of inclusive public goods with strategic complementarities. But to the degree that European integration has ventured into the domain of exclusive collective and pure public goods (especially by moving to Monetary Union), strategic complementarities have come to the fore, which can no longer be solved by more transparent information and policy persuasion. This has led to a gradual erosion of the Commission's credibility and capacity to act, particularly since the signing of the Maastricht Treaty. The weakness of the Commission resides not in personalities, but in the functions it has legitimately been assigned.

The Case for a European Government

There seems to be a large consensus that the avoidance of type-II-inefficiencies and the decentralisation theorem of fiscal federalism would plead in favour of a decentralised federalist polity system characterised by intergovernmentalism and subsidiarity.[142] If the polity levels are to closely reflect the heterogeneous epistemic constituencies within which policy evaluations take place, the subsidiarity principle favours not only decentralisation to the national but also to the sub-national level. As a consequence, the decision-making group will become large and the polity is fragmented unless there is a hierarchy of jurisdictions with a central authority. However, given that such an anarchic system of competing jurisdictions creates policy externalities when policy decisions in one jurisdiction spill over into others, policy co-ordination between autonomous jurisdictions becomes *necessary* to remove type-I-inefficiencies. But this is not *sufficient*. The success of this policy co-ordination depends on the size of the decision-making group. Particularly for European collective goods whose policy domain covers the whole of the European Union, this group will be relatively large. Hence, as we saw, the chances of success for voluntary policy co-ordination will be low. Put differently, the principle of subsidiarity is likely to create policy co-ordination failures over a wide range of collective goods, although it may be appropriate for some inclusive club goods. When decentralising federalism becomes a hindrance, centralisation is the solution. A European government is then the answer.

One may object that the creation of a European government, a centralisation of decision-making, would increase type-II-inefficiencies and carries the cost of insufficient flexibility in adapting to heterogeneous preferences (Alesina et al., 2001). However, the creation of a European government implies more than centralised decision-making. This could also be achieved by administrative rules like the Stability and Growth Pact. A government, by contrast, implies democratic legitimacy. It has to be accountable to individual citizens; it must be subject to potential sanctions by voters and is therefore the focus of public deliberations on policy preferences. Based on constitutional consensus, this open deliberation will transform existing preferences, reduce dissent and tend to a European-wide policy consensus. As a consequence, a European government also contributes to the elimination of type-II-inefficiencies.

Our analysis permits some highly practical conclusions. First, the enlargement of the European Union to a significant number of new member states from Central and Eastern Europe is likely to reduce the EU's capacity to voluntarily provide its members with the optimal amount of European collective goods. The devolution of policy responsibilities under the principle of subsidiarity and without reference to the policy domain would produce the same effect. The reduction of net benefits for old members is quite certain for exclusive collective and pure public goods, because country-specific marginal benefits are likely to fall, while decision-making costs rise. A prominent example is Europe's Common Agricultural Policy (CAP), but the principle has more general validity. The benefits for member states from CAP would not increase by having more countries join, while extending them to new members requires more resource transfers from existing members. Similarly, the benefits of regulating competition or state subsidies in very small countries is marginal for the single market, but the complexity of finding agreement for bargained policy solutions will double with every new member (see Chapter Two, note 44). For inclusive goods, this is less clear. Individual and social marginal benefits may both increase. For example, Poland's accession to the EU may increase Germany's benefit by securing its eastern border, so that it may be willing to provide relevant collective goods (say in terms of net financial contribution). At the same time this fact would allow France or Spain to free ride on Germany.[143] Thus, from the benefit point of view, chances for the provision of these collective goods might increase. On the other hand, the costs of decision-making may also increase. If these costs explode, even inclusive public goods will not be provided optimally (see note 44). A larger Union becomes an inefficient Union, unless it has a central government.

Second, we may loosen the assumption of a non-co-operative game. The necessary condition for the provision of a collective good in the Olson model is that the individual benefits accruing to some members must cover the whole of the cost. This is exaggerated. It derives from the assumption of each group member acting autonomously in a non-co-operative game. However, the analysis can be broadened to include co-operative gains where some members of the group will form coalitions and create binding commitments amongst each other. In this case, institutional or procedural arrangements will produce better outcomes (Olson, 1971:35). The logic of collective action then claims that the required net benefit applies to the whole coalition and must be sufficiently large to provide an incentive to supply the collective good.

During the last fifty years, Europe has frequently benefited from co-operative behaviour of coalitions, particularly between France and Germany. This strategy was considered to be the motor of European integration. Both countries together represent nearly half of the EU's economic force and therefore their joint share in benefits was considerable. Having created a binding mechanism of policy co-ordination in the Elysée Treaty in 1962, the French and German governments co-operated within the framework of the European Union institutions and assured that European collective goods were provided. Hence, these goods were supplied when the Franco-German coalition obtained a share of total net benefits sufficiently large to cover the costs of providing the good. This seems to have worked when the common market, the Common Agricultural Policy, the European Monetary System and EMU were set up, but it failed earlier in 1954 to create a European Defence Community. The Franco-German coalition was not yet sufficiently solidified at that time. Since the political unification of West and East Germany in 1990, the evaluation of benefits by German authorities seems to have changed.[144] Partly this is related to a re-prioritisation of budget commitments to Germany's Eastern *mezzogiorno*. However, from a strategic point of view, the two nations have more to win from co-operation than from competition. Helmut Schmidt has insisted, again and again, that this is a patriotic duty for both French and German politicians. In an important article he wrote (Schmidt, 1999):

> 'It will depend on the leaders in France and Germany, whether, when and how the nations which are united in the EU will draw the consequences from the Union's present situation and from the foreseeable future of the world. True, neither Chirac nor Jospin, Schröder or Schäuble and Stoiber have distinguished themselves as ideological 'Europeans' in their lives to date. Nor is this necessary. It is also not necessary that they become personal friends (although this may be helpful). Necessary is, however, that each of them recognises: a patriot, whether French or German, must strive for the progress of the European Union. Out of national interest, he must correct mistakes in the EU's development as they impede progress. He must convince his national and international colleagues and fellow staff that he takes the details of the Common Agricultural Policy or budget policy seriously, but that he will not endanger the strategic objectives nor the historically unique European Union.

This summer Helmut Kohl has said in the Bundestag: 'Germany and France form a community of destiny (*Schicksalsgemeinschaft*). Without their close co-operation there will be no substantial progress in the process of European unification.' This is correct. The leaders of the political class in France should know: Paris has to decide, once again, between the paling idea of an autonomous national special role in the world and the potential of strategic leadership in Europe. The German political class must know: France disposes over historic, cultural, international and nuclear assets that we Germans do not have. This is why we need the French and owe them priority. Herbert Wehner once reduced it to the shortest formula: 'without France all is nothing'.'[145]

Third, France and Germany often mustered additional members into their privileged coalition and their openness has reinforced the capacity to provide European collective goods efficiently. This analysis proves the shortsightedness of those who wish to 'rebalance' the Franco-German axis. They would be destroying an arrangement that provides them with collective goods and an opportunity to free-ride if they are not part of the coalition.[146] For example, the United Kingdom derives significant free-riding benefits from the existence of a large single currency in the single market, even by not formally joining.

Yet, it is not unlikely that the French-German motor will be losing force after the enlargement of the European Union to a significant number of new countries from Central and Eastern Europe. The reason may be changes in policy preferences after German unification, or simply because individual net benefits will fall in a larger union. The dangers of an insufficient provision of European policies are therefore increasing. The appropriate conclusion is to strengthen the institutional arrangements that contribute to binding agreements between member states. However, in this case the dilemma of type-I-inefficiency versus type-II-inefficiency reappears. By increasing the scope for binding agreements between autonomous member states, without structures of full democratic legitimacy, type-II-inefficiencies will re-emerge because members in the different epistemic constituencies will find their policy preferences frustrated.

This can only be overcome by enlarging the epistemic constituency and by transferring mechanisms for policy deliberations to the European level. But given that in any society disagreement on substantive and distributional issues is the rule, although consensus about procedural issues may exist in the background, enlarging the epistemic constituency implies expanding the polity. Hence, *a European Constitution and therefore the creation of a proper European government* are both desirable and feasible. But the problem of preference heterogeneity will only be overcome, if the delegation of policy-making to the European level takes place in a constitutional context which involves *European citizens and not only governments*. In order to reduce type-II-inefficiencies, the epistemic constituency must be broadened to create structures of mutual respect across Europe. Intergovernmental policy co-ordination is too weak to let a European policy consensus emerge rapidly among citizens. Furthermore, delegating policy-making to the European level broadens the polity with respect to the policy domain, and therefore reduces type-I-inefficiency. Hence, the creation of a democratic European government would reduce or eliminate type-I and type-II-inefficiencies at one stroke. Since European collective goods will not be provided at all or only in suboptimal quantities by voluntary co-operation, they need to be provided at the European level by a centralised institution. *A European government unambiguously improves European welfare.*

This approach has effectively been part of the European method since Jean Monnet, although progress was slow and gradual, with the European Commission at the centre of European policy co-ordination. National governments have transferred some of their sovereignty to the European level, especially with respect to external trade policies, competition and monetary policies. However, the difficulty with the present institutional arrangements is *that the European Commission is an agent of the national governments rather than of European citizens.* The Commission is the guardian of the Treaties which were concluded between governments. In this sense it is the umpire of European policy-making, not an actor. This is also manifest in the appointment modus of the European Commission (article 214 of the Treaty). The President and the Commissioners are appointed by the governments of member states. The European Parliament only approves their decisions. It cannot influence them. This is the old medieval model of approval by acclaim with the European Council acting as the Curia (see note 71). The European Parliament, which represents European citizens is not the choice-making institution that decides policy orientations for the efficient provision of European collective goods. As a consequence, deliberation in the European polity does not, or only partially, allow for the emergence of a European epistemic constituency. National governments have national polities; European policy-making does not have a European polity. Policy preferences are still worked out in the context of national epistemic constituencies.

Therefore preference heterogeneity is a consequence of the EU's present institutional arrangements. The elimination of type-I and type-II-inefficiencies requires transferring policy responsibilities to a European central government. But this means providing and creating institutional structures, which would allow the deliberation on European policy preferences to reflect all individuals in the European Union. Without democracy type-II-inefficiencies cannot be overcome. Hence a *properly structured European polity necessitates that 'the principal' of the European Commission is no longer member state governments, but European citizens.* Transforming the Commission into a government requires that it is legitimised by universal suffrage.

Fourth, a European government does not have to include all member states of the European Union. We can look at the creation of a European government as the provision of a new European public good. The constitutional process is therefore itself subject to the dilemmas of collective action. However, this logic also provides us with guidelines for dealing with opt-outs and reinforced co-operation. One can interpret the creation of a European government as a particularly strong, binding contract amongst members, reinforced by the creation of a European epistemic constituency. Now, let us assume that the European Union consists not only of the jurisdiction administered by the European government but also contains members unwilling to submit and accept the constitution behind such a European government. These opt-out members must consider the *reinforced co-operation* amongst their partners as a *coalition that is willing to provide European public goods from which they may also benefit*. In terms of Olson's model, a European government limited to a restricted number of members, would create a larger net benefit-share in a broader European Union. It therefore turns a 'latent' group with few collective goods into a 'privileged' group where some members in form of the European government provide benefits for all. In this logic, the European government would then provide a larger amount of European collective goods, because it will obtain a larger share of benefits while the number of decision-making member states within the EU has diminished. Effectively this implies that the European government would accept opt-outs as free-riders on the collective goods provided by itself. But it would do so, because the citizens in the polity behind this government value these benefits sufficiently highly that they will provide them on their own. An asymmetric European Union where a European government, based on full democratic legitimacy, provides collective goods to its own citizens would also keep the possibility of intergovernmental co-operative arrangements with other governments open.

This leads us to the question of what kind of institution a European government would enact. Are we creating a super-state within the European community? What are the implications of economic federalism and the logic of collective action for the constitutional system of the European Union?

The Question of a European State

It is often said that realism commands to accept intergovernmentalism as the enduring feature of European integration. For example Weiler (1999: 276) writes:

> 'Intergovernmentalism may be a desirable feature of community and Union governance or a necessary evil, but, whether one or the other, it is a central feature of the system and will, in all likelihood, stay so for the foreseeable future.'

Our analytical approach allows us to go further. What can be said with certainty is that European integration will always have to deal with collective goods, some of which are of inclusive, others of an exclusive or pure public nature. Our theory claims that the likelihood is high for intergovernmentalism to be able to provide inclusive European club goods, although not necessarily in optimal quantities. But the theory also says that other collective goods will not be provided at a sufficient rate as the European Union accepts more and more additional members, the Franco-German motor stutters and the subsidiarity principle prevails. Paradoxically, *the success of European integration is undermining its success.*[147] There is only one strategy possible to avoid the gradual deterioration of policy-making in the Union: not voluntary co-operation between autonomous governments, but binding rules that commit decision-makers and prevent defection. The European Union needs to become a unitary actor. This, of course, raises a controversial issue. Does having a constitution for a European government not imply creating a European super-state?

There are two approaches to discussing such binding rules for unitary policy-making. One is to consider them as *coercive*, i.e. as externally imposed and enforced by brute force. This is the neoclassical explanation of government and the state, which is seen as holding the monopoly of coercive force. The other is an *endogenous* conception of government as a self-enforcing equilibrium among individuals (Basu, 2000:188). The expression of a 'European superstate' has the connotations of the neoclassical model of state. The endogenous state resembles more the classical idea of a *'res publica'*. Government is seen as an instrument to overcome co-operation failure and to internalise externalities for the benefit of all. Of course, political theorists in the tradition of New Political Economy and public choice challenge that governments *actually* operate in such welfare enhancing manners, because politicians seek their own individual benefits. However, like all institution, states have *normative* content because their institutions are based on collective consensus, at least as far as constitutions are concerned. Without going into the details of these different approaches, it is of interest that our model of stochastic consensus is perfectly coherent with the endogenous explanation of the state because consensus on a constitution emerges endogenously from mutual respect and communicative practices. In this perspective, states are a system of institutions, which are based exclusively on public consensus and not on force or coercion. In Basu's (2000:188) words,

> 'The state, in the end is nothing more terrible than the ordinary citizen's belief, that, if he behaves in a certain way, the agents of the state who are simple other citizens will punish or reward him, along with the beliefs of the agents of the state that if a person behaves in a certain way then they ought to punish or reward that person and, if they do not do so, others will punish or reward them and so on. In other

words these beliefs must be self-fulfilling because they result in an outcome that is a subgame perfect equilibrium.'

Similarly Searle (1995:32) has emphasised the consensual nature of institutions, such as money:

'(...) In order that a type of thing should satisfy the definition (...) of 'money', it must be believed to be, or used as, or regarded as, etc., satisfying the definition. For these sorts of facts, it seems to be almost a logical truth that you cannot fool all the people all the time. If everybody always thinks that this sort of thing is money, and they use it as money and treat it as money, then it is money. If nobody ever thinks this sort of thing is money, then it is not money. And what goes for money goes for elections, private property, wars, voting, promises, marriages, buying and selling, political offices, and so on.'

Hence, the rewards and punishments that lead to the emergence of institutions, governments, and states are not necessarily external sanctions by brute force, but they result endogenously from individuals' interactions. This poses two questions: What structures are required for European citizens developing mutual respect and being connected in their policy deliberation? And what is specific about the institution of the state that cannot be achieved by individuals voluntarily co-ordinating their actions?

I will reply to the first question in Chapter Seven. As to the second question, the answer is provided by the theory of co-ordination failures. The state or government is an institution that solves co-operation failure.[148] Benassi et al. (1994) distinguish between weak and strong form co-ordination failure. Silvestre (1993) and Horn (2001) have reframed these concepts. They use the notion of *co-ordination failure* for the strong form, which is due to incomplete information or a failure to react to this information. They call the weak form *co-operation failure*, which is due to the rules of the game (co-operative or non-co-operative). I will stick to their denominations. In the definition of the state by Basu, quoted above, an individual chooses his or her own behaviour *knowing how all or some others will react*. This reaction is what Rousseau meant by *volonté générale* or what Searle called, somewhat differently, the 'collective intentionality' underlying all institutions. It reflects the stochastic consensus whereby individuals 'accept' institutions. However, as I pointed out above, this consensus does not mean everyone thinks the same, nor that everyone acts the same. But if individuals deviate in their behaviour from the general will, they may cause externalities or type-II-inefficiencies for all others. This could create insecurity, lawlessness or simply inhibit the optimal provision of collective goods. The result created by such non-co-operative behaviour will be inferior to a general co-operative solution. There may be good reasons for such behaviour, as the Prisoner's Dilemma in game theory demonstrates, but lack of communication is one condition of the dilemma. The fundamental structure behind co-operation failure is that there is a negative trade-off (a strategic substitutability) between the rewards for the individual and the collective.[149] By appointing government as an agent that imposes sanctions on deviating individuals, society internalises the externality caused by their behaviour. If they cause a loss to the group, their punishment takes away their potential benefit. If they cause a collective gain through their own sacrifice, they will receive a reward. Hence the institution of government overcomes co-operation failure by having an agent acting on behalf of the collective interest.

Why is it necessary to appoint a government, i.e. an independent agent to enforce sanctions on deviating behaviours? Could the same objectives not be achieved by voluntary co-operation of the community?[150] The answer is simple: Providing sanctions on non-co-operating behaviour is itself a collective good that is subject to the logic of collective action. Therefore policing will only take place if one actor (or a coalition of actors) considers that the benefits for themselves from policing others are greater than the costs. However, in a large group the likelihood of dissent increases[151] and therefore the utility of deviating behaviour also rises and so does the disutility of collective sanctions against such behaviour. *Hence, large groups will not be able to police deviating behaviour consistently.*

This logic can be observed quite clearly in the case of sanctions against Euro-member states deviating from the rules of the Stability and Growth Pact. When the European Commission wanted to sanction Germany in spring 2002, the member states vetoed it. The solution to the dilemma of collective action consists in appointing an agent, i.e. *a government that is itself subject to sanctions if it does not sanction others.* This is the basic idea of democratic constitutions. Governments as agents of collective intentionality will not be re-elected if they do not enforce the policies and rules they were charged to implement. But that means that only a democratic government that receives its legitimacy directly from individual citizens who have agreed on the procedures of a constitution can be considered endogenous in the sense described. Such government is powerful. It is endowed with a capacity to act, because it has the agreement of its citizens - if not with respect to detailed regulative issues, at least regarding constitutional procedures. But this fact implies also that the broader public sphere of a European epistemic constituency reduces or eliminates the democratic frustrations that are linked to type-II-inefficiencies. A European Constitution that covers the policy domain of all European collective goods and makes the European government accountable to its citizens does not create a super-state, by systematically violating citizen's preferences. On the contrary, it allows and enables individuals to participate in the formation of European policy preferences. It thereby creates the framework within which a European government will gain endogenously the legitimacy that is required for the efficient administration of Europe's collective goods.

The Open Method of Co-ordination

On the other hand, there is still some room for intergovernmental policy-making when there are strategic complementarities between national governments or spillovers between different governance levels. This argument is linked to our discussion of public goods and collective action failure. Co-ordination failure occurs when the individual and the collective will move in the same direction (strategic complementarity), whilst the outcome remains sub-optimal for reasons of insufficient information, uncertainty or biased incentives.[152] In this case it is sufficient to provide means facilitating the flow of information within the group to ensure Pareto-improved outcomes. We know that the externalities attached to exclusive collective goods and pure public goods imply strategic substitutabilities between individual actors and the group interest. Inclusive goods are characterised by strategic complementarities. Hence, the *efficient provision of exclusive collective and pure public goods requires the action of a unified agent*, a government, to represent the collective European interest. But *inclusive public goods may be provided by voluntary policy co-ordination* between autonomous national governments.

The efficiency of such policies would be improved if there were mechanisms to facilitate the flow of information and understanding between national governments. Hence the institutional mix between centralisation and decentralisation, between policy delegation and intergovernmentalism depends on the nature of collective goods. This is an argument in favour of a bi-cameral parliamentary system, where the provision of inclusive club goods falls into the competencies of a state-representing chamber and European pure goods and exclusive collective goods are subject to a pan-European legislature. In the European context these two functions should be covered by the Council and the European Parliament. For example, the defence of the territory of the European Union is a pure public good. It belongs to the competencies of the Union, as every citizen is concerned and affected by the proper functioning of the European institutions. Hence, citizens have to deliberate jointly about the appropriate policies and the proper representation of European citizens is the Parliament. On the other hand the development of new defence technology may only concern a sub-group of the Union and policy co-ordination between member states may create sufficient synergies to produce the weapon system, which makes it an inclusive collective good. Hence, representatives of national governments should negotiate such ventures in the Council. To be perfectly clear, *national* parliaments as such have no function in the provision of European collective goods. Their task is to control national governments.[153]

These theoretical conclusions are not alien to reality. A European Constitution does not have to re-invent the wheel. We find them expressed in the distinction between the 'Community method' of policy delegation to a supranational authority versus the intergovernmental 'open method of co-ordination'. Delegation means the pooling of sovereignty at the European level in a unified institution. The perfect example is the European Central Bank, which is the unique rule setter for monetary policy. Somewhat less complete, but with similar intentions, the European Commission has been given authority to deal with external trade relations, competition policies and regulation of the single market. Regarding intergovernmental policy co-operation we can distinguish on one side a weak form, which Wallace and Wallace (2000:32) called the 'OECD technique' and which has now been upgraded by the Lisbon summit to the 'open method of co-ordination' (Hodson and Maher, 2001). A stronger form called 'intensive transgovernmentalism' (Wallace and Wallace 2000:33) resembles the coalition building approach in the provision of public goods described above in respect to the Franco-German axis.

The open method of co-ordination clearly focuses on improvements in information flows. The instruments consist in guidelines, benchmarks, performance indicators, targets, monitoring, peer review, and evaluation with the emphasis based on the process of mutual learning (Hodson and Maher, 2001). Helen Wallace has pointed out that this technique of light policy co-ordination 'served as a mechanism of transition from nationally rooted policy-making to a collective regime' (Wallace and Wallace, 2000:32), although recently this approach seems 'being developed not as a transitional mechanism, but as a policy mode in its own right' (p.33). This is not surprising. Given that the ongoing process of integration creates inclusive, exclusive, and pure public goods, the European Union needs to develop a proper governance for inclusive club goods, which is the 'open method of co-ordination'. But it will need to set up better institutions for the efficient provision of all other collective goods. This does not exist today.[154] Although the European Commission is meant to act as the agent of the European 'common concern', it does not have the full democratic legitimacy to impose sanctions on deviating behaviour by national governments. On the one side the Commission owes its authority to the very governments who are supposed to be sanctioned, but only national governments can claim to be legitimised by public vote. In fact, the main role of the Commission and the European Parliament consists in being a voice, in facilitating the flow of information, making proposals, providing analysis, brokering agreements. This is archetypically the agency function to overcome co-ordination failure for the class of inclusive club goods which are subject to co-operation failure. It is not adequate for the provision of exclusive and pure public goods. To repeat, efficient governance for the whole range of policies subject to strategic substitutionability requires a proper European government that draws its legitimacy from an integrated European polity, i.e. from the complete set of European Union citizens.[155]

As I have pointed out, the creation of a European polity does not necessitate a European consensus on substantial policy issues. It simply requires a consensus on a European Constitution, which guarantees equal rights and freedoms to every citizen in the European Union, so that the agreement on procedures allows the individual acceptance of policy decisions, which do not necessarily reflect individual preferences *a priori*. We must now add to this, that such a constitution must set up a European institution, which has the legitimacy and therefore the power to sanction national governments, if they do not conform to European policy decisions. Anything short of this arrangement will not be able to solve the problem of European collective action, nor does it deserve the name European Constitution.

Chapter Six.
The Elusive Policy Mix

The previous chapter has established that voluntary intergovernmental co-operation, even if facilitated by the European Commission, will only produce the efficient provision of European collective goods and policies if they are of an inclusive nature. In this case strategic complementarities create an incentive to co-operate. In all other cases, strategic substitutabilities induce preference dissimilation, free-riding and yield sub-optimal policy equilibria. These problems increase with the number of decision-makers, whether due to EU enlargement or decentralisation according to the subsidiarity principle. Hence, a European government is needed to determine policies for the entire European policy domain of all non-inclusive collective goods. But even for inclusive goods a European government can play a useful part by overcoming information asymmetries and thereby improving the outcome.

The question is now, how should different policies be classified? The answer is not obvious. As Alesina et al. (2002:8) have noted, 'in practice, government functions do not neatly line up on a scale from high to low economy of scale, high to low externality, high to low homogeneity of preferences'. In this chapter I will first take a broad look at these classification problems and then take macroeconomic policy co-ordination as a specific case study. In the next chapter I will draw some conclusions relevant to the writing of a European Constitution.

The Broad Policy Assignment

It is now commonplace that 'the EU has, since its inception, been active in a wide array of policy domains, and indeed has over the decades extended its policy scope' (Wallace and Wallace, 2000:5). The number of Treaty changes has accelerated over time, and the scope of European institutions from the Commission and Council to the European Parliament has become wider, although the powers remain unequally distributed. The European Commission has 24 Directorates-General and corresponding policy areas. But the most important extensions of responsibility have taken place in the Council of the European Union, which meets in numerous different ministerial formations from General Affairs and External Relations, Ecofin, Agriculture to Culture, Tourism and Catastrophe protection. Several hundred committees are active in the implementation of Council decisions and enjoy extensive freedom of discretion (Eriksen, 2000:60). There is no point in going systematically through all these policy domains so as to classify them according to our criteria of inclusive or exclusive goods. These criteria are rather meant as benchmarks to inform deliberation about specific policies.

Table 6.1. The Desirable Allocation of Policy Responsibilities

Policy Domains	Externalities	Pref. Aysmmetry	Devolution
1. International Trade	High	Low	EU/Global
2. Common Market	High	Low	EU/Global
3. Money and Fiscal	Med./High	?	National/EU
4. Education, Res & Culture	Low	High	Local/National
5. Environment	Med./High	High	National/EU/Global
6 Bus. Relations (Sectoral)	Low	High	National
7. Bus. Relations (Non-sectoral)	High	?	EU/Global
8. International Relations	Med./High	Low	National/EU
9. Citizens & Social Protection	Mixed	High	Local/National

Source: Alesina, Angeloni, Schuknecht, 2002

Nevertheless, I will take up from the literature two attempts in classification between national and European policy domains. First, I reproduce as Table 6.1 the allocation of policy responsibility according to externalities from Alesina et al. (2002). It gives 9 policy domains and rates their degree of externalities and preference asymmetry. This gives an indication for the potential size of type-I and type-II inefficiencies respectively. These authors clearly consider the collective goods of international trade, the common market and non-sectoral business relations as European goods, while education, research, culture, and sectoral business relations are classified as local or national goods.

This assignment is relatively uncontroversial because by definition it minimises given inefficiencies of both types. The in-between goods are more problematic. Of course in the environmental field, some externalities are local, like noise protection at an airport, and others are European like the fall-out from nuclear accidents. But even this assignment is only partial. If local authorities legislate on the airport landing and starting hours, they affect also other airports. Similarly, the creation of a European knowledge society concerns education, but there are spillovers from skills and training that may affect European-wide business practices. Hence, simply minimising given inefficiencies is not enough. We have to look at shifting the trade-off curve between type-I and type-II inefficiencies. However, we may retain from the Alesina paper that the nature of externalities and spillovers does indeed constitute an essential criterion for assigning policy to local, national or European levels.

Secondly, an alternative approach is to look at the existing European policy domains as they are defined by the European Treaties. This has been done by Friedrich (2002b). In Table 6.2 I have taken his European policy areas as the basis for the classification of inclusive and exclusive collective goods. I have also added macroeconomic policy-making domains. It turns out that nearly every policy domain in the European dimension has both inclusive and exclusive goods with different strategic implications. This makes a coherent assignment complex, if not impossible. The work of the Convention on Europe's Future has also come to this realisation. Talk of a 'catalogue of competencies' has ceased. In each European policy domain there is scope for the unified action by a European government and the contributions coming from national member state authorities. The proper mix of these community and intergovernmental methods can be demonstrated by looking at macroeconomic stabilisation policy. This is what we will do now.

Table 6.2 Policy Assignment of Inclusive and Exclusive Goods

Policy Areas	Exclusive public good European government	Inclusive public good National or regional government
Single Market	Legislation on freedoms (goods, services, persons and capital), (EC Art. 13-16, 23-31).	Legislation for local cross-border markets without European Dimension
CAP	Market for agricultural products.	Rural development and supportive income policies
Financial service supervision	Unified decision structure	Decentralised information gathering
Territorial infrastructure	Pan-European transport networks	All other infrastructures
Competition policy/ subsidies (Art. 81-93)	Unified decision structure	Decentralised implementation
Industrial policy (Art. 157)	Strengthen competitiveness without distortions	Implementation
Structural policies (Art. 136)	Prevent distortions	Coordinate and implement
Social policy (Art. 136)	Prevent distortions	Coordinate and implement
Direct Taxation	Taxes on highly mobile factors	Taxes on less mobile factors like labour, property, etc.
Indirect Taxation	Prevention distortions in the single market	Possibly share some income for joint policy instruments
Financial market regulation & supervision	Set standards	Surveillance
Macroeconomic policies		
Monetary policy	Maintaining price stability	Supportive supply policies
Fiscal policy	EU government to define aggregate fiscal stance	National governments to implement budgets accordingly.
Exchange rate policy	ECB and EU government as unified external representations	---- None ----
Wage policies	Provide information and general policy orientation	Wage bargaining in national structures.

The Macroeconomic Policy Mix

The theory of fiscal federalism has established that stabilisation policies should be conducted at the centralised policy-making level. The central tenet is, of course, that both monetary and fiscal policies matter. Economists have heatedly debated this issue, but the consensus tends to the verdict that stabilisation policies matter and are welfare improving.[156] Monetary policy matters for output stabilisation definitely in the short term, and for price stability in the long term.[157] Fiscal policy is irrelevant if the Ricardian Equivalence condition holds, whereby individuals reduce current consumption in order to save for future tax and debt repayments, but many empirical studies seem to reject this hypothesis. In the context of the European Monetary Union, fiscal policy is considered important because it can support or endanger the European Central Bank's task of maintaining price stability. This insight has produced an extensive literature on rule-based fiscal policy co-ordination,[158] but the constitutional question of centralisation versus decentralisation of fiscal policy is rarely considered. The strong emphasis on microeconomic incentive systems often neglects the macroeconomic rational of stabilisation policy. Given that price stability is a necessary and sufficient economic (but not political) condition for the long-term sustainability of the European currency (see Collignon, 2002), the proper interaction between fiscal and monetary policy is highly relevant.

According to the theory of fiscal federalism (see Musgrave and Musgrave, 1973) there are at least three major reasons why stabilisation policies should be conducted at the central level. First, the need to keep money scarce, so that it can function as a hard budget constraint, requires monetary policy to be unified at the highest level. This insight was clearly realised by the creation of the ECB. Secondly, in open, small economies within a larger single market, demand effects from increased public expenditures will be easily diluted by import leaks, annulling the multiplier effect.[159] Thirdly, debt issued by small local jurisdictions is largely held by creditors outside the jurisdiction and this can cause problems for the distribution of debt burdens and repayment. I will focus in the following on the demand management functions of fiscal policy because they affect many other policy areas[160] and because they provide a case study of the collective action problems discussed in Chapter Five.

Efficient Stabilisation Policy

The purpose of stabilisation policy is to maintain equilibrium between aggregate demand and supply. In the long term, aggregate supply or potential output, as it is also called, depends on technological factors (productivity) but also on social regulations affecting the supply of labour, capital and innovation i.e. on structural reform policies. In the short run, supply may respond to price surprises when firms cannot disentangle a sudden increase in inflation from improvements in relative prices as formulated in the Lucas supply curve[161]. This offers governments an incentive to create surprise inflation, unless the central bank is independent and committed to price stability. Although there may be reasons why authorities may wish to stimulate supply to increase faster than long-term productive capacity (one reason is the desire to win elections as the political business cycle explains), we will concentrate on stabilisation policies keeping aggregate demand in line with long-term aggregate supply. I will not deal with short-term adjustments in the business cycle, because we are interested in the long-term implications of policy-making. Aggregate demand responds negatively to increases in the real interest rate and positively to higher government (net) spending. Put differently, higher budget surpluses (lower deficits) reduce aggregate demand, and higher deficits increase demand.[162] Furthermore, price stability depends on monetary policy. We know that the European Central Bank is mandated to give priority to the maintenance of price stability, and we assume it uses the real interest rate to achieve its objective, as in the Romer model (1999). Stability requires that if the government reduces demand (increases the budget position) interest rates have to come down to pull in compensating private sector demand.

This can be shown by the efficient-policy-line in Figure 6.1. It is derived from the first two equations in Annexe 3, which describe an economy where two policy objectives (full employment and price stability) are to be achieved by two policy variables, monetary and fiscal policy. In equilibrium both price stability and full employment are realised.[163] But there are infinite combinations or policy mixes along the downward sloping efficient-policy-line in Figure 6.1, where the interaction between fiscal and monetary policy produce the equilibrium position. Any policy mix on the efficient policy line is therefore fully compatible with the ECB's mandate.[164]

A point like B above the line reflects an overly restrictive policy combination. For a given budget position real interest rates are too high and lead to falling prices and rising unemployment. Below the line (point A) aggregate demand is inflationary. Here interest rates are too low, given the governments' deficit position. Hence a policy correction is called for. Stabilisation policy is often associated with policy measures required to return to the equilibrium line after some exogenous shock has occurred. In principle this adjustment can be achieved by using either monetary or fiscal policy exclusively or a combination between the two. Depending on the different impact and use made of the two policies, different positions on the policy line will be reached. For example, I have called a 'monetarist' someone who believes only monetary policy is needed to correct disequilibrium. A stylised 'Keynesian' believes that only fiscal policy is required. Hence, monetarists would reduce excess demand at point *A* by rising interest rates, Keynesians would reduce the deficit. As a consequence monetarists return to equilibrium at point *R*, Keynesians at point *D*. The mirror picture applies in case of a recession (Point *B*). Of course, different combinations between these policy measures are possible.

Figure 6.1 The Efficient Policy Mix

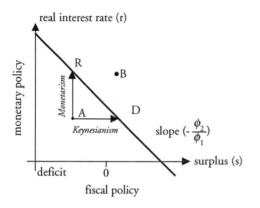

Defining an Optimal Policy Mix

The two policy combinations *R* and *D* are both efficient with respect to the macro-economic balance. But are they also optimal? This, of course, depends on some external standard, naturally a utility or welfare function. Hence, the optimality relevant to the policy mix is maximising welfare. It raises two questions. First, whose welfare is to be maximised? Second, which factors determine the shape of the welfare function?

The first question throws us back to the overarching theme of this book. By definition, welfare functions reflect the collective preferences of epistemic constituencies. Ideally, these preferences translate into the collective choice made by a given polity. In order to make the logic of the subsequent argument more transparent I will now assume that the polity and the epistemic constituencies, which determine the preferences for a given policy mix are congruous. In other words, public choices reflect a broad policy consensus.[165] An optimal policy mix is then the policy combination between monetary and fiscal policy that maximises the welfare of a specific epistemic constituency, given the constraint of macroeconomic balance, with price stability and full employment both achieved.[166]

This leads to the second question. Given that welfare is derived from monetary and fiscal policy, what determines the collective utility, i.e. the form of the welfare function? Individuals in a given epistemic constituency may evaluate the benefits they derive from a given level of interest rates and compare them with the benefits obtained from a given budget position. These evaluations are complex and take other considerations than only the policy mix into account. The interest rate level may be highly relevant for financial institutions, pensioners or corporate investment decisions, as they affect the discount rate of future income streams. Low interest rates may be bad for rentiers, but good for entrepreneurs and economic growth. The budget position affects the burden for taxpayers today and/or in the future. A high budget deficit may stimulate growth because taxes are low today, but strangle it tomorrow when they must be raised. It also may raise equilibrium interest rates and therefore dampen growth.[167] On the other hand, a budget surplus may also release real resources for private consumption and productive investment.[168] Thus, the collective utility of a given policy mix reflects the evaluations of these and other possible arguments through collective deliberation. Our model of stochastic consensus has provided the micro-foundation of collective choice by showing how individual beliefs and preferences can be aggregated into consensual collective preferences. We can use this model here to explain how the parameters of the collective utility function in a given epistemic constituency are determined by this process of public deliberation.[169]

An optimal policy mix maximises a given welfare function at the point where the ratio of marginal social utilities of monetary and fiscal policies equal the slope of the efficient policy line. At that point our given polity maximises the collective preferences for specific levels of interest rates and budget positions. Thus, the two points R and D in Figure 6.1 are representing two different policy mixes and must correspond to two different sets of policy preferences. In the context of the American experience, Dominique Strauss-Kahn has referred to the point R as the Reagan-Volker policy mix (high interest rates, high deficits) and to the point D (low interests, balanced budget or surplus) the Clinton-Greenspan mix. I call them the Republican versus the Democrat choice. Hence, in the American democracy public preferences have shifted over time, taking into account the evidence of previous policy outcomes and the shifting domestic and international context. In any democratic polity, this should be a normal phenomenon. Public preferences are not cast in iron. Yet, this is not so in Europe. Here, defining the optimal policy mix is a highly complex and undemocratic process.

The European Policy Mix under the Stability and Growth Pact

In the EU, macroeconomic policy-making is determined by a hybrid construction, whereby monetary policy is unified, while fiscal policy remains subject to national sovereignty. In principle, this would mean that national parliaments reflect national policy preferences and define their national budget positions accordingly. The European budget position is then the resulting sum of all national positions. However, monetary policy by the ECB is committed to maintaining price stability in Euroland and therefore it is aggregate demand that matters for the ECB's setting of interest rates.[170] National governments cannot expand their deficits or surpluses in an unconstrained way, because the change in anyone's budget position has consequences for the equilibrium level of interest rates affecting all others. Hence, fiscal policy has strong externality effects.[171] In other words, the aggregate fiscal policy stance is a collective good. The policy decision in one epistemic constituency 'produces' a given equilibrium interest rate with consequences for all agents living and working in the whole policy domain called Euroland. It is important to bear in mind that this collective good character is the consequence of economic and monetary unification because European Monetary Union has enlarged the policy domain.

But what kind of collective good is the policy mix? Clearly, it is an exclusive collective good like common property resources. For the 'benefit' of a given interest rate is non-rival, while the costs are rival in the sense that your larger deficit reduces my capacity to borrow without disrupting the equilibrium. This has far-reaching consequences. For as we have seen, it means that voluntary policy co-ordination between EMU member states is unlikely to produce an efficient, let alone an optimal policy mix, unless by pure coincidence the policy preferences in all member states were identical. The reason behind this dilemma is, of course, the very rationale why member states have refused to delegate fiscal policy to the European level: different national polities respond to different epistemic constituencies. Therefore, different collective policy preferences emerge in different member states. European economic policy-makers have attempted to reduce type-II-inefficiencies by keeping the responsibility for fiscal policy at a national level. It is, however, a gross and serious error to believe that this system could operate efficiently and maximise European welfare. For the attempt to reduce type-II-inefficiencies has increased type-I-inefficiencies.[172] *By opting for fiscal subsidiarity, Europe's governments create additional externalities, making the ECB's job more difficult and reducing the likelihood of efficient stabilisation policies.*

One approach to solve this second problem has been the institution of the Stability and Growth Pact (SGP)[173] but it has thrown the baby out with the bath water by maximising type-II-inefficiency. The SGP consists of a set of common fiscal rules and an elaborate multilateral surveillance mechanism, which specify the implementation of the Excessive Deficit Procedure set up in the Maastricht Treaty. They can be summarised as: (1) Keep all budget positions in balance or surplus over the medium term, effectively over the business cycle. Hence, this is a rule to balance structural budgets.[174] (2) Monitor deviations from the rule, and (3) have a range of sanctions from soft public reprimand to hard penalty payments. In terms of our model, this means that there is a rule for the European policy mix consisting in a uniform budget rule ($s_i=0$), applicable to every member state, so that by implication the aggregate fiscal policy stance is also balanced.[175] Monetary policies can then operate effectively as a Stackelberg follower[176] by setting interest rates at the level that corresponds to macroeconomic equilibrium.

There are at least three major difficulties with this approach. First, the fiscal rule is cast in iron, for not applying it would shatter the institutional credibility of EMU. Hence a democratic shift in preferences which may result from policy-learning processes and public deliberation, such as witnessed in the USA, could not take place in Europe. This rigidity poses a major threat to the democratic legitimacy of European stabilisation policies and ultimately to the political consensus behind EMU. For, if democracy has any meaning at all, it is that policy-making should be responsive to public opinion. Secondly, the fact that Euroland's budget policy emerges from national polities and not from a unified European polity implies that national welfare functions are heterogeneous. By superimposing a policy rule of balancing all national budgets, European policy outcomes are by definition welfare lowering. Welfare implies the efficient allocation of scarce resources (here stability-compatible public funds) to satisfy given preferences. This principle is violated if the SGP-rule stipulates an allocation that is not publicly desired. In political economy terms the problem results from the fact that a vote in the Euro-Group or the Ecofin Council reflects the 'median voter' among the 12 (or 15) finance ministers, but not the views of the European median voter. Alesina and Grilli (1992) have analysed the voting procedure in the Council with respect to political/ideological preferences in the appointment of the ECB board. But their analysis also applies to fiscal policy. They found that the decision-making rules in today's 'non-politically-unified-Europe' 'may lead to decisions which could be quite far from the preferences of the European median voter' (p. 69). This problem is structural and dependent on the fact that political representation in the relevant bodies is not reflecting political plurality at the European level, but is composed of only 12 or 15 'districts'. This preference frustration is a cost that lowers the welfare of misrepresented citizens.

Figure 6.2 The Optimal Policy Mix

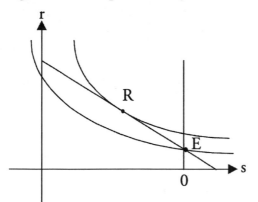

Figure 6.2 demonstrates this case. Suppose the representative voter in one European member state has a Republican preference for the optimal policy mix, while the SGP imposes a balanced budget at point E. The welfare maximising point R lies on a higher indifference curve than the point E. Hence the European policy option will be blamed for the welfare loss. In practical terms this happens when a national government is elected on a tax-cutting program and the European Commission, as the official guardian, demands adherence to the SGP norm. But given that this norm is not sufficiently reflected in the national consensus - otherwise the government would not have been elected - the European Commission's policy request does not seem legitimate, at least not as legitimate as the collective preference expressed by the voters. This lack of legitimacy is also a permanent source of disempowerment of European institutions, as we have seen in Chapter Three.

Third, we have emphasised the need to internalise externalities of exclusive goods by creating a European government that can enforce sanctions. Of course, in principle the SGP foresees penalties. However, the decision-making organ is the Council responding to proposals coming from the Commission. Even if the Regulations of the SGP are rather restrictive and binding on the procedure, they leave a degree of indeterminacy with respect to the substance of Council decisions (Costello, 2001: 129). Hence these decisions are subject to the collective action problem described in Chapter Five (see page 118). Potential poachers act as the principal to the gamekeeper. This may seem too harsh a verdict, but it follows from the fact that national polities reflect national epistemic constituencies and not a European consensus. The unavoidable welfare loss in the present institutional set-up renders every national government into a potential poacher, i.e. it creates an incentive to deviate from the SGP norm.

These are serious allegations not only against the SGP, but also against the whole system of policy-making as it is presently realised in the European multilevel governance. They apply to the complete range of European exclusive and pure public goods. The logical remedy for these problems is the creation of a proper European government.[177] In the next section, I will discuss how a European government would be able to overcome the type-I versus type-II inefficiencies dilemma in fiscal policy. One should note, however, that these conclusions do not affect the provision of inclusive collective good in the same way. In their case, strategic complementarities can produce multiple equilibria outcomes and in order to improve their efficiency, it may be sufficient to facilitate the flow of information. This can be achieved by the European government issuing formal guidelines, passing legally non-binding recommendations and by the Council arguing over benchmarks, best practices and exerting peer pressure. Thus, a European Constitution must provide the space for the *intergovernmental co-ordination of policies concerning inclusive European collective goods*, while at the same time establishing the framework for a *unified governance of exclusive and pure public goods*. I will discuss some practical recommendations for a European Constitution in the next chapter.

Consensual Foundations of a European Welfare Function

Our analysis has brought out the dilemma of the present-day European institutional framework, where policy preferences reflect the consensus formed in national contexts, rather than emerging from policy deliberation in a European polity. We now have to look at the issue of epistemic constitutions and polities more closely. Our theory of stochastic consensus provides us with the analytical tool to understand how preference heterogeneity can be overcome.

Let us discuss the issue of choosing a policy mix for Euroland. For arguments sake, we assume it is derived from people's preference for their retirement arrangements. Those who have invested in private pension schemes may be more interested in higher equilibrium interest rates; those who depend on state pension wish to have balanced budgets to ensure the sustainability of public finance. In order to attain a stochastic policy consensus, two conditions must be met: (1) Mutual respect between the different individuals in an epistemic constituency, meaning that they respect and give weight not only to their own views but also to the arguments advanced by at least one other person. (2) Connectedness, meaning that the pattern of positive respect forms a chain of respect connecting all individuals in the epistemic constituencies in such a way that each member of the group assigns a positive weight to the next member in the sequence and at least one member assigns a positive weight to himself.

Thus, every individual in the group is connected to another through the communication of respect (Lehrer and Wagner, 1981: 27). With these two conditions rational behaviour will ultimately lead to a unanimous preference ranking by each individual adjusting her own beliefs in view of the arguments and evidence produced by others. The process breaks down, if at any point two individuals, or two groups of individuals, refuse respect to eachother (effectively each valuing their own preferences with the weight of one and all others by zero). Although that may frequently happen, individuals may still agree on decision-making procedures, such as voting. In this case we may consider the preference of the median voter as representative for the epistemic constituency's preferences. What matters for our argument, however, is that the median voter's preferences shift systematically towards the consensus as the process of ongoing policy deliberation narrows dissent in the constituency.

Practically, this means that when individuals deliberate on policy issues in a given society, they communicate with other individuals in their immediate environment and life-world. The grandmother will share her worries about her pensions at the family meeting, the young couple discusses the benefits of private pension funds and the cost of mortgage payments with their investment advisor, who attends meetings organised by the bankers' association where a government official may talk about larger policy options and so on. At each communication node, arguments are exchanged whose rationality may be bounded, i.e. not taking into account the broader picture. But because of the connectedness condition a general consensus will eventually emerge (theoretically after an infinite sequence of deliberative iterations but with reasonable degrees of mutual respect much earlier). This outcome does not necessarily conform to any pre-established or universalistic norms, neither ethical nor political nor instrumental. As Stokes (1998) and Przeworski (1998) have rightly pointed out, deliberation may lead people to hold beliefs that may not be in their 'best' interests and that may appear 'perverse' from the perspective of democratic theory. It can create pseudo-preference and pseudo-identities. Yet, a communication process along the described lines by the stochastic consensus model is going on in all societies, regardless of their political regimes and contributes to the legitimacy of collective choices. The outcome of deliberation, whatever it may be, is not independent of the cultural and institutional context in which it takes place. To start with, the bounded rationality of people's preferences is intimately linked to their immediate cultural background and gets only gradually transformed as the broader consensus emerges. Furthermore, institutions create persistence in public preferences, as Jean Monnet saw so clearly. Thus, the debate about retirement schemes will take a different form in a polity where, for example, private pension funds are more widely used than government pensions. As a consequence the policy consensus on the fiscal-monetary-policy mix will also be heterogeneous in different polity contexts. Epistemic constituencies have institutional foundations.

The main reason for the weakness of the European polity and the relative strength of national epistemic constituencies can be found in the fact that structures of cross-border communication remain underdeveloped. This is due to institutional procedures, rather than cultural background factors. It is occasionally argued that linguistic barriers are the main obstacles to the creation of a stronger European polity.[178] But the evidence does not favour this hypothesis. Counterfactual evidence is not only available from multicultural societies like India, China or the Americas. In today's world there are 8000 languages spoken in less than 200 states (Jackson, 1999: 26). More importantly, we observe in Europe that even identical language backgrounds do not ensure policy convergence. French citizens care as little about the policy debate in Belgium, as Germans about Austrians or the British about the Irish. The reason is, that the policy-making process structures are confined to the national constituencies within which policy deliberations are taking place. If the Italian parliament is taking a decision about pension reform, its members are listening to *their* constituency. The median voter is Italian. Similarly, the German or Swedish pension reform will have to reflect the median voter in those countries. But the arguments exchanged in these member states about pension reform are irrelevant to the Italian domestic debate, because retirement age and qualifications are decided by the Italian government.

I am not suggesting that this decision needs to be taken at the European level, but simply that the different national pension reform debates are largely disconnected, although they determine policy preferences on fiscal policy in each polity and *this* is of European concern at least in EMU. I said 'largely disconnected' because it is true that some degree of connectedness and mutual respect takes place in the Council of Ministers and in the related preparatory committees, but this link is weak and the median voter in the Council is likely to represent vastly different preferences from the European median voter. As a consequence of these procedural institutions, it takes a long time for the information originating in some polities to trickle down into other domestic policy debates and to become part of common European knowledge and consensus. Hence, policy dissent between national epistemic constituencies remains dominant.[179]

What is therefore needed is a policy framework, where decisions on the provision of European exclusive collective and pure public goods are subject to legitimation by a European epistemic constituency. This can only be achieved if such policy decisions are taken by a proper European government, which is accountable and subject to the approval by a European electorate. The need to elect a common government would automatically broaden the chain of respect, because the policy debate in another jurisdiction would now become relevant to every individual's assessment of different options. Even if dissent persisted on substantive and distributional issues, consensus on the constitutive rules would unify and broaden the polity by structuring policy deliberation at the level of European citizens. Hence, type-II-inefficiencies would be reduced by a better correspondence between the European polity and the epistemic constituencies, while the broader polity covers a larger range of the policy domain and thereby reduces type-I-inefficiencies. The result is an unambiguous welfare improvement for all European citizens.

Implementing the Optimal Fiscal Policy Stance

The *definition of the aggregate fiscal policy* stance i.e. the determination of aggregate expenditure and revenue programs, is an exclusive collective good because of its externalities on monetary policy as described in the last section. The allocation of *government spending* is a different matter. Most of the expenditure by public authorities is on local and national collective goods whose benefits do not necessarily spill over into other countries. It is true that there are some large-scale European investment projects like transport networks, strategic research (nuclear energy, space technology, molecular biology) or expanding information and communications technology (Soete, 2002), but the bulk of spending is on public goods which are consumed in a local or regional environment. Fiscal federalism has assigned the allocation function for such goods to decentralised levels, while macroeconomic stabilisation was to be decided centrally. This is not necessarily a contradiction, given that in most federations central governments control a large share of general government spending. But in Europe, the Union budget is less than 1.27 per cent of total GDP and less then 3 per cent of general government expenditure. The MacDougall Report (1977) suggested doubling the EU budget to strengthen the stabilisation function in EMU, but this does not seem politically desired, nor is it necessary. What matters for the optimal policy mix is the amount of government net spending, wherever it may originate. This means that the allocation of collective goods is not necessarily a *European* function, although the financing restriction makes the aggregate fiscal stance an exclusive European good. Hence, the budgeting may be done on a national and regional level, while the aggregate fiscal policy stance needs to be set at the European level. This does not exclude that the budget of the European Union could develop over time into a larger item, as genuine European goods are purchased by a European, rather than national governments. I will return to this budget substitution issue below.

The main problem is how to allocate the different expenditure and income shares to national governments. My suggestion to solve the policy mix problem is to assign the function of setting the macro-economic fiscal policy stance to the European government and leave the formulation of the specific spending (and revenue) chapters to national governments. The idea of separating the two functions is not far-fetched. They are already part of budget practices in several European countries, notably France and Italy. In France's Vth Republic, parliament first votes for a given macroeconomic stance by fixing aggregate revenues and expenditure and then proceeds to so-called *arbitrages* between the different titles. An increase of spending in one item needs then always to be financed by a reduction elsewhere. Similarly, in Italy, parliament first votes the *Documento di Programmazione economico-finanziara* (DPEF) in May/June, a macroeconomic document, indicating the targets of budgetary policy over the following three years and their relevance for inflation, growth and employment. A few months later, budgetary policy is implemented by the *Legge Finanziaria* (Finance Act), containing the provisions of the national budget and implementing legislation (*appunto di accompagnamento*). The coherence of the aggregate fiscal policy stance in Europe could be achieved by a similar 'European DPEF' (see also Amato, 2002). It seems to me that the present Broad Economic Policy Guidelines (Article 99) could be developed into such an instrument.

Fiscal policy-making in Europe would then be a process going through several steps. First, a European government would formulate the fiscal policy stance for the whole of the Euro-area in view of the requirements of the business cycle, inflation perspectives, the international environment, economic growth etc. This document would have to be put together by the European government with the input from national governments that would have to produce their own budget drafts beforehand. The European government would broadly accept the local allocations, although it could set some specific European accents with respect to externalities that are relevant to the whole economy. But most fundamentally, it would establish the framework for aggregate fiscal stance, reflecting the policy preferences of European citizens with respect to the efficient policy mix at the European level. But this aggregate deficit may also reflect different national deficit and debt positions, and allows therefore greater regional flexibility than the present Stability and Growth Pact. For example, it could accommodate the point frequently made by the British Chancellor of the Exchequer that a low-debt-country with high infrastructure investment needs should be treated differently than a highly indebted member state. Second, in order to ensure that this document will indeed reflect a (stochastic) consensus about collective policy preferences the integrated European budget plan would have to be debated and voted by the European Parliament. Obviously, the EP representing European citizens could amend the project. All proposals and amendments are public and would fuel a European-wide debate on policy orientations and the provision of collective goods. Institutionally, however the process of deliberation would by definition transcend the national framework. Third, after the vote in the European Parliament, the integrated fiscal document goes to the Council for approval. At this point, arbitrages between national governments under the constraint of the aggregate position are possible. Given that the overall revenue and spending levels are fixed, one government could have a larger share in spending and deficits, if another country accepted a smaller share. In summary, the European government, with the approval by the *European Parliament, fixes the overall 'envelope' of public finance, but the execution is left to national authorities*. It is this aggregate fiscal stance that is then relevant for monetary policy and the European Central Bank.

At this point, the question of budget share allocation arises. Three different approaches for assigning national deficit quota are possible: intergovernmental bargaining, a transfer union or a market solution. The first solution would imply that the Ecofin Council would become some kind of clearing house for different national claims. This has the doubtful advantage that it maintains the intergovernmental form of fiscal policy co-ordination intact, and therefore allows national civil servants to keep their jobs and to travel to Brussels. Hence, their opposition to this proposal may be less strong. But more fundamentally, the drawback is that the annual haggling for budget shares is messy and would hardly contribute to a coherent pan-European view of fiscal policy or to a strengthening of the legitimacy of political choices.

One way to overcome this discretionary bargaining would be to reinforce the European Union's budget, similar to the federal budgets in most developed federations. This is the second option. Such arrangement does not necessarily imply a large budget at the level of central government, but it requires a system of intergovernmental grants and transfers. The theory of fiscal federalism has discussed the implications of such set-ups extensively. It is generally accepted that such grants can contribute to the internalisation of spillovers and externalities from other jurisdictions, facilitate fiscal equalisation and can improve the efficiency of the overall tax system (Oates, 1999). The first function is best addressed by conditional grants in the form of matching finance for specific collective goods when the provision of local services creates benefits or costs for residents of other jurisdictions. Many transfers in the European Union, whether for the Common Agricultural Policy or Structural Funds take this form. Unconditional grants are usually based on an equalisation formula that measures fiscal need or fiscal capacity. In the European Union transfers are never totally unconditional, although the Cohesion Fund clearly has a strong emphasis on fiscal equalisation, especially by identifying Portugal, Spain, Greece and Ireland as deserving support in the run-up to Monetary Union. In all these arrangements, the EU is closer to the German, Austrian or Canadian systems of horizontal transfers between jurisdictions, than to the structures in the USA or India, where equalising grants transfer money from central to state governments. Conditionality allows to restrict transfers on deserving individuals and citizens, while broad support for government budgets always has a strong holistic dimension and is subsequently hard to reduce. But this means that grants are not a very suitable instrument for defining the aggregate fiscal policy stance. For if they are functional and target orientated, they contain an element of 'entitlement' that is inflexible over the short and medium term. If they provide unconditional budget support, like to a large extent in Germany, the greater political, ideological and cultural heterogeneity in Europe would lead to communitarian resentment and demands 'to get my money back'. Hence, in the European context, it seems more appropriate not to expand a European transfer system. Instead, it is recommended that member state governments are responsible for the allocation of national collective goods, and implement the policy choices made by the European government with respect to European policies. Where a European government needs to provide collective goods directly it needs its own resources. But this, of course, implies that a European government stands on its own tax base and is responsible via the European Parliament to the citizens of the Union as a whole.

A third solution for the allocation of shares in the aggregate fiscal policy stance would be the creation of tradable deficit permits, as suggested by Casella (1999, 2001). The idea is derived from the experience in environmental markets where fishing or pollution rights are traded. These markets create property rights for exclusive public goods. In our case, public authorities in EMU countries would be allowed to trade rights to deficit creation after an overall ceiling (the aggregate policy stance) and an initial distribution of permits (for example corresponding to GDP-shares) has been agreed. The virtue of the scheme lies in the definition of property rights for deficits, allowing the internalisation of fiscal externalities and creating an incentive to minimise costs. Here is not the place to discuss the tradable deficit permit scheme in its technicalities. This has been done by Casella. What is, however, of significance is the fact that such an arrangement fits perfectly into our idea that a European government should be in charge of defining the aggregate fiscal policy stance, while national governments are responsible for allocating taxes and expenditure. For the total amount of permits is derived from the aggregate deficit, which is the 'envelope' for accommodating individual countries' deficit needs. In other words, the European government would define the total ceiling of tradable deficit rights. A vote by the European Parliament on the European DPEF would set the legal volume of deficit permits. If any individual jurisdiction, be it a national government, or a regional or local authority or even - why not? - the European government, wishes to issue more debt than is initially allocated, it would have to buy permits from another authority which does not wish to use its own quota. Hence buying permits carries costs that need to be compared with the political costs of domestic fiscal consolidation. *This* is exactly the debate that should be going on in *national or local parliaments*. It confers responsibility to polities, which are by and large capable to take decision in congruence with their respective policy domains. Hence, the 'envelope approach' would allow for the flexible adjustment of the aggregate ceiling in accordance to changing economic requirements. The *stabilisation function* of public finance would be centralised at the European level, as postulated by the theory of fiscal federalism. The *allocation* of deficits through the market mechanism distributes the responsibility for fiscal rectitude in the most efficient manner across different countries at minimum cost.

The advantages of the scheme are its flexibility for individual countries, the correct and efficient evaluation of fiscal consolidation policies, and the regained capacity to pursue active stabilisation policies. Moreover, the perfect transparency in the allocation of national shares by the permit market and the European-wide deliberation on the aggregate fiscal stance would facilitate the emergence of a European policy consensus that is less dependent on national backgrounds and contexts, and more consistent with the requirements of exclusive and pure European public goods. Finally, the allocation of deficit permits through the market is consistent with the normative foundations of individualism and a monetary market economy, breaking the holistic fetters of traditional communitarianism.

I have looked in this chapter at the collective logic of fiscal policy co-ordination as a typical example for the dilemmas and remedies related to the provision of exclusive public goods in Europe. Similar reasoning can be applied to other public goods like competition policy, state aid, the external representation of the European Union, the Common Foreign and Security Policy, immigration etc. I will not discuss these issues here. They require further in-depth studies and will hopefully be addressed by the Convention on Europe's Future. *My purpose was to point at a logical problem in European policy-making.* This problem is simple and requires a simple answer: collective goods and policies that benefit potentially all European citizens require a European government for their efficient provision. Unless a European Constitution addresses this issue, European integration is not sustainable.

Chapter Seven.
Implications for a European Constitution

A lively debate about Europe's future Constitution has developed since the European Convention started its work in February 2002. The idea of writing a constitution now seems generally accepted, even if some deviating interpretations about its meaning persist. Different authors have made recommendations or even written up draft constitutions.[180] The media are also increasingly reporting on the subject. All this is part of the unfolding public deliberation to which this book is meant to contribute. It may seem that some of its ideas are out of line with the emerging policy consensus among Europe's political elites. Some may appear utopian or at least ahead of time. However, my purpose was not to write a constitutional draft, or to formulate a consensus project to which others may agree. I have simply aimed to produce logical arguments and evidence about how a European Constitution must be structured if it is to be consistent with the normative intentions of European integration. Naturally, new ideas question old points of view and this produces dissent. Nevertheless, I believe that intellectual coherence is a necessary condition for sustainable and enduring policy-making. This is my justification for challenging the established policy consensus. In my view, *loyalty to Europe demands dissent* from the weak consensus on the smallest common denominator.

The Convention's President Valéry Giscard d'Estaing has expressed the hope that the new constitution 'will last 50 years' (*Financial Times*, 7 October 2002), but the evidence coming out from the Convention's work does not seem to support his wish. Many proposals do not go far enough, they accentuate the problem of collective action and will actually reduce Europe's capacity to solve its internal and external problems. The Convention's working group on economic governance produced no results. At best, the output of the Convention seems to be another step along the long road of constitutional rule changes since the Single European Act, the Maastricht, Amsterdam and Nice Treaties. The question is whether this Constitution is a final document, or keeping the process of change open. It seems obvious that there is no consensus yet for the far-reaching institutional changes discussed in this book, although I believe they are essential to preserve Europe's future. But our theoretical framework of stochastic consensus allows us not to despair. It tells us that what matters is keeping *the process* of deliberation on European integration going. I consider the sometimes radical policy recommendations in this book, derived from Europe's ideological history and the logic of collective action, as *benchmarks giving direction to smaller pragmatic steps*. But in order to one day reach the final destination, very concrete practical measures have to be implemented today. The most important is the *creation of structures which allow the emergence of a European constitutional consensus*. Europe's civil society, whether individual citizens, academics, business people or politicians have to ponder the arguments for and against constitutive rules and decide what they find acceptable. But they must not be limited by the expediency of political compromise. Agreement among policy-makers should follow deliberation, not precede it. The method of convoking a European Convention has introduced some degree of deliberation into the process. But the composition of its members, and the speed by which it has to conclude does not include European citizens at large. In this final chapter I will look at some concrete implications derived from the general logic of the book. I will first consider four issues of strategic orientations and then three practical consequences.

Creating Constitutional Consensus

Europe consists of highly diversified societies. Although it is quite clear, especially when looking from afar, that some sort of European identity exists, it seems dominated by an obvious heterogeneity of customs, norms, and cultures that are part of Europe's tradition and also its wealth. Yet, in this respect Europe is not unique. Cultural heterogeneity is probably even greater in the Republic of India, in the People's Republic of China, and possibly between the different communities of immigrants in the United States or Canada. *What is unique in Europe is the voluntary delegation of political sovereignty by well established nation-states to common institutions.* Thus what distinguishes Europe from other parts of the world is institutional, not cultural heterogeneity. However, for the EU's common institutions to work effectively a constitutional consensus is required that accepts the ground rules for European policy-making. Even if there is dissent or conflict about certain collective choices on the allocation of public goods, it is paramount that the procedures according to which decisions are made, are fully accepted *by all citizens* of the European Union. This alone will give enduring legitimacy and power to European institutions. When no such constitutional consensus exists, institutions will not last. If the degree of dissent is too high, policy output becomes inefficient.

How can such constitutional consensus be created? Our stochastic consensus model provides some hint. First, the conditions of mutual respect and connectedness between citizens must be met. Second, the deliberative process must converge reasonably quickly so that the narrowing of preference heterogeneity allows taking definite decisions by voting.

(I) Mutual respect emerges quasi-spontaneously from contractual transactions between individuals. We trust those we know. European integration over the last 50 years has greatly expanded the domain of such transactions between European citizens, be it in the business area, cultural and political exchange or on a personal level.[181] This is important because it is the foundation on which Europe's governance must rest. It has also become clear that Monnet's idea of creating institutions to maintain mutual trust is crucial to sustain collective consensus when humans' fickle minds would constantly change. What remains weak, however, is the condition of connectedness in Europe. The matrix of mutual respect will not become 'thick', as long as most policy deliberations take place under a system of two-level governance, where democratic preferences are formed in narrow national debates while policy decisions are negotiated by governments at the European level. We have to *bring citizens into the deliberation process, as it is the rule in all democracies, in order to accelerate the speed of policy preference convergence.*

There are, of course, different governance levels for different collective goods. Local goods should be subject to local policy deliberation, national goods to national and European goods to a unified European deliberation process. When there are spillovers from one level onto another, a forum for the discussion of these externalities among policy-makers is also required. But it is important to establish the principle that with respect to European collective goods and their related decisions *European citizens, not governments, are the sovereign.* And they are equal in the exercise of their sovereign rights. The people are not the property of their governments. It is by creating a European democracy, that a constitutional consensus will become sustainable. If, however, *policy decisions are made by governments who act as representatives of national communities, this mode of decision-making will reinforce national coherence at the expense of individual connectedness across borders and communities.* As a consequence policy dissent and conflict will paralyse decision-making and reduce the power of European institutions. The resulting inferior policy output will further weaken the institutions, leading to a vicious cycle of European disintegration.

To be perfectly clear, *a European Constitution should establish a democratically elected government that takes decisions on European collective goods and policies.* It is by taking the authority for European collective goods out of the hands of national governments and handing it over to citizens, that a constitutional consensus about the procedures of governance will emerge. If this is politically not feasible today, the Convention should at least create structures that open the way in this direction. Three measures are relevant in this respect:

- The European Union has to obtain the status of a single legal personality that makes policy decisions within a unified legal framework. This framework must contain a Charter of Fundamental Rights of European Citizens. Policies on European collective goods are regulated by EU laws which are passed by the European Parliament and in co-decision with the Council where appropriate. Secondary legislation on implementing policies is left to the Commission, but can be delegated to national authorities.

- The European Commission President should be elected by the European Parliament by simple majority. He should be entitled to nominate Commissioners for task orientated portfolios, not as country representatives. The Council may approve of them.

- The Commission must have its own financial resources. Both revenue and expenditure must be approved by the European Parliament. Certain items may be subject to co-decision with the Council.

I will discuss some of these points below in further detail.

(II) Deliberation takes time. African *Kuzungumza*[182] under the Baobab-tree can take forever. Policy-making in Europe does not have this time. It must come to decisions, even if unanimity has not been achieved. Hence, policy decisions are usually taken by voting and not by unanimity. This poses questions of normativity with respect to equality and justice to which I will return below. But it also implies that the acceptance of the constitution itself requires a broad debate and full democratic legitimacy.

How can this be achieved? Several models are imaginable.

- The ratification of the European Constitution can be submitted to national referenda. But if votes are only counted at the level of member state constituencies, as has been customary in previous EU Treaty referenda (Denmark, France, Ireland, UK), this method creates a holistic-communitarian bias that is contrary to the logic of a European Constitution.[183] The European Union will be perceived as belonging to member states, rather than to its citizens.

- Alternatively, the constitution could come into force after a pan-European referendum has approved it. The Constitution would automatically become valid in countries that have approved it. If this is in contradiction to national constitutions, parliamentary ratification procedures would follow the pan-European referendum.[184] If the population of a specific country does not vote in favour of the new constitution, it should have the right to participate nevertheless, if a minimum threshold of EU member states is reached,[185] or to opt out. Of course, this requires appropriate procedures to deal with the opt-outs. The method of a pan-European referendum would provide broad legitimacy to the constitution, although it is not certain that direct democracy is the best instrument to foster mutual respect. A referendum invites individual citizens to express their *given* preference at the moment of voting, but not necessarily to take into account the preferences of others, as representative democracy does. Hence, direct democracy may preserve dissent rather than create consensus. It emphasises static preference heterogeneity rather than dynamic preference convergence.

- An alternative approach would be ratification of the constitution by a European Congress, consisting of an equal number of national and European parliamentarians. This solution takes into account the desire to give national parliaments a greater say in important European policy decisions. The number of national and European members of Parliament should be equal in order to prevent any bias in favour of national or European governance. However, the drawback of this method is that it does not necessarily mobilise cross-border public debate, deliberation and commitment, unless it is linked to a major election, say of the European Parliament.

Either of the last two methods of ratification would probably provide a sufficient foundation for the legitimacy of a European Constitution. In the case of conventional European Treaty ratifications through national constituencies, this is more doubtful. Recent Treaty changes were legitimated by the existing constitutional arrangements in each member state, but public opinion and the disenchantment with European integration after the Maastricht Treaty are an indication that the ratification process did not increase mutual respect among European citizens. A European Constitution requires a new approach to legitimation. It should aim at the largest possible mobilisation of European citizens.

Structures for Policy Deliberation

Even if a constitution has been fully accepted by Europe's citizens, the institutions for policy-making require a structure that allows the creation of policy consensus on substantive issues which are relevant at the European level. This requires, first of all, European-wide public deliberation for collective preferences to emerge and then, secondly, collective choice rules for public decision-making. It is

148 | Stefan Collignon

important to keep the two aspects separate. The first is about constructing a public sphere, the second is about efficient government, although the two are obviously linked.

(I) The construction of a European public sphere requires that there is *something for a European public to deliberate*. This concerns both, the object of deliberation (preferences for European goods) and the process of deliberation, i.e. the role of the nation-state in preference formation. The object is given by the assignment of European competences, as discussed in Chapter Six. As for procedures, it is now generally understood that today policy-making in Europe is a form of multi-level governance (Wallace and Wallace, 2000). Citizens are forming their preferences in the national context, while governments bargain or vote on European issues. As we have seen, this creates structural difficulties for the acceptance of policy choices. Alesina and Grilli (1992) have shown that the likelihood for the median voter and the median government in the Council to diverge is high in the present day institutional framework. This creates preference frustration and type-II-inefficiencies in policy-making. But it is also an incentive for political demobilisation of public opinion. If citizens are excluded from policy decisions because decisions are a bargained outcome between governments, citizens are also unlikely to argue what is best. In the conservative model of government they will humbly and gratefully accept the wisdom of the rulers; in the revolutionary model they will 'stand up for their rights', but hardly listen to the other side's arguments. In the first model conformism, in the second large and persistent dissent and conflict dominate consensus. A European Constitution that emphasises the power and role of member state governments by favouring the Council in policy-making errs on the conservative side and risks the revolutionary backlash, at least in its populist form. The crucial question is: to whom is a European executive accountable – to governments or citizens? Only direct accountability to European citizens (or their parliamentary representatives) allows the construction of a European public sphere where public policy deliberation will lead to collective policy preferences.

However, in this context, representative democracy should be favoured over direct democracy, because the latter falls more easily prey to temptations of populism.[186] This puts the European Parliament into the centre of policy deliberation. It is the natural place for the representation of citizens' policy preferences. If the European Parliament is responsible for European policy legislation on European collective goods and for providing political legitimacy to the Commission as an executive organ, this will contribute to the strengthening of both the mutual respect and the connectedness condition. This does not preclude the option of associating the Council with the legislative process, representing legitimate interests of national *administrations*. But what is important is the fact that individual citizens can assume their civic responsibility by electing direct representatives who are *exclusively accountable for decisions regarding European collective goods*. This is fundamentally different from today's procedures, where national governments are accountable to their 'own' people and where they justify the entire bundle of their policies (national and European) primarily with reference to *national* collective goods.

(II) Structures for policy deliberation are also affected by who makes policy decisions and translates public preferences into actions. This question is related to the *choice between parliamentarian and presidential democracies*. Several models are worthy of consideration. Recent studies have also focused on the impact of government regimes on economic policies, in particular the different effects of parliamentary majoritarian versus proportional representation (see Person and Tabellini, 2002 for an overview). They find that presidential regimes lead to smaller governments than parliamentarian regimes; majoritarian parliamentary elections ('winner takes all') lead to smaller governments and smaller welfare programs than proportional representation. These empirical effects seem to be robust, although we do not know the transmission effect through which constitutions operate on government spending. Are they direct or via altered political representation? Person and Tabellini (2002:5) point to the fact that 'constitution selection is not random, and countries with different constitutions also differ in many other respects'. One crucial distinction, it seems to me, is the degree of preference heterogeneities between different epistemic constituencies. We saw in Chapter One that federations tend to more consensual models of substantive decision-making because the constitutional consensus on procedures is weaker, so that substantive policy issues in federations require more policy consensus. This can be achieved by the greater representativity of *proportional representation*. This electoral regime also implies higher degrees of mutual respect and consensus than is prevalent in majoritarian regimes, where non-majority preferences are zero-weighted. Hence, parliamentarian regimes with proportional representation are not only *reflecting* higher degrees of consensuality, but they actually *produce* them.

However, as Dur and Roelfsema (2002) show, if all the costs of public goods are shared through a common budget, this may create an incentive to delegate decisions to 'public good lovers' and cause an oversupply of public goods. On the other hand, if the costs can not be shared, conservatives will dominate government and under-provision persists. One answer to remedy this problem is to incorporate checks and balances by separating the powers of parliament from those of the head of the executive (President). The President may then veto legislators' strategic behaviour. For some observers this makes the presidential regime attractive. Hix (2002) also points out that it prevents the fusion of legislative and executive powers in the EU. Yet, in terms of the creation of constitutional consensus, we do not have robust knowledge as to which regime is preferable. But the evidence from the Americas (North and South) seems to tilt in favour of a directly elected president. In order to get elected, a presidential candidate has to create a policy consensus around a platform that represents the median voter. Because the presidential constituency consists of every individual elector, this regime provides a strong incentive to reinforce connectedness and mutual respect. This is an argument against Hix's (2002) conjecture that European elections are fought on national issues by national parties with little public interest and debate. By contrast, voting in parliamentary constituencies alone, as in Canada, maintains a lower degree of connectedness, with the consequence that the constitutional consensus is weaker and the influence of local, heterogeneous communities, hence dissent and conflict are more dominant. This reasoning would recommend the election of the President of the European Commission by universal suffrage, as suggested at one time by the Belgian Prime Minister Guy Verhofstadt and the German Foreign Minister Joschka Fischer.

But, in the meantime the holistic-communitarian ideologies seem to have won the day. The direct election of the Commission President is often rejected with the argument that under universal suffrage, German voters would dominate every or most winning policy coalitions and this would be 'unacceptable' to other nations. The argument is about as 'stupid'[187] as it is widely believed. It either implies that European policy preferences reflect the preferences for local and thus not for European collective goods, or it is subject to the naturalistic fallacy whereby preferences are exclusively derived from the cultural context, and that European citizens are not capable of understanding and agreeing with the arguments of their neighbours. However, I have demonstrated that rational arguments and mechanisms of public trans-border policy deliberation are transforming primary desires and will lead to the rational *acceptance* of European policy preferences rather than to the suppression of national views. Human beings are not Pavlov's dogs; they are capable of transcendent rationality, as we have been aware of since Kant. If they are connected and trust each other, it is a matter of intellectual coherence and rationality for them to consider other views and change their own. I am not denying that common knowledge and traditions influence individual identities and preferences, but I insist that a European Constitution must provide mechanisms to overcome them. More intellectual creativity in this respect is needed. In the meantime, the election of the Commission President by the European Parliament seems the politically most acceptable solution.

Voting and Equality

Institutional arrangements are not only essential for providing a framework for policy deliberation, but also for political legitimacy and justice. The principle of political equality is, together with freedom, one of the founding norms of modern democracies.

Given that reaching full social consensus may take a long time, especially when mechanisms of public policy deliberation are underdeveloped, voting is the solution. What should be the voting modalities in the European Union? Again the main distinction is between modern-individualist and holistic-communitarian ideologies. The modern norm of equality is 'one (wo)man, one vote'. The holistic version is: 'all communities are equal' (although some may be more equal than others). In the European Union, voting does not follow these pure principles. In the Council the votes are weighted to reflect the size of countries, in the European Parliament not all members represent the same number of citizens. Table 7.1 shows the different distributions as agreed by the Treaty of Nice for the EU of 27 member states.

Table 7.1 Voting Distributions Agreed by the Treaty of Nice

	Population		Council votes		EP seats		Ratios	
	mio (1)	per cent	no.(2)	per cent	no.(3)	per cent	(2)/(1)	(3)/(1)
Malta	0.4	0.08%	3	0.87%	5	0.68%	10.7	8.4
Luxembourg	0.4	0.09%	4	1.16%	6	0.82%	12.8	9.0
Cyprus	0.8	0.16%	4	1.16%	6	0.82%	7.1	5.0
Estonia	1.4	0.29%	4	1.16%	6	0.82%	4.0	2.8
Slovenia	2.0	0.41%	4	1.16%	7	0.96%	2.8	2.3
Latvia	2.4	0.50%	4	1.16%	8	1.09%	2.3	2.2
Lithuania	3.7	0.77%	7	2.03%	12	1.64%	2.6	2.1
Ireland	3.8	0.79%	7	2.03%	13	1.78%	2.6	2.2
Finland	5.2	1.07%	7	2.03%	12	1.64%	1.9	1.5
Denmark	5.3	1.10%	10	2.90%	17	2.32%	2.6	2.1
Slovakia	5.4	1.12%	12	3.48%	20	2.73%	3.1	2.4
Bulgaria	7.9	1.65%	12	3.48%	20	2.73%	2.1	1.7
Austria	8.1	1.68%	7	2.03%	13	1.78%	1.2	1.1
Sweden	8.8	1.84%	7	2.03%	13	1.78%	1.1	1.0
Hungary	10.0	2.07%	10	2.90%	17	2.32%	1.4	1.1
Portugal	10.0	2.08%	10	2.90%	18	2.46%	1.4	1.2
Belgium	10.2	2.13%	12	3.48%	22	3.01%	1.6	1.4
Czech Republic	10.3	2.13%	12	3.48%	22	3.01%	1.6	1.4
Greece	10.6	2.20%	12	3.48%	22	3.01%	1.6	1.4
Netherlands	15.9	3.29%	14	4.06%	33	4.51%	1.2	1.4
Romania	22.4	4.66%	13	3.77%	25	3.42%	0.8	0.7
Poland	38.6	8.01%	27	7.83%	50	6.83%	1.0	0.9
Spain	39.9	8.28%	27	7.83%	50	6.83%	0.9	0.8
Italy	57.5	11.94%	29	8.41%	72	9.84%	0.7	0.8
France	59.2	12.29%	29	8.41%	72	9.84%	0.7	0.8
United Kingdom	59.4	12.33%	29	8.41%	72	9.84%	0.7	0.8
Germany	82.0	17.02%	29	8.41%	99	13.52%	0.5	0.8
TOTAL	481.8	100%	345	100%	732	100%	1	1

Political equality implies, every country's voting rights would represent its population share. This is not the case. The EU has a bias in favour of small member states. Malta and Luxembourg with less than half a million people and less than one per mille of the EU27 population have over ten times as much voting power in the Council and over eight times the representation in the European Parliament than they deserve for their population share. Germany with roughly 17 per cent of the population has only half the weight in the Council and only 13.5 per cent of the seats in parliament. These distortions have always been present in the EU policy-making system and they will change only marginally after enlargement. One way to measure inequality is the Gini coefficient.[188] This coefficient ranges from 0 to 1, where 0 represents perfect equality, and 1 total inequality. Thus, 'one (wo)man, one vote' represents a coefficient of zero, 'all communities are equal' implies a coefficient of one.

Table 7.2 shows that political equality is fairly evenly distributed in the EU, both before and after enlargement. Equality in Council weights improves by 3 per cent and deteriorates by 7 per cent for the European Parliament. Nevertheless, the Gini coefficient for Council representation is nearly twice as high as for the EP, although in absolute terms it remains rather low. This fact emphasises our point that the Council is a representation of national *administrations not citizens*. The inequality is justified if, and only if, the Council represents member state governments rather than citizens. It should therefore have legislative competencies that are relevant to national collective goods and their interdependence with European policies, not for policies that are relevant for the entire European policy domain. The European Constitution should therefore distinguish between domains of legislation that require co-decision because of spillovers from European and national policy decisions, and a proper European policy domain, where every citizen is concerned by policy decisions and should therefore be represented equally. Whether this requires changing the voting weights at some future point should be open for debate. But the proposal of introducing a double majority of member states and population as the criterion for qualified majority voting in the Council would not only increase the efficiency of the decision-making process, it would also improve the transparency of arguments in the process of policy deliberation. If the Council votes according to the principle of equal government and the European Parliament according to the equality of citizens and a majority in both chambers is required for legislation, the two chambers would emphasise very different arguments in the process of deliberation.

Table 7.2 Gini Coefficient for Political Inequality

Gini Coefficient	Council	European Parliament
EU15	0.291	0.149
EU27	0.282	0.160

The Question of Borders

Another open question is where the borders of the European Union are to be drawn? Often this is addressed in terms of geography. Valéry Giscard d'Estaing has pointed to the obvious when he said: 'Turkey is not a European country' (Financial Times, 11 November 2002). 95 per cent of its population live outside the European continent, its capital Ankara is not in Europe. The fact that a small part of its territory lies on the European continent does not make Turkey European, just as Spain, which owns the Parsley Islands 200 meters off Morocco's coast, is not African or the UK is not Latin American because it owns the Falklands. However, it can be argued, that even Romania or Serbia are not part of Europe's cultural heritage (see footnote 27 above). The argument here is essentially that there is a degree of cultural heterogeneity which affects policy preferences in such a way that efficient policy-making is becoming difficult if not impossible. This view deserves respect. Although I have insisted throughout this book that it is possible to overcome communitarian borders of distrust towards others, realism commands to acknowledge that cultural differences may be too large to be bridged within a time span that matters for policy-making. It is often claimed that geostrategic objectives of stabilising Europe would require us to first take Turkey, followed by the Ukraine, Russia[189] and one day, why not, Morocco or Israel into the European Union. By the same logic one could justify also admitting Iraq, Iran, Pakistan, India etc. to the European Union, 'once they have democratic governments' and fulfil the 'Copenhagen criteria'. It may be wiser to remember Napoleon who had learned a lesson when he said:

'Empires die of indigestion.'[190]

Where are the limits of the European Union? If we follow the logic outlined in this book, the limits appear by auto-selection of those who want to play by the set of Europe's constitutive rules. These rules must be structured in such a way that they enable coherent and efficient policy-making by providing desired collective goods and legitimacy into the policy process. These rules are very stringent. They do not allow decisions to be taken as the smallest common denominator, but rather as the least common multiple.[191]

The first question regarding the admission of new countries must be, whether the externalities of policy decisions are such that the polity should be enlarged to the size of the policy domain. The incidence of policy externalities on a particular set of people is partly dependent on the policy decisions themselves, partly on technical constraints. For example, by setting up European Monetary Union, most macroeconomic policy variables have become European collective goods, requiring unified governance. But if trade integration is not well advanced and per capita income is low, there are only limited monetary flows and the benefits from belonging to such a currency area are limited (Collignon, 2002). Hence, technically such a country would not be part of the policy domain and there is no point of integrating it into the polity. However, the size of the policy domain is not a clear-cut criterion, as some policy decisions may create externalities which extend the reach of the policy domain. In fact, the criterion must be whether the will to provide European collective goods coincides with the capacity to provide them, without falling prey to the logic of collective action. As I have pointed out, this means centralising important policy areas at the European level and subordinating their governance to a European government, which is accountable to its citizens. Hence, the question of who is a citizen of the European Union is not one of cultural background, but it depends on the acceptance of the European Constitution.

If the Constitution provides efficient structures for policy-making that minimise the cost of public decisions but also open up the public sphere for collective European policy deliberation, cultural background will become transformed. The resultant acceptance of European policy decisions by European citizens will then strengthen the Union's legitimacy and power. Hence the border of the European Union is the epistemic constituency of its Constitution. Yet, if the cultural heterogeneousness is too large, this acceptance will not be forthcoming within a reasonable timeframe. Such countries will and should remain outside. As the case of Switzerland demonstrates, this may not necessarily have damaging consequences. Lessons from international development assistance also show that economic progress and stability depend on domestic conditions and cannot be imported. As the World Bank (2002:xxii) observed:

> 'The international development community has recognised that assistance is most effective when recipient countries are the primary drivers of their own reforms and institutional development'.

The experience of Ireland and Greece in the European Union seems to confirm this assessment. As a consequence of these observations, international aid organisations have become much more selective about their contributions. The Copenhagen European Council has established criteria for the enlargement of the EU. But although this was a step in the right direction, these criteria were rather general, easily fudgeable and, most importantly, not linked to Europe's internal governance. The European Convention now has the chance to remedy this mistake for future applicants.

The Value Content of Europe's Constitution

Another open issue is the normative content of a European Constitution. Although there seems to be consensus that the democratisation of institutions is desirable, there is disagreement as to whether there is a need to go beyond procedural rules. From the political left there is a demand to enshrine the model of a social market economy, or a Social Union in the constitution. The political right resists such attempts. Unfortunately, the debate about this issue has turned into a clash of economic programs for government, rather than a deliberation of rules for Europe's economic governance. As a result, the Convention's working group on economic governance has failed. It may be useful to go back to basics.

In Chapter One I have insisted that constitutions have normative content and Chapter Four has shown the historic link between a monetary market economy and liberal republican forms of democracy.[192] The essential distinction is between holistic/hierarchical communities, where the individual is subject to the collectivity and individualism of modern societies that is the essence of liberal democracies. However these ideological poles are not either-or alternatives. Each society articulates and integrates them in its own particular form. What matters is which principle dominates or incorporates the other. The political values of modernity are expressed in the republican values: *liberté, égalité, fraternité*. However, they do not only establish the dimensions of the modern political space, they also formulate a ranking of these values. Individualism is based on the predominance of two fundamental norms, which are related to the contractual nature of the modern economy: the right to freedom and equality. Freedom implies that individuals are free to enter into contract relationships, equality means that they are equal in accepting or refusing the terms of the contract. By contrast, holistic ideologies persist and survive in the modern context either as communitarian values, such as fraternity, or in the hierarchical institutions of the state. What matters, however, is that they are subjugated in modern societies under the two dominant principles of freedom and equality.[193] Solidarity is a modernist articulation of fraternity when the formal freedom of individuals requires collective action to preserve or re-establish substantial equality. A modern constitution must articulate these fundamental principles as individual rights.

It is therefore not only coherent with the political foundations of European integration to formulate a Charter of Fundamental Rights of the individual citizen, but it is also an expression of the economic principles of a monetary market economy that are its foundation. A Charter that protects European citizens against the holistic claims by governments and communities, whether national or European, and protects the formal and substantive equality of their individual rights must be part of the normative content of a European Constitution. Such rights must enable citizens to have access to the European Court of Justice, to participate in the political process of law-making, and preserve the freedom to negotiate contracts, including wage bargaining. It must also give guarantees for the protection of individuals' rights as equals. These are the basic principles of a social market economy. However, it would also be contrary to the spirit of a modern constitution to give priority rights to communities, even if expressed through national governments. Obviously, this does not mean that national governments, as the trustees of local citizens in dealing with local public goods, must not have rights with respect to the European authorities. Checks and balances between the different levels and branches of government are crucial to preserve freedom and equality. But it does imply that nobody in the European Union should have a privileged status or rights on the grounds of belonging to a specific community or representing a specific institution.

By embracing individualism as a fundamental norm of modernity, a democratic European Constitution does not necessarily have to take a position with respect to the two twin principles of modernity, i.e. liberty and equality, although both need to be preserved and protected. Traditionally, these have been the guiding stars of the political right and the political left in democratic societies.[194] Economic liberals (*laissez-faire* liberalism) emphasise the freedom of entrepreneurship, while social democrats emphasise the substantive equality between individuals that is easily lost under the dynamics of unfettered markets. Thus, for the political right a European Constitution must preserve the functioning of efficient markets. For the left, high levels of employment and social protection are a substantive condition of political equality and economic freedom. In modern democracies, policy preferences swing between these two major poles reflecting the outcome of different weights in arguments during public policy deliberations. It would therefore be wrong to limit the outcome of these deliberations by constitutional norms, although it is essential to ensure that both these fundamental norms and values are respected by the constitution. For only the respect of both, freedom and equality, allows consensual policy preferences to emerge. Therefore a catalogue of constitutional rights of European citizens should formulate how European institutions are to preserve the principles of freedom and equality of all European citizens rather than the actual outcomes. This should be the normative platform of Europe's social model.

The Structure of Government

Political debates and policy deliberation are focussed on the election of a government. It is the task of governments to administer collective goods. Given that the European Union now covers a large range of collective goods, a European government has become a necessity. Especially after enlargement, the traditional role of the European Commission as an initiator, guardian and umpire is no longer sufficient for the efficient management of common concerns. By giving European citizens the right to elect a European government, a public sphere for policy deliberation is created that will contribute to the emergence of consensual collective policy preferences. It has been argued that there is 'no lack of representative bodies in the EU' (Eriksen, 2000:56). However, most of these bodies, with the exception of the European Parliament, represent partial constituencies and not all European citizens. This causes, as we have seen, type-II-inefficiencies, i.e. preference heterogeneity and democratic frustration. Hence, a European Constitution must design *European citizens as the ultimate constituency for policy deliberation* and for the accountability by its elected representatives.

Who should this government be? It cannot be the same as the European Commission is today. The European Commission has been conceived as a high authority, an umpire, whose task it was to guard over the common interest of Europeans. Even if in recent years the European Commission has become more accountable to the European Parliament, its ultimate source of legitimacy and power resides in the member states. This is evident not only from its mode of designation but also from the endless debates around the European Council in Nice regarding the right of every member state to send at least one Commissioner to Brussels. The logic of collective action implies that a proper European government must take responsibility for the provision of collective European goods, although structures for regulating the spillovers from the provision of European goods on to local and national goods are also needed. A Commission which is seen as a representative body for national interests rather than an executive institution for European policies,[195] cannot overcome the dilemmas of collective action that lead to the sub-optimal supply of collective goods. This requires a profound transformation of the role and functioning of the European Commission as well as its relationship with the Council of Ministers and the European Council.

Transforming the Commission into a government requires that the Commissioners are no longer representatives of member states but agents of European citizens. As a consequence, the Commission must be elected by and accountable to the European Parliament. However, this only makes sense if it has powers to act and a President who provides orientation for the general policy direction. Otherwise, why should European citizens bother to vote? The Commissioners must be responsible for the provision of specific European collective goods. The Commission's services and staff are then the administration of such a political executive. It therefore should be the responsibility of the Commission President to establish who is in charge of what and whether regional interests are sufficiently represented and balanced. In this respect the restructured European Commission should be modelled on the European Central Bank, where the Executive Board is task orientated and the Governors meeting in the Governing Council do not represent individual countries but the common interests of the Euro-area.[196]

If the Commission is to become a clearly defined European executive, it needs democratic control. This is the task of the European Parliament. Parliament must therefore have the right to vote the Commission in and to revoke it. For only the European Parliament is able to *directly* reflect the European policy preferences of citizens. By voting for parties and members of parliament every citizen has the possibility of participating in the political orientation of European policies. Of course, the accountability of Commissioners vis-à-vis the Parliament would contribute to a politicisation. But this is a desired side-effect, for it is likely to increase public participation in policy debates throughout Europe. It is therefore the accountability of the European government to the European Parliament that is simultaneously creating and reinforcing a public European space. Hix (2002:16) has objected that the European Parliament cannot provide legitimacy for choosing the Commission President, because elections to the European Parliament are 'second order national contests'. However, this argument only holds under present day constitutional arrangements where the European Parliament has only limited powers and the Commission is not a government.[197]

Even if there is a range of European collective goods, which can clearly be distinguished from national goods, there is also a wide field of interdependences and spillovers from national to European goods as we have seen in Chapter Six. This assigns a clear role to the European Council and the Council of Ministers. It means establishing the Council as a second legislative chamber which co-decides with the European Parliament on European secondary law. However, the implementation provisions of this European secondary legislation should be left to the authority of the European administration who may delegate it to national authorities. This would greatly simplify the procedures of European legislation by taking away the bureaucratic bargaining between national administrations over the detailed application of European legislation that contributes to the over-regulation and bureaucratisation in the European Union today.

A European government must be in charge of European collective goods. However the delimitation between European and national collective goods is not always clear. The debate on the European Constitution started as a debate about the assignment of competencies. But such assignment is far from being unambiguous, as we saw in Chapter Six. An authority of last resort is therefore required to settle disputes. Some have suggested that this should be the European Court of Justice. However, as an arbitrator of legal disputes the Court could only take decisions if the Constitution contained a clear assignment or formulation of the subsidiarity or decentralisation theorem. Yet, as we have seen, this principle is itself subject to a large ideological debate. Formalising a 'subsidiarity imperative' within the Constitution, as some have postulated, is unlikely to produce efficient government. Given the nature of collective goods and therefore also of European policy competences that may change character with technological progress, it might be a better idea to assign the responsibility of deciding at which level policy decisions should be taken to a European Congress, consisting of an equal number of members of national and the European Parliament. This Congress would therefore be the authority of last resort in constitutional rule setting and have the competence of competence transfers. It would have the exclusive role of dealing and deliberating and deciding constitutional issues. In this capacity it may decide to decentralise certain policies as and when the technical, economic and political developments require such decision and when certain policy issues should be delegated to the European level. It should be possible that both the European Commission, subject to a vote by the European Parliament, as well as the European Council (but maybe even the Committee of the Regions with a two-thirds majority) can call the European Congress into session. The European Court of Justice's role would then be to ensure that the decisions by the Congress would be coherent with the other principles of the European Constitution.

Another difficulty in the delimitation of tasks between a new-style Commission and member states relates to joint tasks, when there are spillovers from one level to the other. This is where the European Council and the Commission could jointly assume executive functions. But who would be the driving force? Two systems are under discussion: a bicephalous executive, like in the French Constitution, assigning different tasks to the President and the Prime Minister; or a double-hat where the Commission president also chairs the European Council. Which system is more likely to strengthen Europe's constitutional consensus? The present system of rotating presidencies in the EU has the advantage of re-enforcing mutual respect across Europe, as each Presidency makes special efforts to prove its European commitment. In peripheral countries, this is a beneficial side effect and helps mobilising public interest for European affairs. However, the short durations (six months) are handicapping continuity, especially for small countries that are constrained by their administrative capacity. After enlargement eight member states will represent populations of less than 5 million. It has therefore been recommended that a more permanent administrative structure be created for policy issues which require continuity, such as foreign affairs. In my view, given the European character of the policy issues involved, this continuity is best provided by the administrative services of the Commission, although relevant political decision-making can be reserved to the European Council. In this case one could preserve the rotating presidencies of the EU to allow member states to provide impetus into certain policy areas (Portugal did this successfully at the Lisbon meeting in 2000), while the Commission President could act as a General Secretary of the European Council and give his telephone number to Mr Kissinger.[198] This could provide an efficient middle path between the bicephalous executive and the double hat solution.

Economic Governance

With the advance of economic integration the largest share of Europe's collective goods relates to economic governance. Prior to the start of European Monetary Union a large debate took place about the need to establish an Economic Government for the Eurozone. This issue was particularly emphasised by French authorities who rightly insisted on the need to define a coherent macroeconomic framework when monetary policy was unified. However, the question of regulating financial markets should also be raised here. The proposal was resisted by German authorities, who saw it as an attack on the independence of the European Central Bank. However, this discussion has missed the essential point. Most economists, including central bankers, are aware that monetary policy alone cannot guarantee price stability. The independence of a central bank is about whether governments can force it to accommodate inflationary pressures. The Statutes of the European Central Bank unambiguously prevent this. The real issue about the economic government is about who should exercise the function of giving sense and orientation to macroeconomic policies. The French government's idea of an Economic Government for the Eurozone was exclusively designed as an *intergovernmental* form of macroeconomic co-ordination. At one stage, ideas were floated of setting up an independent secretariat and all attempts to give greater macroeconomic policy authorities to the European

Commission have always been resisted. If one were to progress with these ideas, the economic governance of the European Union or at least of the Eurozone would be seriously hampered by the logic of collective action and the lack of democratic legitimacy.

The experience of the first four years of EMU has demonstrated this. The informal Euro-group, where finance ministers of the Eurozone meet regularly ten times a year, has been the meagre realisation of earlier French ideas. Yet, the group's role has gained weight. The Euro-group has played a useful role in allowing finance ministers to better understand their colleagues' policy objectives and constraints and has therefore fostered mutual respect amongst these policy-makers. However, this emerging ministerial consensus does not necessarily spill over into society at large. The Euro-group functions therefore more like an epistemic community, i.e. a circle of experts, rather than as an institution that responds to an epistemic constituency.[199] The informal character of the Euro-group also prevents the ministerial consensus from becoming policy consensus in member states. This has been most apparent in the case of dealing with the oil price increases in the year 2000, or the windfall incomes from rapid economic growth in France (*cagnotte*). When the French finance minister agreed with his colleagues that these unexpected revenues should be used for debt reduction, he was overruled by his Prime Minister who was very much aware of the forthcoming presidential elections. Similarly, binding fiscal policy co-ordination with an eye to anti-cyclical fiscal policy has been impossible.[200] Hence, as I pointed out in the previous chapter, the necessary power for macroeconomic policy-making in the European Union can only come from a fully and democratically legitimated government which reflects the collective preferences in the European constituency. This implies, of course, that the *gouvernement économique* cannot be an independent intergovernmental structure, but its tasks have to be assigned to the new-style European Commission which would be responsible to European citizens. Ideas, which are particularly attractive to academics, of setting-up independent expert groups are also counterproductive. They may resemble Plato's philosopher-kings, but they are incompatible with an open society, as we have known since Popper (1995).

Establishing the European Commission as a proper European government with executive functions also means that it will have to command its own resources.[201] In order to manage collective goods, a European government needs its own administration, even though it may remain small for the foreseeable future. At present its resources are derived from member state contributions. Although the European Parliament has some limited impact on the expenditure side of the European budget (it can approve discretionary expenditure, but not entitlements), it has no authority over the collection of income for the European budget. A proper financial constitution for the European Union requires: (1) full budget authority from the European Parliament, on both the income and expenditure side. This does not exclude the possibility that the Council may have co-decision rights with respect to certain issues, but the autonomy of a European government with respect to the provision of European collective goods is indispensable. (2) This implies that the European Parliament must have the authority to authorise the new Commission to raise a European tax. The principle of jurisdictional congruence requires such taxing capacities to be subject to the full representation of European citizens at the level of the European Parliament. A European tax does not necessarily imply heavier tax burdens for European citizens. Part of the funds raised for a European budget would eliminate transfers that were previously coming from national budgets and may therefore even reduce the tax burden in some countries. The Council is the forum where distributional transfer issues must be discussed and decided jointly with the Commission.

The criteria for choosing which kind of taxes may be suitable for European purposes must be related to the European single market with the purpose of avoiding distortions. This implies that the appropriate tax base for European government revenue should be related to the free circulation of goods, services and factors. In practical terms, this refers to goods and capital markets: (1) On goods and services, a proportion of VAT could be assigned to the European level while member states collect the other part. The European VAT rate would be uniform throughout the single market (say 2 per cent) whilst national rate variations would reflect local policy preferences. (2) The uniform taxation of highly mobile factors of production, such as capital, is also imperative in order to prevent distorting unfair tax competition. However, all other taxation such as wage contributions, income tax, property taxes, etc. can and should remain under the authority of national governments, as harmful tax competition is unlikely to take place in this domain. National member state governments could then voluntarily co-ordinate their policies in the framework of the Council while the Commission as the European government would have tax authority for the specific revenue incomes assigned to it for which national governments would no longer have the right to veto. Decisions of occasional reallocations in the tax base between the European and the national level would be submitted to the European Congress.

Conclusion

This book has tried to look at what it takes to make the process of European integration sustainable, efficient and democratically legitimate. Because European integration is based on market integration in a monetary economy, we have focussed on economic issues, which have both, a normative impact on constitutional rules and a need for efficient policy-making institutions. As we have seen, the logic of collective action in the context of the enlargement of the European Union to new members, and the decentralisation of certain policy-making issues to lower levels of government, leads to problems in providing collective goods optimally. They can be solved by creating a European government. It has also become clear that a European Constitution has normative content which must reflect the fundamental values of modernity as they have arisen from Europe's history. They require the primacy of the republican values of freedom and equality over fraternity. An efficient European Constitution will have to ensure the normative coherence of the constitutional rules with the functional requirements of the modern monetary market economy. I call this a European Republic.

My insistence on creating a European government may not seem to fit into the present intellectual climate of subsidiarity, the exhortation of local values, intergovernmental co-operation and the affirmation of national identities. But the apparent ideological consensus surrounding these issues does not remove the logical dilemmas that I have exposed in this book. All it may achieve is an incoherent set of rules, which will ultimately destroy European integration. I therefore appeal to the reader to give due consideration and respect to my arguments and to discuss them with others. By doing that we would fulfil the two minimal conditions of our stochastic consensus model. I would then have hope that the present European policy consensus can be moved in the direction of constitutional arrangements, which will ultimately ensure the sustainability of European integration.

Annexe 1.
Stochastic Consensus

I will present here a formal model of stochastic consensus that can be used in economics and political science for the explanation of collective preference formation. Collective preferences are formed in a 3-step process. Each step is considered separately under ceteris-paribus assumptions. In reality the time-sequence may approach simultaneity.

Step I: Desires and Naturalistic Preferences

Standard decision theory (see Jeffrey, 1983) analyses acts, which individuals perform under certain conditions because their consequences are desirable. Desirability is measured by assigning some numbers to the consequences of acts. Economic theory usually *assumes* that consumers have preferences when they are able to order bundles of desirable consumption goods, but it remains silent about the origin of preferences. Here, we want to look at how preferences come about.

We first distinguish between desires and individual preferences. A preference is an accepted desire subsequent to its positive evaluation. Therefore desires are prior to preferences. I define desires as mental states of individuals whose intentionality is directed toward the objects of desires. They can be expressed through language in the form of propositions. The sincere expression of a desire is a first evaluation of the mental state, because it accepts the desire as worthy of communication.[202] But it is not a preference until it is accepted as worthy of action. The objects of desire are projected future states of the world S, called options. Conventional decision theory models desires as desirable consequences of acts under specific conditions. But this does not explain desirability, because it assumes what needs to be explained. It looks at the evaluation (the choice) of intentional acts, given the probability distribution of potential states of the world. Hence it is a theory of preference and not of desire.

The mental states of desire are conditional on a given background or context, which may be physical or structured by culture, convention, habit, common knowledge, cognitive frames etc. However, our knowledge of the background is usually incomplete. As a consequence, mental states appear as random. For example the lack of liquid may induce my mental state of thirst, but whether I desire water or tea may depend on the temperature of the weather. With complete knowledge of the context ('I am thirsty and it is hot'), my desire for water is deterministic. But an incomplete specification of context, say by only focussing on being thirsty, would describe my desire for water or tea as random, with the distribution reflecting the temperature of weather. Hence, we may assign a *probability that a given individual will express a sincere[203] desire* for a certain state of the world rather than another, given the context. We may call this probability the intensity of desire. Formally, if s is the set of k available options, i.e. $s = \{s_j : j=1,...,k\}$, the intensity of desire δ_{ij} is the probability of option s_j being (truthfully) expressed by an individual i, given B[204]:

(1) $\delta_{ij} = p(s_{ij}|B)$

In a deterministic world, individuals' desires are perfectly determined by their background and $\delta_{ij}=1$. The person wants water and that is it. But when the knowledge of the context is incomplete, different options may be ranked according to their desirability, i.e. according to their intensities or degrees of desire. If the probability of me saying 'I want tea' is higher than saying 'I want water', given identically described contexts, we say my desire for tea is higher than for water.

However, the randomness of desire makes rational choice impossible. If in a given (incompletely described) context a person chooses x over y, and at other times but in the same (incompletely described) context y over x, he is considered incoherent. Of course, most of us behave in this way most of the time, but we can construct a coherent personality referring to 'expected desire'. This means individuals can be regarded as 'lotteries of desires', where a person's normal desire is the expectation (probability-weighted average) of the individuals' desires for different states of the world. This expected desire is analogous to the well-established notion of expected utility. It means, *ceteris paribus,* that given the fact of a person living in cold climate, we can expect her to ask for tea when she is thirsty. I will therefore call a person's expected desire for state j a *naturalistic preference,* because the background is assumed to be given exogenously, i.e. 'by nature'. Naturalistic preferences are the building stones of what individuals call their 'identity'.

Step II: Rational Preferences

A rational decision-maker will not act on all desires. She will re-evaluate and actualise her desires in the light of alternative evidence, arguments, or *any kind of information*. We will call *rational preferences* (π_j) for option j the evaluated desires, which an individual accepts as worthy of action. The evaluation can be modelled by Bayes' theorem:

$$(2) \ \pi_j = p(s_j | B \text{ and } E) = p(E | s_j \text{ and } B) \ \frac{p(s_j|B)}{p(E|B)} = \frac{p(E|s_j \text{ and } B)}{p(E|B)} \ \delta_j$$

The rational preference for state j by a given individual corresponds to the intensity of desire, modified by the likelihood $p(E|s_j \text{ and } B)$ or reliability of the argument E and normalized by the probability of the argument arising given the background. Hence a rational individual's preference reflects the posterior probability of desire δ_j for option j being accepted, given the argument or evidence E and the background B. We may interpret $p(E|B)$ as the value of an argument providing new information,[205] while $p(E|s_j \text{ and } B)$ reflects the probability assessment or weight that is attributed to the *reliability* of an argument (or statement) given the background. Hence, the modification of naturalistic desires depends on the reliability of an argument and its innovation over the existing informational background in the process of evaluation.

With rational preferences rational choice is possible, because equation (2) allows a ranking of preferences for different options. A possible rational choice rule from the set of s options is: $C(s) = \max_j \pi_j$.

Step III: Social preferences

The third step is to extend the conversation to other members of a group or society. First we note that different individuals have different backgrounds and therefore also different desires and individual preferences. Hence we re-write (2) with an index i for individual i:

$$(3) \ \pi_{ij} = p(s_{ij} | B \text{ and } E) = p(E | s_{ij} \text{ and } B) \ \frac{p(s_{ij}|B)}{p(E|B)} = \frac{p(E|s_{ij} \text{ and } B)}{p(E|B)} \delta_j$$

The individual preferences can also be written in matrix form as Π^0 with dimension $n \times k$, where the n row vectors represent each individual's preferences and the k column vectors the set of preferences for each option. Individuals have different preferences due to their different desires, their individual backgrounds and the evaluations of arguments and evidence accessible in this context. As social beings, they communicate about their differences. This communication leads to part of the individual backgrounds becoming common knowledge, and this will reduce the variance of individual preferences.[206] But in the process of communication and reflexive deliberation they will also reconsider the reliability of their own assessment in light of other individuals' opinions and preferences. This will lead to *preference change.*

We can assume that the adjustment process consists in modifying one's previous preference by a fraction of the difference between their own and someone else's individual preference intensities.[207] However, they will not attach the same weight to all other individuals' opinions. There will be some individuals that they trust and respect more than others. As a consequence, they will change their own preferences to a larger or smaller degree. The speed of preference change depends on the weight of respect that individuals attribute to each other. In order to keep the mathematics simple, we will first demonstrate the two-person case. Hence, individual one ($i=1$) adjusts his preference for option ($j=1$) as follows:

(4a) $\pi_{11}^1 = \pi_{11}^0 - \alpha(\pi_{11}^0 - \pi_{21}^0)$

and person two does something similar:

(4b) $\pi_{21}^1 = \pi_{21}^0 - \beta(\pi_{21}^0 - \pi_{11}^0)$

Thus, person 1 adjusts his previous individual preference by the fraction α of their difference in opinion and person 2 by the fraction β. We assume α and β to fall into the interval $0 \leq \alpha, \beta \leq 1$. If the adjustment coefficient is zero, the person does not change his opinion; if it is 1, he totally aligns his views on the other person's previous preference. Equations (4a) and (4b) can be rewritten as:

(5a) $\pi_{11}^1 = (1 - \alpha)\pi_{11}^0 + \alpha \pi_{21}^0$

(5b) $\pi_{21}^1 = \beta \pi^0{}_{11} + (1-\beta) \pi^0{}_{21}$

In this form, the adjustment coefficients in the process of deliberation reflect the relative weights that members of a group attribute to each other's opinions and preferences. This statement is easily generalized to a group of n members forming an $n \times n$ weight matrix $\mathbf{W}$. Social preference assignments over the set of k options s are represented by the product of the weight matrix $\mathbf{W}$ with the individual preference matrix Π^0. The result is an $n \times k$ matrix, where the n row vectors reflect the adjusted preferences of the n individuals and the k column vectors represent the set of new preferences for each option:

(6) $\Pi^1 = \mathbf{W} \, \Pi^0$

We assume for simplicity and without loss of generality that $\mathbf{W}$ is constant. The social preference matrix $\prod^t$ reflects both the variety of individual preferences based on background and evaluative capacities, but also a judgement about each other's backgrounds and capacities.[208] As long as different individuals take each other's opinion into account, they attribute a positive weight to each other including themselves, and this means they respect each other. We therefore call the condition $0 < \alpha, \beta < 1$ *mutual respect*. Mutual respect is a necessary, but not sufficient condition for social preferences to converge to a unique equilibrium, which we call consensus.

Consensus

Equation (6) describes a dynamic system of preference adjustment. For, as soon as one individual's preference has been changed, all those who respect her will also adjust their preferences because they trust her evaluation of new evidence. This is the nature of deliberation. It does not matter whether the initial change originates in new evidence ($p(E|s_j$ and B)), or in a change in reputation[209]. Either way, all social preferences will be affected. But how? De Groot's (1974) algorithm shows that if the weight matrix $\mathbf{W}$ is a stochastic matrix (a square matrix whose columns or rows are probability vectors adding to 1)[210] in a system of first-order difference equations, the system converges under certain conditions to a unique equilibrium vector. Multiplying the matrix of rational individual preferences by the consensual weight matrix yields social consensus on preferences. This can be shown as follows:

Given the weight of respect individuals assign to each other's opinions, a first round of deliberation must be followed by a second round because the change in opinion of one individual requires the change of opinion of those who respect her assessment. Hence:

(7) $\prod^t = \mathbf{W} \prod^{t-1} = \mathbf{W}^t \prod^0$

Given our assumption of non-negative entries and unit row sum, (7) describes a stochastic process known as finite homogenous Markov chain. As is well known, with $t \to \infty$ the process tends to converge to a unique weight matrix $\lim_{t \to \infty} \mathbf{W}^t = \overline{\mathbf{W}}$ *with identical rows*, which lead to the consensual preference assignments:

(8) $\prod^t = \overline{\mathbf{W}} \prod^0$

The consensual social preference for option s_j reflects the weighted mean of all individual preferences. We call $\overline{\mathbf{W}}$ the consensual weight matrix, because it consists of n identical equilibrium vectors indicating the consensual weights of respect within the group. It summarizes available information about each individual's expertise and reliability within that group. Thus, different people may receive different consensual weights, but every individual will use these same consensual weights in his evaluation of himself and others.[211] This vector is a numerical summary of background knowledge. However, in this formulation, background does not only reflect naturalistic conditionings but also an evaluation of evaluative capacities.

The consensual preference matrix Π^* has n rows for each individual and k identical columns for the number of available options. The unique feature of this equilibrium matrix is that each row contains identical values for the probability assessment of accepting a given option. Hence, in equilibrium (and only in equilibrium) there is unanimity about collective preferences – and given the choice rule also about choices.[212] In equilibrium the process of preference adjustment is complete, because there is no new information forthcoming, which would make people reconsider their preferences.

The necessary conditions for convergence to the equilibrium to take place are, in the terminology of Lehrer and Wagner (1981): (1) mutual respect and (2) connectedness. We may also add (3) the general condition of rational behaviour with respect to the processing of information. Condition (1) requires the weight matrix W to be a stochastic matrix and condition (2) implies a 'chain of respect' such that each individual can be shown to be connected by positive respect to at least one other (and himself). This condition is required to avoid that the group splits into two disjoint subgroups (Lehrer/Wagner 1981:137). Condition (3) is a consistency argument, for if a person refuses to aggregate the knowledge about other individuals' beliefs and preferences into his own preference evaluation, although assigning a positive weight to other members in the group, he is acting as if he were assigning a weight of one to himself and a weight of zero to every other member of the group (Lehrer/Wagner, 1981:22). Provided these three conditions hold, social *consensus* can be modelled as the equilibrium value of a stochastic process. It is not the same as actual unanimity, as deterministic consensus models assume.

Dissent and Conflict

Deviation from the equilibrium weights is a sign of disagreement or dissent, indicating that the exchange of information has not yet been optimised. Thus, in our model dissent is the result of *incomplete deliberation*. Technically this implies that dissent could be measured by the variance of the values from the equilibrium value in a column vector of the social preference matrix at the tth round of deliberation Π^t. Alternatively, if conditions (1-3) are not fulfilled, *no equilibrium* exists. In this case the chain of mutual respect is broken, the group splits into separate subgroups and conflict prevents the emergence of consensus. I define *conflict* as the impossibility of equilibrium, i.e. as the existence of disjunctive sets of preferences, while *dissent* reflects the deviation from equilibrium at any given moment of time.[213] Overcoming conflict requires establishing conditions of mutual respect and connectedness. The rationale of communication logically leads then to the dynamic process of preference adjustment. As deliberation progresses, individual preferences converge to the unique consensus equilibrium and dissent will vanish. This can be shown as follows.

Equation (7) describes a system of first-order difference equations, which has the general solution for each column vector *j*:

(9) $\pi_j^t = c_1 r_1^t v_1 + c_2 r_2^t v_2 + \ldots + c_n r_n^t v_n$

where c_i (i=1,…n) are constants, r_i are the eigenvalues of W and v_i the respective eigenvectors. Since it is a characteristic of Markov processes that $r_1 = 1$, and $0 < r_i < 1$ for $i \neq 1$, the system converges to the consensual equilibrium vector $\pi_j^* = c_1 v_1$ as t→∞, with π_j^* indicating the unanimous preferences in the *n*-member group for option *j*.

Hence in our specific case of equations (4) and (5) the equilibrium vector is:

$$\pi_1^* = \begin{pmatrix} \dfrac{\beta}{\alpha+\beta} & \dfrac{\alpha}{\alpha+\beta} \\ \dfrac{\beta}{\alpha+\beta} & \dfrac{\alpha}{\alpha+\beta} \end{pmatrix} \begin{pmatrix} \pi_{11}^0 \\ \pi_{21}^0 \end{pmatrix}$$

Hence the consensual preference depend on individuals' original preferences and their weighting by the respective degrees of trust they have for each other.

The speed of convergence of each individual's opinion to consensus (i.e. the number of iterations necessary to reach an infinitesimal deviation) depends on the characteristic equation of the weight matrix - i.e. an *nth*-degree polynomial equation. Convergence requires that the other roots of the characteristic equation are less than 1 in absolute value. The closer they are to zero, the faster is the speed by which consensus is obtained. In general this means that *fast convergence and little dissent require a high degree of reciprocal weights of respect*.[214] In the specific case of the 2-person and 1-option system in equation (4) and (5), the eigenvalues are

$r_1 = 1$, $r_2 = 1 - (\alpha + \beta)$

so that the solution is:

$$(10) \ \pi_1^t = \pi_1^* + c_2 v_2 \ (1 - \alpha - \beta)^t$$

and more precisely:

$$(10a) \ \pi_{11}^t = \frac{\alpha \pi_{21}^0 + \beta \pi_{11}^0}{\alpha + \beta} - \frac{\alpha(\pi_{21}^0 - \pi_{11}^0)}{\alpha + \beta}(1 - \alpha - \beta)^t$$

$$\pi_{21}^t = \frac{\alpha \pi_{21}^0 + \beta \pi_{11}^0}{\alpha + \beta} + \frac{\pi_{21}^0 - \pi_{11}^0}{\alpha + \beta}(1 - \alpha - \beta)^t$$

As t→∞, the system converges to the consensual preferences π^*. The vector $c_2 v_2$ reflects initial disagreement. There are several possible approaches to describe dissent. One would be to measure the average squared deviation from consensus at time t. In our special case of $j=1$ options and $n=2$ members:

$$(11) \ \text{Diss} \left(\pi_1^t \right) = \frac{1}{n} \sum_{i=1}^{2} (\pi_{i1}^t - \pi_{i1}^*)^2 \ = \frac{1}{n} \ c_2^2 \ (1 - \beta)^{2t} \langle v_2, v_2 \rangle^2$$

With the number of deliberative steps increasing (t→∞), initial dissent will disappear. If both individuals have a high degree of reciprocal respect, i.e. if the expression $(1 - \alpha - \beta)$ is close to zero, convergence is fast; if they have no or little respect for each other, i.e. the bracket is close to one, convergence is slow and dissent is high. Yet, as long as the general conditions of mutual respect and connectedness are fulfilled, communicative action and the process of deliberation will tend to create consensus.

The occurrence of new evidence can be interpreted as a stochastic shock, which will increase dissent. But it will also 'disappear' in the background, as it becomes part of the common knowledge in the process of deliberation. Contrary to conflict, a high degree of (tolerated) dissent is therefore a sign of intellectual creativity, while a highly consensual society converges toward conformism. The 'noise' created by new evidence manifests in dissent, and may overshadow consensual collective preferences. Although the nature of deliberation is such, that ultimately consensus will be reached, it may appear that a consensual equilibrium is far from being achieved if the noise is high.

Voting

Because collective choice requires taking a decision at some stage, procedures may be necessary to shorten the process before unanimity is attained. With full consensus on collective preferences over the set of s options, the choice rule $C(s) = \max_j \pi^*(j)$, where $\pi^*(j) = \pi_{1j}^* = \pi_{2j}^* = ... = \pi_{nj}^*$ is a formality. Any individual's preference ranking over the k options would be identical. With stochastic noise, the visibility of collective preferences is blurred and consequently choice makers (governments) may pick from a range of options that do not necessarily maximize everyone's preferences. *Voting* is a standard procedure to terminate the deliberative process *before* full convergence to equilibrium is achieved: when the consensual weighted *mean* of the preference distribution for k options is unobservable due to dissent, the preference ranking of the *median* voter may be second best.[215] The choice rule may then become: $C(s)=\max \pi^t_{mj}$, where m=median votes. Hence the voting process decides on picking the median row vector from the social preference matrix Π^t and the choice rule would maximize the preferences of the median voter over the s options.

A simulation of structural dissent in the EU

Institutional arrangements have important consequences for the degree of trust and respect, the emergence of collective preference, and the speed of convergence to consensus. We look at three distinct cases.

1. The *intergovernmental model* consists of two identical countries, which are linked by a symmetrical, mutual degree of trust between governments, but not between citizens. (See Figure Annexe 1.1a). The only difference between the two countries is that citizens in country A have preference values 1, 0.9, 0.7, 0.6 and the government takes the median position; in country B citizens preference values are 0.4 to zero. The numbers next to the arrows indicate degrees of trust. Every actor gives a weight of 0.5 to himself and spreads the rest among the other members he is connected with.* The results are robust for variations of these parameters within a reasonable range.

2. Today's *EU model* with the European Commission adds one layer of policy-making to the intergovernmental structure, but the Commission functions as an umpire in a median position between governments and is not accountable to citizens. (Figure Annexe 1.1.b).

3. This is changed in the *European Republic*, where a European government is directly connecting citizens and gives some low degree of respect to national governments. (Figure Annexe 1.1c). Figure Annexe 1.2 a-c shows the corresponding convergence of preferences to a European Consensus.

It is clear that the convergence to a European policy consensus is most rapid in the European Republic and slowest in the intergovernmental system. This is also documented by figure Annexe 1.3, which shows the vanishing policy dissent (as calculated in equation (11)) under the three regimes. Consensual collective preferences are most efficiently obtained in the European Republic, or put differently preference frustration by voting is highest in intergovernmental regimes and lowest in a Republic.

---

* Due to rounding, the weights shown in the graph may not add to 1.

Figure Annexe 1.1: Structures of Respect

a. The intergovernmental model.

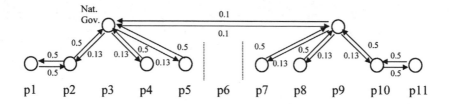

b. The EU-model with the European Commission.

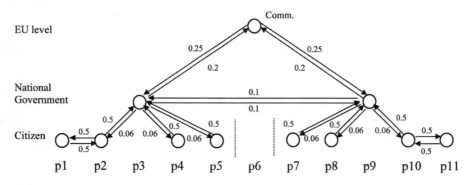

b. The European Republic model.

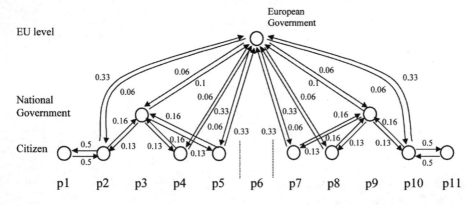

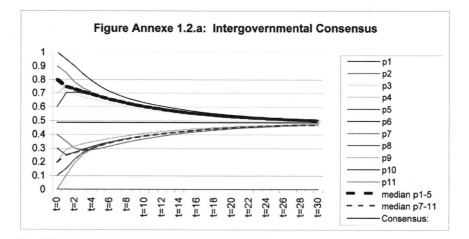

Figure Annexe 1.2.a: Intergovernmental Consensus

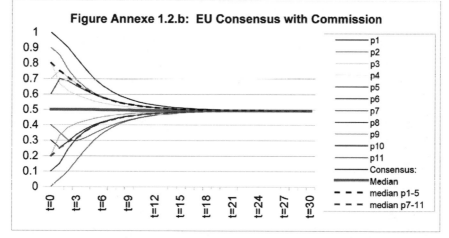

Figure Annexe 1.2.b: EU Consensus with Commission

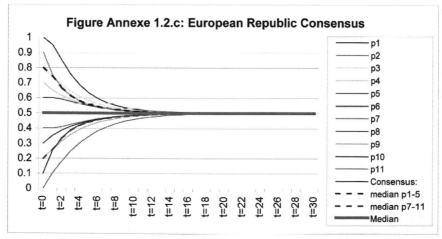

Figure Annexe 1.2.c: European Republic Consensus

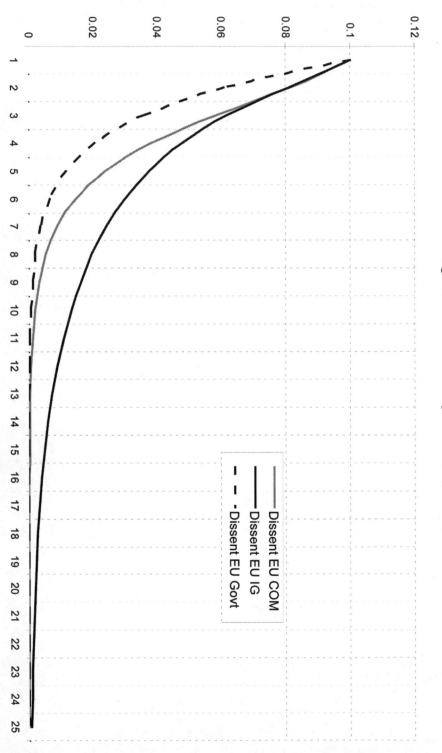

Figure Annexe 1.3: Policy Preference Dissent

Annexe 2.
The Logic of Collective Action

The logic of collective action (Olson, 1971) explains the conditions, which determine

1. the optimal amount of a collective good for each individual to buy, if he/she is to buy any.

2. whether any member or members of the group would find it advantageous to provide this good at the optional quantity at all.

We will first explain the framework within which these conditions are determined and then discuss the implications.

We assume, that the quantity of a collective good provided by a government programme can be measured by a discrete variable, x (such as kilometres of roads built, numbers of jobs created by the government programme etc.) and that the cost and benefit of the government policy can be measured in monetary terms. The provision of the policy will depend on the difference between benefits and costs of the policy. We assume that the cost of the government programme will depend on the level or amount of the collective good (policy) provided and also on the size of the group:

(1) $C = C(x, n)$

The total cost curve is increasing in x, but the average cost curve, i.e. the average cost per unit of public good has the conventional U-shape because of economies of scale at first and later of diminishing returns. The response of cost to group size is in principle indeterminate, but given that costs of bargains and coalition building exponentially increase, [217] the probability is very high that costs will be high for large groups and marginal costs increase with the size of the group.

These costs need to be compared with the benefits derived from the policy. Every member of the group will evaluate the benefits he or she will derive from the provision of the public good individually. However given the public nature of collective goods, the benefits may also depend on the number of other members in the group. It is important to distinguish between individual and social benefits. If you and I look at Mona Lisa in the Louvre, your doing so does not reduce or increase my joy (assuming we go on a weekday to the Louvre). But the total joy in the world has increased.[218] We may therefore write the utility accruing to an individual i member of the polity group by:

(2) $U^i = u^i(x,n)$ for i=1,2,...n

Because we assume that benefits can be measured in monetary terms they are additionable and we can translate individual utilities into the maximum amount that an individual would be willing to pay in order to gain outcomes that he views as desirable (Boardman et al., 1996:70). The formulation in equation (2) allows us a precise classification of public goods discussed in Table Annexe 2.1. Let us first look at the benefits for each member of the group and their change if the size of the group changes. The effect depends on the class of collective goods, discussed earlier. *The individual marginal benefits (IMB) to the individual i from an increase in the group will be negative for each individual in the group if the collective good is an exclusive good.* Because the total benefit of these common property resources is fixed, an additional member to the group will reduce the benefit accruing to each member. In the case of pure public goods the size of the group that consumes the public good is irrelevant and therefore the marginal benefits to any individual within the group are zero. Finally in the case of inclusive collective goods (club goods) the benefits from an increase in the number of group members are positive.

Table Annexe 2.1 A Formal Classification of Collective Goods

	Individual Marginal Benefits (IMB)	Social Marginal Benefits (SMB)	Change in benefit share $\propto^i$
exlusive public goods	$u_n^i < 0$	$V_n = 0$	$\dfrac{\partial \propto^i}{\partial n} < 0$
pure public goods	$u_n^i = 0$	$V_n > 0$	$\dfrac{\partial \propto^i}{\partial n} < 0$
inclusvie public goods	$u_n^i > 0$	$V_n > 0$	$\dfrac{\partial \propto^i}{\partial n} \lessgtr 0$

The total or social benefit derived from the provision of collective goods to the group as a whole is the *sum of all individual benefits* given the number of members in the group.

$$(3) \quad V(x,n) = \sum_{j=1}^{n} u^j (x,n)$$

We may also call this the total social benefit (TSB) derived from a public good given *n* members of the group. It follows that the social marginal benefit from increasing the membership in the group by one person is given by:

$$(4) \quad V_n = \sum_{j=1}^{n} u_n^j (x,n)$$

The social marginal benefit (SMB) with respect to an additional group member *n* is equal to the *sum of the marginal utilities* with respect to *n* for every individual in the group. For exclusive public goods (common property resources) the sum of individual marginal benefits is zero, because the gain of group member *n* is the loss of all others. In the case *of pure public goods social marginal benefits are positive because the additional member has a benefit without taking anything away from others. The same applies to the case of inclusive goods (club goods).*

Next, we have to look at the incentives to group members to provide these collective goods. Each individual will get some share of the total social benefits:

$$(5) \quad \alpha^i = \frac{u^i (x,n)}{\displaystyle\sum_{j=1}^{n} u^j (x,n)}$$

The nature of collective goods is such that the goods are available to all. The optimal amount of collective goods requires maximising the net benefit i.e. the difference between cost and benefits for a given amount of goods. The net benefits to an individual consumer from buying different amounts of the public goods are

$$(6) \quad NB^i = u^i (x,n) - C(x,n)$$

Olson argued that if $NB^i > 0$ for some **i**, the likelihood that one member of the group will provide the good is high. He therefore called such groups privileged. If $NB^i < 0$ for all **i**, the group is latent and is likely to fail unless selective (non-collective) incentives are available to induce contributions or binding agreements between coalitions of members.[219]

Holding the number of participants in the group constant and maximising the individual net benefits yields the optimum amounts of collective goods (x*). The necessary condition for this optimum is that the share of individual benefits in the social benefits α^i is equal to the marginal social cost-benefit ratio.

(7) $\alpha^i = \dfrac{\partial C}{\partial x} \Big/ \dfrac{\partial V}{\partial x} = \dfrac{\partial C}{\partial V}$ (Condition I)

The second condition which needs to hold is that at least one member (or a coalition of members) derives sufficient amount of individual benefits from the provision of the public good that they are willing to cover the necessary cost. This condition for a privileged group is expressed in equation (8).

(8) $\alpha^i \cdot V(x^*, n) \geq C(x^*, n)$

(8a) $\alpha^i \geq \dfrac{C(x^*, n)}{V(x^*, n)}$ (Condition II)

Equation (8a) reveals that the individual share of social benefits has to be higher than the total social cost-benefit ratio if the collective good is to be provided by voluntary co-operation between members of the group. A privileged group is crucial for the successful provision of collective goods. The smaller α^i is, the lower is the probability that the collective good will be voluntarily supplied by the group, provided the cost-benefit ratios remain constant. This implies that in a non-co-operative game voluntary action would not be sufficient to provide an optimal amount of European policy goods. Olson (1971:28) argued that large groups have a tendency to provide themselves with no collective goods at all, whereas small groups tended towards a sub-optimal provision of collective goods.

However, this statement has been challenged by authors, who claim that there is no logical connection between the size of the group and its likelihood to provide public goods (Drazen, 2000: 384). In fact it can be shown that the response of the individual benefit share α^i to the number of group members depends on the nature of public goods. By differentiating equation (5) with respect to n we obtain equation (9).

(9) $\dfrac{\partial \alpha^i}{\partial n} = \dfrac{u_n^{\ i} \cdot V(x, n) - V_n \cdot u^i(x, n)}{V(x, n)^2}$

For α^i to remain constant, we obtain the condition:

(10) $\dfrac{u_n^{\ i}}{V_n} = \dfrac{u^i(x, n)}{V(x, n)} \Leftrightarrow \dfrac{IMB}{SMB} = \dfrac{IB}{TSB}$

meaning that the ratio of individual marginal benefits to social marginal benefits has to be equal to the ratio of the individuals' benefits to the total social benefits. If the marginal benefit ratio is smaller than the total benefit ratio, α^i will fall, as Olson assumed. Referring back to table Annexe 2.1 and given that total individual and social benefits are always positive, we obtain an unambiguous fall in α^i for any additional group member, provided the collective goods are exclusive or pure private goods. The result is less certain in the case of club goods. If the inclusive good resembles a pure public good, the benefit share would fall as well. If there is, however, a club member who will draw a higher benefit from the new member than the rest of the group (including the new member), then it is possible that the individual benefit share will increase and the club member will voluntarily provide the collective good.

In fact, the analysis can be substantially simplified by arguing in terms of absolute net benefits accruing to group members, rather than in benefit shares. By differentiating equation (6) with respect to n, we obtain:

$$(11) \quad \frac{\partial NB^i}{\partial n} = u_n^i - c_n$$

The net benefits to any group member i will increase with the admission of a new member n if the individual marginal benefits to one member of the group exceed the marginal cost from admitting new members. But given that the cost of collective goods are related to the complexity of decision-making in bargaining between autonomous actors, *marginal costs are likely to increase with group size.* On the other hand, u_n^i are zero for pure public goods and falling for exclusive goods. Hence the *non-excludable collective goods in boxes II and VI in Figure 5.1 are unlikely to be supplied by voluntary co-ordination between autonomous actors.* Large groups have a tendency to become 'latent' in Olson's sense. Only in the case of inclusive club goods is there a possibility that the net benefits for some i will increase, but the probability is low for very large groups, unless decision-making costs and procedures are greatly simplified.

Annexe 3.
Defining the Optimal Policy Mix

Efficient Policy Mixes

An extremely simplified model of stabilisation policy can be formulated in the context of the IS-MP model formulated by D. Romer (1999), augmented by fiscal policy. We assume aggregate supply (y*) as exogenously given. Aggregate demand responds negatively to real interest rates and an increase in the budget position. s is the budget surplus (s<0 $\Leftrightarrow$ deficit) and ϕ_0 stands for some autonomous demand (animal spirits). In the Monetary Union $s = \frac{1}{y} \Sigma s_i$, i.e. the aggregate fiscal stance is the sum of each member state budget position. We then have the output gap as a measure of excess demand.

(1) $y - y^* = \phi_0 - \phi_1 r - \phi_2 s$

Monetary policy targets inflation. If inflation exceeds the central bank's target π^*, the ECB raises the real interest rate, if it falls below, it cuts rates.

(2) $r = r^* + \varphi(\pi - \pi^*)$

r* is the equilibrium or 'natural rate of interest' (Wicksell) where price stability is preserved. This equilibrium interest rate is not necessarily constant. In this model it depends on fiscal policy. An efficient macroeconomic policy mix yields simultaneously price stability ($\pi - \pi^* = 0$) and full employment of productive resources (y - y* = 0). This gives us the condition at which the interaction of fiscal and monetary policy will yield macroeconomic equilibrium:

(3) $r^* = \phi_0 - \frac{\phi_2}{\phi_1} s$

Hence the equilibrium interest rate is positively correlated to fiscal deficits (s<0) or negatively to fiscal consolidation. The impact of fiscal policy on monetary policy depends on the elasticities by which output responds to either interest rates (ϕ_1) or changes in fiscal policy (ϕ_2). It is described by the slope of the efficient policy line in *Figure 6.1*. In this most elementary model, the relationship between efficient monetary and fiscal policy is a linear trade-off. If we admit risk-averse behaviour by investors who are holding the public debt, the efficient policy line would be concave. If Ricardian Equivalence holds, $\phi_2=0$ and the efficient policy line is a horizontal line. Fiscal policy is then totally inefficient. This is also true, if the interest response of output is perfectly elastic ($\phi_1=\infty$). Monetary policy would be totally inefficient when the interest elasticity of output equals zero. This is what Keynes called the liquidity trap. The policy line is then vertical.

The Utility Function of the Policy Mix

The optimal policy mix obtains when the slope of the efficient policy line ($-\frac{\phi_2}{\phi_1}$) is equal to the ratio of marginal utilities of fiscal and monetary policy. The utility function can be formulated as a Cobb-Douglas function:

(4) $U = r^{\alpha} s^{(1-\alpha)}$

α is the constant share that monetary policy contributes to the collective welfare. It measures the partial elasticity of collective utility to changes in interest rates.

The optimal policy mix implies

(5) $-\dfrac{\phi_2}{\phi_1} = \dfrac{1-\alpha}{\alpha} \dfrac{r}{s}$

Hence, *different preference weights imply different combinations of r and s, i.e. of monetary and fiscal policy.* An aggregate policy stance requires a single collective weight assignment for α.[220]

How is α determined? We can use our model of stochastic consensus to explain how the collective assessment of the utility shares are found. Each individual assigns an individual weight to the utilities of these policies. Through public deliberation under the conditions of mutual respect and connectedness the collective weights α and $(1-\alpha)$ emerge as the consensual equilibrium vector (see Annexe 1).

Notes

1 Emphasis added.

2 An overview of European integration theory is given by Rosamond 2000. For a critical discussion of integration theory see Collignon and Schwarzer, 2003.

3 Quoted in Burgess 2000:33.

4 See Wittgenstein, (1984), Searle (1998), Giddens (1993), Habermas (1984 and 1987). Collignon and Schwarzer (2003) discuss the implications for European integration theories.

5 Epistemology is the science of knowledge. By 'epistemic ingredients' I mean the conditions which allow us to make informed and knowledgeable decisions.

6 For a full discussion, see Chapter Five.

7 This fact is usually taken for granted. An exception is Buchanan and Tullock (1962:19), who explicitly state their model's assumption that 'the same basic values motivate individuals.'

8 Buchanan (1991:61) has called the first aspect the *interest component*, and the second the *theory* or *cognitive component* of rational choice.

9 The precise definition refers to the model of stochastic consensus. An *epistemic constituency* is the set of all those individuals, who form a chain of respect, i.e. fulfil the two conditions of connectedness and mutual respect with respect to accepting a constitution. See Annexe 1. I deliberately avoid the notion of *epistemic community* in this context, as it has a more narrow focus on experts in the literature. For further details see Collignon and Schwarzer, 2003.

10 Elazar (1987:2-4) identifies three basic ways in which polities come into existence: conquest, organic development and covenant i.e. agreement. At least in the last two, polities and epistemic constituencies overlap.

11 In stateless communities, the importance of epistemic consensus is even more important than in modern societies, where the institution of the state permits a degree of dissent. Taylor (1982:2) has argued 'that in the absence of the state social order can be maintained only if relations between people are those characteristic of community'. He then defines the core characteristics of the 'almost complete consensus on a wide range of beliefs and values' (p 26). I will return to these concepts below.

12 Of course, rational decisions *are* possible if there is a rational decision-making *procedure*, such as voting. In this case the agreed standard of evaluation becomes the number of votes. But this is not the same as a rational choice derived from the evaluation of options and picking 'the best'.

13 This was also Hobbes' view. See Chapter Three.

14 I discard the paternalistic argument that I may know better than you what is good for you.

15 Technically, the value of this procedure is equal to the expected utility of the policy choice, or the fair value of betting that my preference will prevail.

16 Such agreement on procedures can be described as Nash equilibrium in mixed strategies.

17 The reasons may be that actors prefer cooperation under constitutional terms over anarchistic results. However, in a two-stage social contract with incongruous decision-making and policy domains, this argument can also be used to explain constitutional decline. See Cullis and Jones 1998:366.

18 This argument of fairness with respect to constitutions is particularly strong in the 'contractarian' tradition of justifying governments, such as Buchanan and Tullock (1962) and Rawls (1971). See also Mueller (1996:63-64).

19 This is the definition used by Cullis and Jones, 1998:366. For reasons that will become apparent below, I prefer this definition over the formulation as sets of 'rules and principles governing the legitimate exercise of public power...and the allocation of this power between different public authorities' (Harden, 1995:1). This definition assumes power as exogenously given, but power needs to be assigned to an authority and the constitution is this mapping. My approach in this book is an endogenous approach to power.

20 Bellamy and Castiglione (2000:69) have called this fact Europe's 'splintered' or 'mixed' polity.

21 For example through most of the 1990's, German trade unionists and opposition politicians were opposed to the Kohl government's restrictive macroeconomic policies, favouring an approach that was much closer to what was part of the policy debate in France. But these voices were given little, if any, weight in European deliberations on policy-making. 'Germany' was perceived as a monolithic bloc that was in favour of restrictive monetary and fiscal policy and exchange rate appreciations. The cost for economic growth and unemployment were high. For a formal analysis of median voter preferences in the EU see Alesina and Grilli, 1992.

22 Interestingly, we find a similar, although nastier, phenomenon in Spain during the 16th and 17th centuries. Because the different kingdoms of Spain remained splintered polities with different laws, institutions, currencies and even languages, the State remained weak. There was a lack of constitutional consensus which required focus on substantial issues and the suppression of dissent. This function was accomplished by the Holy Inquisition. See Pérez, 2002.

23 In fact, majority voting allows the possibility that several incongruous epistemic domains add their votes to form a majority. This phenomenon is frequently observed in voting on referenda. For example, in the French referendum on the Maastricht Treaty it was never clear whether the 'No' vote reflected a refusal of the Treaty or a rejection of the Mitterrand presidency. Strictly speaking, this is inconsistent public choice. The French policy domain was effectively split into several epistemic constituencies. For details on the ratification debates in several EU countries, see Collignon and Schwarzer, 2003.

24 Technically, the policy deliberation is a stochastic process where the utility or preference variables of individuals change with a given probability distribution, which is determined by the weights different individuals attribute to each other. See Annexe 1.

25 In the first half of the 20th century the racist view that biological background directly determines collective preferences was highly influential. From a logical point of view, today's communitarians stand in this tradition.

26 They are 'naturalistic' because in their case 'ought' is derived from 'is' and because it seems 'natural' to act as everyone else.

27 This is certainly true for Turkey, Russia, Ukraine and Belarus, probably also for the Balkan States, including Bulgaria, Slovakia and even Romania. See Schmidt 2000:211-227.

28 In Annexe 1 this modification of preferences is modelled using Bayes' rule.

29 Italics added.

30 This seems to be one of the necessary conditions of 'community' according to Michael Taylor, 1982. In formal terms it implies a symmetric weight matrix. See Annexe 1.

31 Technically, the difference is that under reciprocity they give each other the same weights of respect, while in the Lehrer and Wagner model they can respect each other to different degrees.

32 On holism see Chapter Three.

33 If the weight matrix in Annexe 1 is symmetrical (the weights are reciprocal) consensus is instantaneous.

34 We may measure dissent in a given population as the variance from the equilibrium. See Annexe 1

35 Italics added.

36 See also Tönnies, 2001.

37 Walzer (1994:101), a leading communitarianist, explicitly acknowledges that 'Tension and conflict seem to be inherent' in the communitarian model. Gambetta, 1998, has linked low respect for others to holism, which also explains why communitarianism is more conflictual, given the close association between communitarians and holism.

38 Taylor (1994:53) reports, for instance, that the Meech amendment to the Canadian Constitution proposed to recognise Quebec as a 'distinct society'.

39 For a fuller treatment of this statement see Dumont, 1991. See also below pp. 63-64 and Chapter Four.

40 For a discussion of the concept of a hard budget constraint in a monetary economy, see Kornai (1980), Riese (1990) and Maskin (1999).

41 This is a convenient abstraction. In reality it is a range of short-term interest rates.

42 Strictly speaking there can be an indirect effect of consideration of neighbours on domestic policy preferences, if voters care about the welfare of other nations. Although such altruism is less infrequent than one may expect when raised in Hobbesian hard-nosed models of social choice, the indirect respect for others takes a long time to enter the domestic consensus, while it increases domestic dissent in the meantime.

43 The regression equation is: Modelling L (EU membership is a good thing) by OLS

(L indicates log; EU member is a dummy with 1= EU member state and 0 for accession countries)

	Coefficient	Std.Error	t-value	t-prob	Part.R^2
LGDP/EU	-0.130673	0.1895	-0.690	0.497	0.0194
LTrust	1.28334	0.1675	7.66	0.000	0.7097
EUmember	-0.306896	0.2935	-1.05	0.306	0.0436
sigma 0.374788		RSS 3.37117682			
log-likelihood -10.2236		DW 1.98			
no. of observations 27		no. of parameters 3			

44 For any single issue, the number of potential combinations of yes/no votes is 2^n where n is the number of negotiators. This implies that the complexity of intergovernmental decision-making *doubles with every new member.*

45 Ireland approved the Nice Treaty in a second referendum, Denmark also approved Maastricht in a second referendum, but not EMU.

46 See Moore, 1993

47 For a deeper analysis see Gargarella, 2000.

48 Economists and game theorists model this intergovernmental bargaining by 'minimising national loss functions'. But for ordinary citizens, a loss is a loss, even if minimised.

49 The four freedoms are the freedom of circulation for goods, services, capital and labour.

50 For an application of Searle's theory to sovereignty in the context of international relations, see Sørensen, 1999.

51 'Collective agreement about the possession of the status is constitutive of having the status, and having the status is essential to the performance of the function assigned to that status' (Searle, 1995:51).

52 See for example his discussion with Jean-Marc Ferry, in Habermas, 1990.

53 See also Mann, 1974:22: 'The German state did not serve any nation: the nation had no state'.

54 See footnote 19 above.

55 This is the modified definition given by Russel,1938:25. See Wrong 1997.

56 'Status hominum *extra* societatem civilem' (see Hobbes, 1988:94). The natural state is *outside* civilised society, not prior to it.

57 'Bellum omnium in omnes'. Hobbes, 1988:128.

58 'Bellum enim quid est, praeter tempus illud in quo voluntas certandi per vim verbis factisve satis declaratus? Tempus reliquum Pax vocatur'. Hobbes, 1988:132.

59 See Taylor, 1982; Nozick, 1974. I discuss the concept of the State in Chapter Five.

60 This formulation is owed to de Jasay, (1998:76). Przeworski (1991:54) quotes a definition by Lamournier: 'acquiescence motivated by subjective agreement with given norms and values'. Weber (1972:16) also excludes reward and punishment from the concept of legitimacy.

61 There may be, of course, indirect rewards in the form of unintended consequences resulting from rule following, such as improved reliability in an uncertain world. However, the creation of these externalities is the purpose of institutions as commitment devices and requires an explanation why individuals would follow rules in the first place.

62 The concept of legitimacy seems to be absent from modern economic theory. For economists, rational behaviour seems to follow mainly stimulus and response. The *homo economicus* is hardly distinct from Pavlov's dogs. As a consequence, neoclassical economists find it rather difficult to deal with issues of legitimacy, which is, at best, reduced to a positive net balance of costs and benefits. However, more recently economists have argued that economic rationality implies 'coherent behaviour' with respect to some outside standard (see Sen, 1987, Basu 2000). But what determines these standards in the first place? For Talcott Parsons (1949) the answer was found in the legitimacy of institutions: '[Institutions] are normative patterns which define what are felt to be, in the given society, proper, legitimate or expected modes of action or of social relationship' (p. 190) and ' it is precisely around social institutions that, to a very large extent, the content of self interest is organised' (p.197).

63 See also Habermas, 1992:49: 'Die Rechtsgültigkeit einer Norm - und darin besteht ihr Witz - besagt nun, dass *beides zugleich* garantiert ist: Sowohl die Legalität des Verhaltens im Sinne einer durchschnittlichen Normbefolgung, die erforderlichenfalls durch Sanktionen erzwungen wird, wie auch die Legitimität der Regel selbst, die eine Befolgung der Norm aus Achtung vor dem Gesetz jederzeit möglich macht'.

64 The naturalistic interpretation of the nation-state has been well formulated by Herder, an eminent thinker of German romantic communitarianism: 'Every nation contains its own central point of felicity, just as every sphere has its centre of gravity' (Quoted by Habermas, 2001b:3).

65 One of the first theorists of sovereignty, Jean Bodin 1583 (1993:118) expressed this idea as follows: 'disons que signifient ces mots, PUISSANCE ABSOLUE. Car le peuple ou les seigneurs d'une République peuvent donner purement et simplement la puissance souveraine et perpétuelle à quelqu'un pour disposer des biens, des personnes, et tout l'état à son plaisir...' Johannes Althusius, his younger contemporary and one of the founders of communitarian federalism, defined sovereignty as follows: 'What we call this right of the realm [i.e. the right of sovereignty] has as its purpose good order, proper discipline, and the supplying of provisions in the universal association. Towards these purposes it directs the actions of each and all of its members, and prescribes appropriate duties for them. Therefore, the universal power of ruling (*protestas imperandi universalis*) is called that which recognises no ally, nor any superior or equal to itself. And this supreme right of universal jurisdiction is the form and substantial essence of sovereignty (*majestas*) or, as we have called it a major state. When this right is taken away, sovereignty perishes...' (Althusius, 1964:64-65).

66 Nevertheless, Goyard-Fabre (1989:136) rightly points out: 'La souveraineté, en tant que forme de la République, est *la norme* d'une politique que Bodin met à l'épreuve en traçant la figure de meilleur gouvernement.' (emphasis added)

67 Buchanan and Tullock (1962) have called the phenomenon of holism the 'organic view of society'. See also Tönnies 2001 who has described the two concepts of holistic communities and individualistic societies.

68 A clear formulation was given by Adolf Hitler in his notorious memorandum on the Four Year Plan in 1936: 'The nation does not live for the economy, for economic leaders, or for economic and financial theories: on the contrary, it is finance and the economy, economic leaders and theories, which all owe an unqualified service in this struggle for the self assertion of our nation'. (quoted in Nicholls, 1994:61).

69 In traditional societies, individualism lives in the other worldly freedom of religion (Dumont, 1991). In modern societies, individualism has become inner-worldly because it was integrated into the constitutive principles of monetary market economies. Autonomous individuals are here linked through contracts, and credit contracts are at the origin of markets and money (See Chapter Four).

70 Present day Communitarians seem to forget this distinction. See for example Charles Taylor (1995:276): 'The idea underlying popular sovereignty is that people who are sovereign *form some kind of unit*' (emphasis added by author).

71 The classical model is the election of the Pope. He is elected *unanimiter et concorditer* and approved by popular acclamation ('*fiat, fiat, justum et dignum est*'). Arguably the only difference to modern European Council decisions is that nowadays the media proclaim: '*nec justum nec dignum est*'.

72 Article 6 of the Declaration of Human Rights states explicitly: 'La loi est l'expression de la volonté générale. Tous les citoyens ont le droit de concourir personnellement, ou par leur représentants à sa formation'. Rousseau made an unfortunate step back by *identifying* rational individual will with general will. This Rousseauan-Jacobin virus has corrupted the French program of modernity ever since.

73 For the historic emergence of the modern concept of the sovereign citizen see Rosanvallon 1992; for the atavistic survival of the traditional views in the modern approach see Habermas 2001b, Chapter One: What is a People?

74 For a discussion of these issues, including communitarian interpretations of the 'non-existent European *demos*', see Eriksen, 2000.

75 See next chapter.

76 'La souveraineté donnée à un Prince sous charges et conditions, n'est que les conditions apposées en la création du Prince, soient de la Loi de Dieu ou de nature', Bodin (1993:119).

77 See Gierke, (1902:96 and 297). See also Dumont (1980) who emphasises the distinction between authority (sovereignty) and power (rulers) in traditional societies. Authority stands here for constitutive rules and power for regulative (distributive) rules.

78 I refer here to the definition of Baumol (1986:19): 'A distribution is fair if it involves no envy by any individual of any other'. For a discussion of models of fairness, see also Sen, 1999.

79 I share Rawls modernist emphasis on pluralism and tolerance as the foundation of political liberalism: 'The problem of political liberalism is to find out how a stable and just democratic society, which is composed of free and equal citizens, but profoundly divided by mutually incompatible religions, philosophy and moral doctrines, can be sustained.' (Rawls, 1993:10).

80 This is how I translate Dumont's (1991) '*englobement*', which describes the principle of hierarchisation. It bears some resemblance with Hegel's notion of *Aufhebung*.

81 For a controversial view setting the European Model against the American Dream, see Hutton (2002).

82 See for example his debate with Joschka Fischer in *Le Monde*, 21 Juin, 2000.

83 As Sacha Guitry put it: 'le contraire de la vérité est déjà très près de la vérité' (Todd, 2002:22).

84 This is one reason why Mitrany's functionalism was later transformed into the neo-functionalism of European integration theory.

85 I call *republican federalism* the tradition where individual citizens are the sovereign. It is not to be confused with 'New Federalism' which has become the catchword for the reform of federalism in the USA under the Republican administration of Ronald Reagan. See also note 192.

86 See also King (1982:19).

87 For an excellent discussion of the apparent *'absurdité'* of a compromise of sovereign rights between a federation and its constituent states, see the introduction in Chopin (2002).

88 See also Elazar (1987:34): 'Federal polities are characteristically non-centralized; that is, the powers of government within them are diffused among many centres, whose existence and authority are guaranteed by the general constitution, rather than being concentrated in a single centre.' From this point of view the EU is a federal polity without a centre.

89 For Elazar (1987:33) this is even the defining criterion for federalism: 'Federalism has to do with the need of people and polities to unite for common purposes yet remain separate to preserve their respective integrities. It is rather like wanting to have one's cake and eat it too.'

90 (In Buchanan et al. 1990:4) claims that Madison's grand design of limiting the range and scope of political authority over the liberties of citizens failed. Yet this American failure looks like a bright success when compared with European nation-states which sometimes seem to have an attitude of keeping citizens like rabbits in a cage.

91 On fundamental rights and fundamental boundaries, see Weiler, 1999, Chapter Three. Buchanan (1990:5) argues that ' the threat of potential secession offered a means of ensuring that the central government would, indeed, stay within those boundaries of political action defined by the general interest of all citizens in the inclusive territory.' European experience with opt-outs does not support this proposition. It is rather an invitation for *states* to blackmail and free-ride.

92 For a detailed analysis of Helmut Schmidt's and Valéry Giscard d'Estaing's European strategies, see Collignon and Schwarzer (2003).

93 The idea of a 'composite state' goes back to Althusius' *res publica composita* which was distinguished from the *res publica simplex* which dominated Bodin's line of thinking. See Gierke (1902:245).

94 As Tullock (1994:14), an American decentralising federalist, put it succinctly: 'It seems that people, on the whole, like living with other people who are similar to them'.

95 The Catholic Social Movement in the 19th century, which partly emerged as a reaction to the creation of the Italian state, also reflected this ideology (Kelikian, 2002).

96 See in particular Philpott, 1999. Sørensen (1999:169) observes: 'The world did not change over night at a specific point in time; elements of the old system remained in place for a long period. There was no momentous change from one day to the next in 1648. Still it is justified to look at 1648 as a crucial point in the transition from feudal to modern authority.' I believe this may be appropriate for the discussion of sovereignty in international relations, but not for the concept as such.

97 See Burgess (2000).

98 According to Kriegel (1998:77) 'l'émergence du concept date de la proclamation de Jean Bodin, aux premières lignes de son oeuvre majeure: 'République est un droit gouvernement de plusieurs mesnages et de ce qui leur est commun avec puissance souveraineté.''

99 Another approach to this problem was 'to falsify moneis' (Bodin, 1993:512) by debasing them. This observation led Bodin to link the quantity of money to inflation and effectively established Bodin as one of the first economists in the modern sense (Groyard-Fabre, 1989:35). The first clear exposition of the quantity theory of money was, however, given by Martin de Azpilcueta in 1556, a writer of the School of Salamanca. See Elliot 2002:191-192.

100 Some authors like Guth (1982) even argued that the early modern period was a transition from the 'Age of Debt' to the 'Age of Contract'. See also Muldrew (1998:132).

101 On individualism and modernity, see Dumont, (1991).

102 Anti-Semitism by the Spanish Inquisition was an early attempt by Isabelle de Castille and Ferdinand d'Aragon to keep control over public debt. See Pérez, 2002:13.

103 See also Macpherson (1962). Bodin described his contemporary situation lucidly: '...a Republic has no other foundation than trust *(foi)*, for without it neither justice, nor any society could last. Trust only arises when promises and legitimate agreements are honoured. If these obligations are broken, contracts annulled, debts abolished, what else can one expect but the total subversion of the state? For none would any longer have any confidence in another.' (Bodin 1993:431; my translation). Modern capitalism still operates under the same law!

104 R. J. Knecht (2000:54-5) reports that in the mid-1500s merchants turned to Protestantism as well as the lower orders in towns, particularly artisans. Bankers remained close to the establishment, while peasants stood at the sidelines of religious division. For an overview on recent research of the sociology of French Protestantism see also Holt (1995).

105 This is clear from the assignment of weights in the model of stochastic consensus. See Annexe 1.

106 Dumont (1991:163) has explained totalitarianism as a 'disease of modern society which results from the temptation to subordinate individualism to the primacy of society defined as a totality'.

107 While anti-semitic programs in Spain may have inspired the massacre, the number of victims do not seem to be comparable. See Pérez, 2002:145.

108 In *Leviathan,* Hobbes (1973: Chapter Two) Hobbes lists six 'infirmities' that weaken the Common-wealth, the first five describe the dangers of individualism and the sixth 'that the Sovereign Power may be divided. For what is it to divide the power of a Common-wealth but to dissolve it; for powers divided mutually destroy each other.'

109 'A Common-wealth is said to be instituted, when a multitude of men do agree, and covenant, every one, with every one, that to whatsoever man, or assembly of men, shall be given by the major part, the right to present the person of them all (that is to say, to be their representative).' Hobbes, 1973:90.

110 Dumont, 1985:73

111 To do full justice to these early thinkers it would be important to distinguish between 'power' and 'authority', as Dumont 1985:19 and 1980:167 has pointed out.

112 Weiler, 1999 Chap.1 develops an interesting comparison of the Jewish Covenant with European integration.

113 It is not by coincidence that Calvinist Geneva was ruthless in enforcing the new religion and in eliminating dissenters. By 1564 the Devine State of Geneva had executed 58 dissidents including the Spanish doctor Michael Servetus, who discovered blood circulation and was burnt on a scaffolding in Geneva in 1553.

114 'The numbers of a realm, or of this universal symbiotic association, are not, I say, individual men, families or collegia, as in a private [...] association. Instead, members are many cities, provinces and regions agreeing among themselves on a single body constituted by mutual union and communication. Individual persons from these group members are called natives, inhabitants of the realm and sons and daughters of the realm. *They are to be distinguished from foreigners and strangers who have no claim upon the right of the realm.* Althusius, 1965:62 (my italics)

115 I return to the implicit hierarchy of these republican values in Chapter Seven.

116 The dominant role of the Catholic Church in Italy and Spain mentioned above prevented an early development of protestant individualist ideologies as well as federalist communitarianism in these countries.

117 There is some evidence that the synthesis was less inspired by European political thought, but by American Indians (See Burgess, 2000)

118 Hueglin, (1999:152). Hueglin also reports that this resolution was acknowledged by a European Commission research team reporting to President Delors as the earliest formulation of the principle of subsidiarity eventually entrenched in article 3b of the Maastricht Treaty, respectively in article 5 of the Amsterdam and Nice Treaty.

119 The Vatican did not recognise the reality of the United Kingdom of Italy until 1929.

120 The French presidential elections of 2002 have given a clear message in this respect.

121 In a different context, the point has been made by Buchanan, (1958:36): 'In an individualistic society which governs itself through the use of democratic political forms, the idea of the 'group' or the 'whole' as a sentient being is contrary to the fundamental principle of social organisation.'

122 In the German Constitution of the Reich the Länder were formally the owners of the Reich.

123 Fiscal federalism is a sub-field of public finance, dealing with the provision of public goods and services by different levels of government. As Oates (1999) mentioned, the term is unfortunate as it suggests narrow concern with budgetary matters. I will refer to 'economic federalism' as the broader range of policy-making issues encompassing the vertical structure of the public sector and, to 'fiscal federalism' when I have established theories in mind. The theory of collective action focuses on the conditions under which autonomous and self-interested individuals are willing to commit themselves to the voluntary provision of collective goods shared by a group.

124 Technically, if X is total consumption of a good by n individuals, and x_i is individual i's consumption, then for a private good we have:

$$X = \sum_{i=0}^{n} x_i \text{ and for a public good: } X = x_1 = x_2 = x_3 = \ldots = x_i = \ldots x_n$$

125 In Collignon (2002) I have applied similar considerations to determine the size of an optimal currency area.

126 A more restrictive definition of externality stipulates that the external effect must not be compensated because of 'missing markets'. This restriction is not crucial to our argument here.

127 Formally, this is described by a utility function of the form:

$$U^A = U(x_1, x_2 \ldots x_n; y^B)$$

Where the utility of A depends on a range of goods $(x_1, x_2 \ldots x_n)$ over which A has the capacity to choose and an action by B (y^B) over which he has a priori no control. A change in B's action may increase (positive externality) or decrease (negative externality) the welfare of A. With symmetric information B would take into account the effects his own action has on A's welfare and could pay or ask for compensation. See Cullis and Jones (1998): 31; Baumol and Oates (1975): 17-18; Coase, (1960). But a change in y^B may not only affect A's overall utility, but also the marginal utilities of the goods A chose autonomously.

If $\dfrac{\partial^2 U(x)}{\partial y^{B^2}} > 0$, we speak of *strategic complementarities* between the two goods or actions. If the expression is negative, we have a case of *strategic substitutabilities*.

128 Olson (1971) has emphasized *'selective incentives'*, but this requires obviously also some form of regulation.

129 A formal model for preference change is given in Annexe 1.

130 See note 124. In fact, Samuelson's argument focussed on the optimal supply of pure public goods *relative* to private goods, so that the condition states that the sum of marginal rates of substitution between private and public goods must be equal to the marginal rates of transformation between the two goods.

131 We ignore the impact of ERM II which presently applies only to Denmark.

132 Pareto-efficiency implies that there is no technically feasible use of resources which would improve the benefits to any one individual without reducing those of any other.

133 I am well aware that this is a simplification. When dissent prevails and decisions are taken by votes, there is always a degree of preference frustration. However, it is contained by the mutual respect and tolerance for other opinions, if it is based on constitutional consensus. See Annexe 1.

134 Technically the welfare loss can be measured in terms of the reduction in consumer surplus. The individual in the smaller group suffers as a result of what may be for him an other-than-desired level of consumption of the good. See Oates, 1999:41.

135 Alesina, Angeloni and Etro (2001) have argued that multilevel governance (a 'two-step procedure') with majority voting defines a 'flexible union' which is a Pareto-improvement over a 'rigid Union' with a uniform policy for each country. However, this result is dependant on the assumption of exogenous preferences where policy deliberation is confined to the nation-state. In the next chapter, I will argue that this describes the dilemmas of the Stability and Growth Pact correctly. But their model does not take into account the effects on union-wide policy deliberation for the emergence of a stochastic consensus for European policy preferences.

136 I thank Keith Lehrer for pointing this out to me.

137 'In advocating the reintroduction of a mass of special legal statutes in place of the single status of uniform citizenship that was the achievement of the Enlightenment, multiculturalists seem remarkably insouciant about the abuses and inequalities of the *ancien régime* which provoked the attacks on it by the Encyclopaedists and their allies. It is not so much a case of reinventing the wheel as forgetting why the wheel was invented and advocating the introduction of the sledge' Barry, 2001:11.

138 Alesina et. al (2002) argue that the provision of European collective goods should be assigned to the 'central level', i.e. the Union, when type-I-inefficiencies dominate and to national member states or local governments if type-II-inefficiencies are prevalent. However, this does not solve the dilemma, because if spillovers exist, structures and mechanisms for collective preference formation are required if preference heterogeneity is to be overcome.

139 Hence, we assume implicitly that governments represent the preferences of an epistemic constituency which is identical with the member state's polity.

140 Olson (1971:22) explicitly acknowledges the possibility that each individual in a group may place a different value upon a collective good. He avoids the valuation problem by dressing his argument in qualitative terms of the cost and benefit functions. Alternatively, one can circumvent the problems resulting from different epistemic constituencies by defining the value by individuals' or member states' willingness to pay. See Boardman et al. 1996.

141 For a discussion of EMU as an optimal currency area from a similar perspective, see Collignon, 2002.

142 For an academic treatment see for example Alesina et al. 1999 and 2002.

143 I thank Sebastian Dullien for bringing this point to my attention.

144 A leading German government official once remarked to me: 'The enlargement of the EU to Central and Eastern Europe will liberate us from our Babylonian imprisonment with France.'

145 Translation by the author.

146 Of course, it is also possible that splitting such coalition may be motivated by the wish of not seeing the collective good being provided.

147 Werner Weidenfeld (2000:10) uses the expression 'Erfolgsfalle' for this paradox.

148 See Cooper and John, (1988) for the underlying theory of coordination failure.

149 See Benassi et al. (1994) for the formal model. It is, of course, also possible that deviating behaviour creates positive externalities, by greater creativity or innovation. I will discuss these pristine externalities and associated strategic complementarities below.

150 Basu (2000:117) even develops a 'Core Theorem': 'Whatever behaviour and outcome in society are legally enforceable are also enforceable through social norms.'

151 For a precise formulation of this statement see Annexe 1. Dissent reflecting the variance from consent, the likelihood of dissent depends on the roots of the characteristic equation of the weight matrix.

152 Technically, coordination failure of this form is characterised by multiple Pareto-rankable Nash equlibria. See Benassi et al 1994:348.

153 Hix (2002) has proposed that the Commission President is elected by national Parliaments, because this is what epistemic constituencies focus upon. This idea would increase type –I-inefficiencies.

154 For an analysis of the functioning of the EMU-polity, see Friedrich, 2003.

155 I have given a formal exposition of this statement in Collignon 2002a.

156 See Romer, 1996: chapter 9.

157 In Collignon (2002) I have shown that monetary policy may also have long-term output capacity consequences.

158 For an overview see Schelkle, 2001:54-62.

159 Local or decentralised public expenditure must therefore focus on the allocation function and not the stabilisation function.

160 Including the sustainability of public debt, see Collignon and Mundschenk, 1999

161 In this Lucas supply curve, firms make output decisions with respect to relative prices. But because they cannot disentangle a relative price increase from a change in the general price level, their long run supply is determined by structural factors and monetary policy only affects inflation.

162 Hence our model does not assume Ricardian equivalence whereby households save today to pay for higher taxes in the future. Ours is a more realistic description of the world which is supported by empirical evidence.

163 Effectively, it corresponds to the full employment of the scarcest resource. If previous investment was insufficient to create the capital stock required to employ all labour willing to work, natural unemployment would still be high. See Collignon, 2002, Chapter 8.

164 Permanent deficits along the efficient-policy-line are also compatible with the sustainability of public debt, provided nominal GDP-growth is sufficiently high. See Collignon and Mundschenk 1999 for details.

165 We could also make this argument by separating the polity into different epistemic constituencies and let the median voter decide the collective preference.

166 To avoid misunderstandings I would like to emphasise that, because we consider a long-term supply curve, there is no Phillips-curve trade-off between unemployment and inflation in this definition of optimality.

167 Gros and Hobza, 2002 produce some empirical evidence for this thesis.

168 Remember we are arguing in the neoclassical world of full employment when we are on the efficient policy line.

169 Technically we can model the welfare function as a Cobb-Douglas utility function where the contribution of monetary and fiscal policy is weighted by constant shares adding to one. These weights can be obtained from the equilibrium vector of our stochastic consensus model (see Annexe 1 and 3).

170 In Annexe 3 equation (6.2) remains unchanged, but (6.1) is re-written as

(6.1a) $y - y^* = \phi_0 - \phi_1 r - \phi_2 \sum_{i=1}^{n} s_i$, where s_i is the ratio of national net borrowing to EMU-GDP.

171 Gros and Hobza (2002) have examined the question of spillovers from fiscal policy and did not find strong evidence. But their focus is on a different question. They measure the regional demand spillovers into different jurisdictions. Here we are interested in the spillover from fiscal to monetary policy.

172 See Chapter Five.

173 See Harden, (1999) and Brunila/Buti/Franco, (2001).

174 Structural budgets or deficits are cyclically adjusted budget positions. Because our efficient policy line represents macroeconomic equilibrium, any budget position s on the line is simultaneously reflecting the structural and the actual position.

175 In the notation of Annexe 3 the SGP-rule is $s_i = 0 \forall i$ so that $\Sigma s_i = 0$.

176 In a sequential game, a Stackelberg follower does the second move with the intention to maximise his objectives.

177 Alesina and Grilli (1992:68) come to a similar conclusion.

178 Nearly 1 out of 2 European citizens (47 per cent to be precise) speak a foreign language, of which English is the most well-known (48 per cent speak it well enough to follow a conversation). 69 per cent consider English, 37 per cent French a useful language to know (Eurobarometer 55, Spring 2001). Surely, these figures could be improved if governments made some effort (In Thailand, for example, English is regularly taught in primary school. Why not in Europe?). I suspect that the language argument against an integrated European polity is mainly due to the fact that too many national leaders have spent their careers at home and do not speak foreign languages well.

179 To give an example: In 2000 I was part of a fact finding group on pension reform by the German Ministry of Finance. We first went to London where we met with City people and Treasury colleagues. At the end of the day we had learned that one third of the British population will one day live in poverty and the head of the German delegation concluded, ' This is not how we should do it.' A few weeks later, we travelled to Stockholm to learn about the ideal model of a generous and sustainable pension reform with great flexibility for individual choice. This time, the head of the delegation observed, 'They have shown us how to do it; but of course in Germany we are heading in the opposite direction'. The reason for this 'coordination failure' lay in the institutional constraints of German national party politics that inhibited the integration of non-national evidence into the domestic policy debate.

180 For official input into the work of the Convention, see http://european-convention.eu.int

181 For a fuller analysis of this statement see Collignon and Schwarzer, 2003.

182 Swahili for deliberation.

183 The same argument applies if nation-states ratify the constitution by parliamentarian procedures. I will not discuss them separately here.

184 For example, the German Constitutional Court has insisted on the Bundestag's role in transfers of sovereignty. By accepting a pan-European referendum as consultative at a higher level, but taking the formal decision by the constitutionally relevant institutions, it should be possible to combine the two.

185 For example Bavaria did not ratify the constitution of the Federal Republic of Germany in 1949, but it did participate in the new state.

186 See Collignon and Schwarzer 2003, Chapter 5, for an analysis of European populism.

187 I take the liberty of this adjective after Commission President Prodi has used it to characterise the Stability and Growth Pact.

188 The Gini Coefficient is based on the Lorenz Curve, a cumulative frequency curve that compares the distribution of a specific variable with the uniform distribution that represents equality. The greater the deviation of the Lorenz Curve from the equality line, the greater such inequality is. The Gini Coefficient aggregates this information.

189 These ideas are less popular in the present EU15, but often heard among policy-makers in the Eastern European accession countries.

190 This is the often cited English version of the quotation: 'D'ordinaire les empires conquérants meurent d'indigestion.' (Hugo, 1987 :936)

191 The least common multiple is the least quantity that contains two or more given quantities exactly.

192 The language here is ambivalent. The economic dimension of liberalism is now mainly covered by the prefix *neo*-liberal. My use of the word liberal has a broader, political dimension in the sense used by Rawls that includes social democracy. The word 'republican' has a different meaning in the US-context compared to Europe. I use it in the French tradition of *valeurs républicaines*. In a German context it would be addressed as *democratic*.

193 Although the last Constitutions of the Ancien Régime referred to *fraternité* in the context of national festivities, none of the four constitutions of the First Republic in France mentioned the notion. It only appears as the third term of the republican slogan with the revolution of 1848, when it was put forward by anarcho-communitarians revolutionaries and Christian communists. See Duclert et al., 2002:178.

194 In non-democratic societies either the political right (fascism) or the political left (communism) fused with communitarian ideologies.

195 This attitude is substantiated by the claim that every country needs its 'own' Commissioner.

196 This relation is not without tension, as Artus and Wyplosz, (2002) show. It is also clear that a Governing Council with 27+5 members is too wieldy.

197 For a critical assessment of Hix' article, see also Hoffmann, 2002.

198 It is reported that Henry Kissinger once asked whom the USA should call in Europe when there is an international crisis.

199 For the discussion of epistemic communities see Haas, 1992 and Collignon and Schwarzer, 2003. For the distinction between epistemic constituencies and communities, see above note 9.

200 In 1999 I witnessed three finance ministers making such an attempt within the Euro-group, but they were not endorsed by their colleagues.

201 See also Emmerling and van Ackere, 2002.

202 In essence this evaluation of the mental state is about whether it fits into a specific discursive context. Kuran (1997) gives numerous examples for such considerations. In step II we discuss more sophisticated evaluations leading to the acceptance of preferences based on evidence and logical or ethical principles.

203 Sincerity implies that the mapping of the mental state into language is a one-to-one relation so that the proposition reflects the mental state correctly.

204 To be precise, we should write the statement about the projected state of the world as: $s_i(S_j)$. To avoid the clumsiness of this denomination, I will write s_{ij} for the statement by i about state S_j.

205 If $p(E|B)$ is high, we may interpret the evidence E as reflecting knowledge implied in the background. If $p(E|B)$ is low, it adds significantly new evidence to the existing body of knowledge.

206 In the logically extreme case where the whole background consists only of common knowledge, individual desires would be identical. We may interpret this as a preference-theoretical formulation of Kant's categorical imperative.

207 A change in preference intensity may actually lead to changes in preference *ranking*, i.e. an overwriting of individual by social preferences, but this is not necessarily so.

208 The formation of the weight matrix may itself be subject to Bayesian probability revisions.

209 A change in the weight matrix W.

210 This is our condition of mutual respect.

211 The matrix multiplication converges toward a matrix with every row the same, though the columns may differ. See Lehrer and Wagner, 1981: 24.

212 One may object that 'the fact that all members of a community come to *accept* a certain social situation does not necessarily mean that it is unanimously *preferred* to other social alternatives'. Sen, 1970: 26. However, this dichotomy is implied by our modeling of collective preferences as being derived from

naturalistic desires, but subsequently re-evaluated by evidence and mutual respect for others. The point is that consensus does not require unanimity in desires, beliefs and feelings, but a commitment to evaluate all available information in society (including institutions, ethical norms etc.) in the context of mutual respect and trust, as this yields unanimity in assessments.

213 My distinction of dissent and conflict is different from Lehrer/Wagner (1981), who amalgamate the two notions. For analytic reasons it is important to distinguish between the *variance* from equilibrium and the *non-existence* of equilibrium.

214 In the limiting case of perfect reciprocity, the weight matrix is symmetrical and consensus is instantaneous.

215 There are of course other choice rules. Dictatorship, for example, implies maximising the ruler's preferences.

216 See Chapter Two and footnote 24.

217 This statement must not be confused with note 24, which referred to the amount or quantities of goods. Here we deal with values.

218 See also Hardin, 1982:20.

219 For a formal analysis of the weighting process in a model of multilevel governance see Collignon 2002a.

Bibliography

Alesina, A. and Grilli, A. 1992.: *The European Central Bank: reshaping monetary politics in Europe*; in: M. Canzoneri, V. Grilli, P. Masson: Establishing a Central Bank: Issues in Europe and lessons from the US. Cambridge University Press, Cambridge.

Alesina, A. and Wacziarg, R. 1999: Is Europe Going Too Far? National Bureau of Economic Research. C.A. Mass.

Alesina, A. , Angeloni, I., Etro, F. 2001: *Institutional Rules for Federations*. National Bureau of Economic Research. C.A. Mass.

Alesina, A. Angeloni, I. Schuknecht, L. 2002: *What does the European Union do?*

Althusius, J. 1603/1965. *Politica* (The Politics of Johannes Althusius. An abridged translation by Frederick S. Carney). London: Eyre & Spottiswoode.

Amato, G. 2002: Verso un DPEF europeo? In: *nens-nuova economia, nuova società*, anno II, Luglio 2002, No. 4.

Aron, R. 1987. *Sur Clausewitz*. Bruxelles: editions complexe.

Arrow, K. J. 2nd ed 1963. *Social Choice and Individual Values*. London: Chapman & Hall.

Artus, P. and Wyplosz, C. 2002. *La Banque centrale européenne* Conseil d'Analyse Économique. Paris.

Bakunin, M. 1953. *Scientific Anarchism*. ed. G.P. Maximoff, Glencoe: III. Free Press.

Barry, B. 2001. *Culture and Equality. An Egalitarian Critique of Multiculturalism*. Cambridge, UK: Polity Press.

Basu, K. 2000. *Prelude to Political Economy. A Study of the Social and Political Foundations of Economics*. Oxford: O.U.P.

Baumol, W. J. 1986. *Superfairness. Applications and Theory*. Cambridge Mass: MIT Press.

Baumol, W. J. and Oates, W.E. 1975. *The Theory of Environmental Policy: Externalities, Public Outlays, and the Quality of Life*. Englewood Cliffs; London: Prentice-Hall

Benassi, C., Chirco, A. and Colombo, C. 1994. *The New Keynesian Economics*. Oxford: Blackwell Publishers.

Bellamy, R. and Castiglione, D. 2000. The Uses of Democracy. Reflections on the European Democratic Deficit. In: Eriksen, E. O. and Fossum, E. 2000. *Democracy in the European Union. Integration through Deliberation?* London: Routledge.

Boardman, A. et. al. 1996. *Cost-benefit Analysis: Concepts and* Practices. New Jersey: Upper Saddle River, Prentice Hall.

Bobay, F. 2001. Émergence d'un nouvel équilbre européen à Nice. Analyse de la réforme du Conseil de la Union européenne à partir de la théorie des jeux. In *Association Française de Science Economiques* 20/21 Septembre.

Bodin, J. 1583/1993. *Six Books of the Commonwealth*, Oxford: Blackwell.

Bohman, J. 1996. *Public Deliberation, Pluralism, Complexity and Democracy.* Cambridge, Mass: MIT Press.

Bossi, T. 2001. Die Grundrechtecharta - Wertekanon für die Union; in: W. Weidenfeld (Hrsg.): *Nizza in der Analyse.* Verlag Bertelsmann Stiftung.

Brunila, A., Buti, M. and Franco, D. (ed.). 2001. *The Stability and Growth Pact: The Architecture of Fiscal Policy in EMU.* New York: Palgrave

Buchanan, J. and Tullock, G. 1962. *The Calculus of Consent: Logical Foundations of Constitutional Democracy.* Ann Arbor: University of Michigan Press.

Buchanan, J. 1991. *The Economics and Ethics of Constitutional Order.* Ann Arbor: University of Michigan Press.

Buchanan, J., Poehl, K., Price, V., Vibert, F. 1990. *Europe's Constitutional Future.* London: Institute of Economic Affairs.

Buchanan, J. 1958. *Public Debt.* Homewood, Illinois : Richard D. Irwin, Inc.

Buchanan, J. 1965. An Economic Theory of Clubs. In *Economica 32*, 125. p1-14.

Burgess, M. 1993. Federalism and Federation: A Reappraisal. In Burgess, M. and Gagnon, A.G. *Comparative Federalism and Federation. Competing Traditions and Future Directions.* New York and London: Harvester Wheatsheaf.

Burgess, M. 2000. *Federalism and European Union: the building of Europe, 1950-2000.* Routledge, New York.

Burgess, M. and Gagnon, A.G. 1993. *Comparative Federalism and Federation. Competing Traditions and Future Directions.* New York and London: Harvester Wheatsheaf.

Casella, A. 1999.Trade-able Deficit Permits: efficient implementation of the Stability Pact in the European Monetary Union. *Economic Policy*, Oct 1999.

Casella, A. 2001. Trade-able Deficit Permits: in Brumila, A., Buti, M and Franco, D. 2001. *The Stability and Growth Pact, The Architecture of Fiscal Policy in EMU.* London: Palgrave.

Chopin, T. 2002. *La République 'une et divisible'. Les fondements de la Fédération américaine.* Paris: Plon.

Coase, R.H. 1960. The Problem of Social Cost. In *The Journal of Law and Economics* 3 (October), pp.1-44

Collignon, S. 1999. *Why Do Poor Countries Choose Low Human Rights?* Download from: www.StefanCollignon.de

Collignon, S. 2002. *Monetary Stability in Europe.* London: Routledge.

Collignon, S. 2002a. Les conditions politiques et institutionnelles d'une coordination des politiques économiques dans l'Euroland. *Revue Economique et Financière.* Paris. An earlier English version was published as: Economic Policy Coordination in EMU: Institutional and Political Requirements. Center for European Studies, Harvard University, May 2001

Collignon S. and Mundschenk, S. 1999. '*The Sustainability of Public Debt in Europe*', Economia Internazionale LII,1;101-59.

Collignon, S. and Schwarzer, D. 2003: *Private Sector Involvement in the Euro. The Power of Ideas.* London: Routledge.

Cooper, R. and John, A. 1988. 'Coordinating Coordination Failures in a Keynesian model' in *Quarterly Journal of Economics* 103, August 1988, p. 441-463; reprinted in: Mankiv, G. N. and Romer, D (eds.) (1991) *New Keynesian Economics, vol. 2: Coordination Failures and Real Rigidities*, The MIT Press, Cambridge, MA and London, UK.

Cowles, M. G., 1995. 'Setting the Agenda for a New Europe: The ERT and EC 1992', *Journal of Common Market Studies*, 33, 4: 501-26.

Costello, D. 2001. The SGP: How did we get there? In Brumila, A., Buti, M and Franco, D. 2001. *The Stability and Growth Pact, The Architecture of Fiscal Policy in EMU.* London: Palgrave.

Cram, L. 1998: The EU institutions and collective action. Constructing a European interest? In: J. Greenwood and M. Aspinwall (eds): Collective Action in the European Union. Interests and the new politics of associability. Routledge, London and New York.

Cullis, J. and Jones, Ph. 1998. *Public Finance and Public Choice*. Oxford: O.U.P.

De Cecco, M. 2002: The economy from Liberalism to Fascism. In: A. Lyttleton, Liberal and Fascist Italy, 2002, Oxford University Press, Oxford.

De Groot, M. H. 1974. 'Reaching Consensus'. In, *Journal of American Statistical Association*. 69.

Downs, A. 1957. *An Economic Theory of Democracy*. New York: Harper and Row.

Drazen, A. 2000. *Political Economy in Macroeconomics*. Princeton, NJ: Princeton University Press.

Dryzek, J. S. 2000. *Deliberative Democracy and Beyond. Liberals, Critics, Contestations*. New York: Oxford University Press.

Duchêne, F. 1994. *Jean Monnet. The First Statesman of Europe*. New York: W. W. Norton & Company.

Duclert, V. and Prochasson, C. 2002. *Dictionnaire critique de la République*. Paris, Flammarion

Dumont, L. 1980. *Homo Hierarchicus. The Cast System and its Implications*. Chicago and London: The University of Chicago Press.

Dumont, L. 1985. *Homo Aequalis (I). Génèse et épanouissement de l'idéologie économique*. Paris: Editions Gallimard.

Dumont, L. 1991. *Essais sur l'individualisme. Une perspective anthropologique sur l'idéologie moderne*. Paris: Editions du Seuil.

Dur, R.A.J. and Roelfsema, H.J. 2002. *Why does Centralisation Fail to Internalise Policy Externalities?* Tinbergen Institute Discussion Paper TI 2002-056/3

Elazar, D. J. 1987. *Exploring Federalism*. Tuscaloosa, AL: University of Alabama Press.

Elliot, J. H. 2002: Imperial Spain. 1469-1716. Penguin Books, London.

Emmerling, T. und van Ackere, S. 2002. *Kompetenzordnung und Finanzverfassung in Europa – Überlegungen zur Konventsdiskussion*. C·A·P Working Paper, München 10/2002

Engerman, S. 1965. Regional Aspects of Stabilization policy. In Musgrave, R. (ed) *Essays in Fiscal Federalism*. Washington D.C.: Brookings Institution.

Englander, S. and Egebo, T. 1993: Adjustments under fixed exchange rates: application to the European Monetary Union. OECD Economic Studies, 20.

Eriksen, E. O. 2000: Deliberative supranationalism in the EU. In: E.O. Eriksen and J.E. Fossum (ed): Democracy in the European Union. Integration through Deliberation? Routledge, London.

Eurobarometer 2002: Candidate countries, March 2002, http://europa.eu.int/comm/public_opinion/archives/eb/eb56/eb56_en.htm.

FAO 2002. Food, Security, Justice and Peace: Multi-stakeholder Dialogue. World Food Summit, 10-13-June 2002.

Featherstone, K. 1994. Jean Monet and the 'Democratic Deficit' in the European Union; *Journal of Common Market Studies*, Vol.32, No 2 June, p.149-170.

Ferry, J. M. 2000. *La question de L'État Européen*. Paris: Gallimard.

Fischer, T. and Schley, N. 1999. *Europa Föderal Organisieren*. Europa Union Verlag, Bonn.

Fotion, N. 2000. *John Searle* Princeton, Oxford: Princeton University Press.

Friedrich, C. J. 1974. *Limited Government: A Comparison*. New Jersey: Englewood Cliffs.

Friedrich, H. B. 2003 (im Erscheinen). *Modernisierung und Integration. Die Folgen des Euro für die politische Handlungsfähigkeit der Mitgliedstaaten. Eine Analyse aus deutscher Sicht*, Schriftenreihe Münchner Beiträge zur Europäischen Einigung, Europa Union Verlag, Bonn.

Friedrich, H. B. 2002a. *Eine Wirtschafts- und Finanzverfassung für Europa*, in: HWWA Wirtschaftsdienst, 82. Jg., Heft 6, Juni 2002, S. 329-334.

Friedrich, H. B. 2002b. *A European Economic and Financial Constitution*, Convention Spotlight No 5, CAP / Bertelsmann Foundation, Gütersloh.

Friedrich, H. B. 2001. *Probleme und Folgefragen des Euro*, CAP Working-Paper, München.

Galli della Loggia, E. 1998: *L'identità italiana*. Il Mulino, Bologna.

Gambetta, D. 1998. 'Claro!': An Essay on Discursive Machismo. In Elster, J. (ed): *Deliberative Democracy*. Cambridge: Cambridge University Press.

Gargarella, R. 2000: Demanding Public Deliberation. The Council of Ministers: some lessons from the Anglo-American History. In: E.O. Erikson and J.E. Fossum: Democracy in the European Union Integration through Deliberation? Routledge, London.

Giddens, A. 1985 *A Contemporary Critique of Historical Materialism;* Vol. II, *The Nation-State and Violence,* Cambridge: Polity Press.

Giddens, A. 1993. 2nd Ed. *New Rules of Sociological Method. A Positive Critique of Interpretative Sociologies.* Oxford: Polity Press.

Gierke, O. 1902. *Johannes Althusius und die Entwicklung der naturrechtlichen Staatstheorien.* Breslau. 2nd Edition.

Goyard-Fabre, S. 1989. *Jean Bodin et le droit de la République.* PUF, Paris.

Gray, J. 1995: *Liberalism;* (2nd ed.), Open University Press, Buckingham.

Greenwood, J. and Aspinwall, M. 1998. *Collective Action in the European Union.* London and New York: Routledge.

Gros, D. and Hobza, A. 2002: *Why Coordinate Fiscal Policy?* Paper presented at the conference, Economic Coordination in EMU. College of Europe, Bruges 28 June 2002.

Guth, D. J. 1982. The Age of Debt, the Reformation and English Law. In Guth, D. J. and McKenna. J. W. (eds.). *Tudor Rule and Revolution: Essays for G.R. Elton from his American.* Cambridge.

Haas, E. B. 1958. *The uniting of Europe: political, social and economical forces, 1950-1957.* London: Stevens.

Haas, P. M., 1992. Introduction, Epistemic communities and international policy coordination. International Organization, 46, 1–35.

Habermas, J. 1984. *The Theory of Communicative Action. Vol.1. Reason and the Rationalization of Society.* London: Heinemann Education.

Habermas, J. 1987. *The Theory of Communicative Action. Vol.2. Lifeworld and System : a Critique of Functionalist Reason.* Trans. McCarthy, Thomas. Boston: Beacon. Cambridge: Polity.

Habermas, J. 1990. *Die Nachholende Revolution.* Frankfurt: Suhrkamp.

Habermas, J. 1992. *Faktizität und Geltung. Beiträge zur Diskurstheorie des Rechts und des demokratischen Rechtsstaats.* Frankfurt: Suhrkamp.

Habermas, J. 1999. *Die Einbeziehung des Anderen.* Frankfurt: Suhrkamp.

Habermas, J. 2001a. *Zeit der Übergänge.* Frankfurt: Suhrkamp.

Habermas, J. 2001b. *The Postnational Constellation, Political Essays.* Oxford: Polity Press.

Halliday, F. 1996. *Islam and the Myth of Confrontation: Religion and Politics in the Middle East.* London & New York : Tauris Publishers.

Harden, I. 1994. *The Constitution of the European Union.* Public Law, 609-624.

Harden, I. 1995. *The European Union and its Influence on Constitutional Reform in the UK.* LSE Public Policy Group Seminar Series (October); http://www.lse.ac.uk/Depts/ppg/pdf/8-harden.pdf

Harden, I. 1999. The Fiscal Constitution of EMU. In Beaumont, P. and Walker, N (ed). *Legal Framework of the Single European Currency.* Oxford-Portland: Hart Publishing.

Hardin, R. 1982. *Collective Action.* Maryland: Johns Hopkins University.

Head, J.G. 1962. Public Goods and Public Policy. In *Public Finance,* XVII, No. 3 pp 197-219.

Hindley, B and Howe, M. 2001. *Better off out? The Benefits and Costs of EU Membership.* London: Institute of Economic Affairs.

Hix, S. 2002. *Linking National Politics to Europe: next generation democracy.* The British Council and Weber Shandwick Adamson. London.

Hobbes, T. 1973. Leviathan. London: J.M. Dent & Sons Ltd.

Hobbes, T. 1988 *De Cive*; reprint: Verlag Dr. J. Königshausen + Dr. Th. Neuman, Würzburg 1988.

Hodson, D. and Maher, 2001. The Open Method as New Mode of Governance: The Case of Soft Economic Policy Co-Ordination. *Journal of Market Studies,* Vol 39, No 4, November 2001.

Hoffmann, L. 2002. *Linking National Politics to Europe - an opposing argument.* Federal Trust for Education and Research. London.

Holt, Mark P. 1995. *The French Wars of Religion, 1562-1629.* Cambridge: Cambridge University Press.

Horn, G. A. 2001. *Koordinationsmängel als Ursachen konjunktureller Krisen am Beispiel der USA und Deutschland.* Berlin: Habilitationsschrift TU.

Hueglin, Thomas O. 1999. *Early Modern Concepts for a Late Modern World. Althusius on Community and Federalism.* Waterloo, Ontario: Wilfred Laurier University Press.

Hugo, V. 1987. Choses vues. Histoire / Oeuvres complètes. Paris, Robert Laffont - Bouquins.

Huntington, S. 1993. The Clash of Civilisations? *Foreign Affairs,* Summer Vol.72, No.3, pp22-49.

Hutchinson, J. and Smith, A. (ed.). 1994. *Nationalism.* Oxford: Oxford University Press.

Hutton, W. 2002. *The World we're in.* London, Little, Brown.

Jackson, R. 1999. Sovereignty in World Politics: a Glance at the Conceptual and Historical Landscape. In Jackson, R. (ed): *Sovereignty at the Millennium.* Oxford: Blackwell Publishers.

De Jasay, A. 1998. *The State.* Indianapolis: Liberty Fund.

Jeffrey, R.C. 1983. *The Logic of Decision.* Chicago: University of Chicago Press.

Kavka,G. 1986. *Hobbesian Moral and Political Theory.* Princeton, New Jersey: Princeton University Press.

Kelikian, A. 2002: The Church and Catholicism. In: A. Lytlelton, *Liberal and Fascist Italy.* 2002, Oxford University Press, Oxford.

King, P. 1982. *Federalism and Federation.* London & Canberra: Croom Helm.

Klug, F., Starmer, K. and Weir S. 1996. *Three Pillars of Liberty. Political Rights and Freedoms in the United Kingdom.* London: Routledge.

Knecht, R. J. 2000. *The French Civil Wars, 1562-1598.* London/New York: Longman.

Kornai, J. 1980. *Economics of Shortage.* Amsterdam: North Holland.

Kriegel, B. 1998. *Philosophie de la République.* Paris: Plon.

Krugman, P. 1991. Geography and Trade. MIT Press, Cambridge, Mass and London, UK.

Kuran, T. 1995. *Private Truth, Public Lies – The Social Consequences Of Preference Falsification.* Cambridge Mass.: Harvard University Press.

Kymlicka, W. 1993. Community. In Goodwin, R and Pettit, M (ed.) 1993. *A Companion to Contemporary Political Philosophy*. Oxford: Blackwell.

Ladurie, E. 1987. *L'État Royal 1460-1610*. Paris, Hachette.

Lehrer, K. and Wagner, C. 1981. *Rational Consensus in Science and Society*. Dordrecht, Holland: D. Reidel Publishing Company.

Lehrer, K. 2001. Individualism versus Communitarianism and Consensus; in: *The Journal of Ethics*, vol. 5 No. 2 pp.105-120.

Lewis, D. 1969. *Convention*. Cambridge, Mass.: Harvard University Press.

Lijphart, A. 1999. *Patterns of Democracy. Government Forms and Performance in Thirty-six Countries*. New Haven and London: Yale University Press.

MacDougall, D. et al. 1977: *Report of the Study Group on the Role of Public Finance in European Integration*. Economic and Financial Series, A13, April. Commission of the European Communities, Luxemburg.

Macpherson, C. B. 1962. *The Political Theory of Possessive Individualism*. Oxford : O.U.P.

Mann, G. 1974: *The History of Germany since 1789*. Penguin Books, Harmondsworth.

Maskin, E. S. 1999. Recent Theoretical work on the Soft Budget Constraint. *American Economic Review*. Vol 89, No 2, May 1999.

McKay, D. H. 1999. *Federation and European Union: A Political Economy Perspective*. Oxford: Oxford University Press.

Monnet, J. 1978. *Memoirs*. New York: Doubleday.

Moore, G. E. 1993 *Principia Ethica* (edited by Thomas Baldwin), Cambridge University Press.

Moravcsik, A. 1998. *The Choice for Europe: Social Purpose and State Power from Messina to Maastricht*. Cornell University Press.

Mueller, D. 1996 *Constitutional Democracy*. Oxford University Press, Oxford.

Muldrew, C. 1998. *The Economy of Obligation: The Culture of Credit and Social Relations in Early Modern England*. Basingstoke, UK: Macmillan Press.

Musgrave, R. A., 1959: *The Theory of Public Finance*. NY. McGraw-Hill.

Musgrave, R. A. and Musgrave, P. B. 1973. *Public Finance in Theory and Practice*. N.Y. and London: McGraw-Hill.

Nicholls, A. J. 1994. Freedom with Responsibility. The Social Market Economy in Germany 1918-1963. Oxford, Oxford University Press.

Nozick, R. 1974. *Anarchy, State and Utopia*. Oxford: Blackwell

Oates, W. 1972: *Fiscal Federalism*. New York/Chicago: Harcourt Brace Jovanovich Inc.

Oates, W. 1999: An Essay on Fiscal Federalism. *The Journal of Economic Literature*, Vol. XXXVII, (September 1999 pp. 1120-1149).

Olson, M. 1969: The Principle of 'Fiscal Equivalence': The Division of Responsibilities among Different Levels of Government.: in: *American Economic Review*. Papers and Proceedings, 59, pp.479-87.

Olson, M. 1971. *The Logic of Collective Action. Public Goods and the Theory of Groups*. Cambridge, Mass: Harvard University Press.

Overman, H. 2001. *Globalisation and Integration: Implications for the Location of Economic Activity across the EU*. In: I. Tsoukalis (ed): Globalisation and Regionalism. A double challenge for Greece. The Hellenic Observatory of the European Institute, at the LSE and ELIAMEP, Athens.

Parsons, T. 1949. *Structure of Social Action*. Free Press.

Pérez, J. 2002. Brève Histoire de l'inquisition en Espagne. Paris, Fayard.

Person, T. and Tabellini, G. 2002: Political Institutions and Policy Outcomes: What are the Stylised Facts? Centre for Economic Performance, London School of Economics.

Philpott, 1999. Westphalia, Authority, and International Society. In Jackson, R. (ed): *Sovereignty at the Millennium*. Oxford: Blackwell Publishers.

Popper, K. 1995: The Open Society and its Enemies. Routledge, London.

Przeworski, A. 1991. *Democracy and the Market. Political and Economic Reforms in Eastern Europe and Latin America*. Cambridge: Cambridge University Press.

Prezorswki, A. 1998. Deliberation and Ideological Domination: in Elster,J. (ed) *Deliberative Democracy* Cambridge University Press, Cambridge.

Puterman, M. 1994. *Markov Decision Processes: Discrete Stochastic Dynamic Programming*. Wiley-Interscience.

Rasmussen, D. 1990. *Universalism vs. Communitarianism. Contemporary Debates in Ethics*. Cambridge Mass: MIT Press.

Rawls, J. 1955. Two Concepts of Rules. Reprint in: John Rawls, Collected Papers (edited by Samuel Freeman); Harvard University Press, Cambridge, Mass, 1999, pp.20-46.

Rawls, J. 1971. *A Theory of Justice*. Oxford: Oxford University Press

Rawls, J. 1993. *Justice et Démocratie*. Paris: Editions du Seuil.

Rawls, J. 1996. *Political Liberalism*. New York: Columbia University Press.

Riese, H. 1990. *Geld im Sozialismus*, Marburg: Metropolis.

Rodrik, D. 1997. *Has Globalization Gone Too Far?* 1997. Washington D.C.: Institute for International Economics.

Romer, D. 1999. *Short–Run Fluctuations*. August 1999, http://eurlab.berkely.edu/users/dromer/paper/short_run_fluc_paper.pdf.

Romer, D. 1996. *Advanced Macroeconomics*. New York: McGraw Hill.

Rorty, R. (ed.) 1992. *The Linguistic Turn: Essays in Philosophical Method*. Chicago and London: University of Chicago Press.

Rosamond, B. 2000. *Theories of European Integration*. Basingstoke: MacMillan, New York: St Martins Press.

Rosanvallon, P. 1992. *Le sacre du citoyen*. Paris: Gallimard/folio.

Russel, B. 1938. *Power: a New Social Analysis*. London: Allan and Unwin.

Saint-Simon, C. H. 1814. *De la Réorganisation de la société Européenne, ou de la Nécessité et des Moyens de rassembler les peuples de l'Européen un seul corps politique, en conservant à chacun son indépendance nationale*. Paris.

Samuelson, P. 1955. *Readings in Economics*. New York: McGraw Hill.

Sandholtz, W. and Zysman, J. 1989. '1992: Recasting the European Bargain', *World Politics*, 42, 1:95-28.

Schelkle, W. 2001. *Monetäre Integration. Bestandsaufnahme und Weiterentwicklung der neueren Theorie*. Heidelberg: Physica Verlag.

Schmidt, H. 1998. *Auf der Suche nach einer öffentlichen Moral. Deutschland vor dem neuen Jahrhundert*. Stuttgart: Deutsche Verlags-Anstalt.

Schmidt, H. 1999. *Patrioten setzen auf Europa*. Die Zeit, No. 33, p.8: 12.08.1999.

Schmidt, H. 2000. *Die Selbstbehauptung Europas: Perspektiven für das 21. Jahrhundert*. Stuttgart: Deutsche Verlags-Anstalt.

Searle, J. R. 1998. *Mind, Language and Society.* New York: Basic Books.

Searle, J. R. 1995. *The Construction of Social Reality.* Harmondsworth: Penguin.

Sen, A. 1970. *Collective Choice and Social Welfare.* Amsterdam, New York, Oxford: North Holland.

Sen, A. 1987. *On Ethics and Economics.* Oxford: Basil Blackwell.

Sen, A. 1999. *Development as Freedom.* Oxford University Press.

Silvestre, J. 1993. *The Market-Power Foundations of Macroeconomic Policy.* Journal of Economic Literature.

Smith, A. 2001: *Nationalism.* Polity Press, Cambridge, UK.

Soete, L. 2002. The Challenges and the Potential of the Knowledge Base Economy in a Globalised World. In Maria Joao Rodriguez. 2002. *The New Knowledge Economy in Europe: a Strategy for International Competitiveness and Social Cohesion.* Cheltenham, UK: Edward Elgar.

Sørensen, G. 1999. Sovereignty: Change and Continuity in a Fundamental Institution. In Jackson, R. (ed): *Sovereignty at the Millennium.* Oxford: Blackwell Publishers.

Stokes, S. 1998. *Pathologies of Deliberation.* In Elster, J (ed) *Deliberative Democracy.* Cambridge: Cambridge University Press.

Taylor, C. 1994. *Multiculturalism : examining the politics of recognition.* Princeton, N.J. : Princeton University Press

Taylor, C. 1995. *Philosophical Arguments.* Cambridge, Mass: Harvard University Press.

Taylor, M. 1982. *Community, Anarchy and Liberty.* Cambridge, UK: Cambridge University Press.

Tiebout, C. M. 1956: A pure theory of local expenditures. In: *Journal of Political Economy,* 64, 5 pp. 416-24.

Todd, E. 2002: *Après l'Empire.* Gallimard, Paris.

Tönnies, F. 2001: *Community and Civil Society*; Cambridge University Press, Cambridge. (First published in Germany in Leipzig, 1887 as *Gemeinschaft und Gesellschaft*).

Treaty on European Union, 1992. In *Official Journal of the European Communities,* August, 1992.

Tsoukalis, L. 1997: *The New European Economy Revisited.* Oxford, Oxford University Press.

Tullock, G. 1994: *The New Federalist.* Fraser Institute, Vancouver, BC.

Van den Doel, H. and van Velthoven, B. 1993. *Democracy and Welfare Economics* (2nd ed) Cambridge, UK: Cambridge University Press.

Von Hagen, J. 1993: Monetary Union and Fiscal Union: a Perspective from Fiscal Federalism. In: P.R. Masson and M.P. Taylor, 1993: *Policy Issues in the Operation of Currency Unions.* Cambridge University Press, Cambridge.

Von Hagen, J. and Pisani-Ferry, J. 2002: *Why is Europe different from what economists would like?* Paper prepared for the Vth Congress of the French Economic Association – AFSE, Paris, 19-20 September 2002.

Wallace, Helen and Wallace, William. (eds.) 2000. *Policy-Making in the European Union.* Oxford: O.U.P.

Walker, N. 1996. European Constitutionalism and European Integration. *Public Law.* 266-290.

Walzer, M. 1983. *Spheres of Justice. A Defence of Pluralism and Equality.* Oxford: Basil Blackwell.

Walzer, M (ed) (1994) *Towards a Global Civil Society.* Providence, RI. Oxford. Berghahn Books.

Weber, M. 1972. *Wirtschaft und Gesellschaft.* (5th ed.) Tübingen: J.C.B. Mohr (Paul Siebeck).

Weidenfeld, W. 2000: Europäische Einigung im historischen Überblick. In: Weidenfeld, W. and Wessels, W. (eds.) 2000. *Europa von A bis Z. Taschenbuch der Europäischen Integration.* Bonn: Europa Union Verlag.

Weiler, J. 1999. *The Constitution of Europe: „Do the new cloth have an Emperor? „ and Other Essays on European Integration.* New York: Cambridge University Press.

Wicksell, K. 1990. *Allgemeine Volkswirtschaftslehre*. München: Vahlen.

Wittgenstein, L. 1984. *Philosophische Untersuchungen*. Frankfurt am Main: Werkausgabe Band I, Suhrkamp.

Woodcock, G. 1975. *Anarchism*. Penguin Books, Harmondsworth UK.

World Bank, 2002. The Role and Effectiveness of Development Assistance: Lessons from World Bank Experience. http://econ.worldbank.org/files/13080_Development_Effectiveness.pdf.

Wrong, D.H. 1997. *Power. Its Forms, Bases and Uses*. New Brunswick (USA) and London (UK): Transaction Publishers.

WWF, *Living Planet Report 2002* edited by Jonathan Loh.

Index